JOHN ROGERS OF MARSHFIELD AND SOME OF HIS DESCENDANTS

Published @ 2017 Trieste Publishing Pty Ltd

ISBN 9780649027521

John Rogers of Marshfield and Some of His Descendants by Josiah Hayden Drummond

Edited by Trieste Publishing Pty Ltd.
 Cover @ 2017

www.triestepublishing.com

JOSIAH HAYDEN DRUMMOND

JOHN ROGERS OF MARSHFIELD AND SOME OF HIS DESCENDANTS

John Rogers of Marshfield

AND

SOME OF HIS DESCENDANTS

BY

JOSIAH H. DRUMMOND

Published by Rhoda B. Ellis
West Hanover, Mass.

PORTLAND, MAINE
SMITH & SALE, PRINTERS
1898

PREFACE.

In the preparation of the article on "The John Rogers Families of Plymouth and Vicinity," I gathered many facts in relation to the family of John Rogers of Marshfield. Correspondence with Miss RHODA B. ELLIS, a descendant, developed the fact that she had material of the same character, gathered partly from the Scituate Friends' records, which I had never examined. These materials seemed worth preserving by publication; and it was concluded to publish them (with additions furnished by Miss ELLIS or obtained from records of wills and deeds) under the title of " Some Materials for a Genealogy of John Rogers of Marshfield."

We contemplated a small pamphlet of some forty pages. But when our design became known other descendants desired Miss ELLIS to enlarge the work, offering to aid in furnishing material and in other ways. We acceded to these requests, and the consequence is that the pamphlet has grown to nearly five times its contemplated size.

While very many have aided in the collection of material, I am under special obligation to Charles C. Whittier, Esq., 40 Dartmouth Street, Boston, and to Col. Hiram A. Oakman of North Marshfield, for results of examination of public and family records; and to Miss Minnie K. Bachelder, of the Probate Office, at Plymouth, for skillful examination of probate records, and accurate reports thereon.

The arrangement may be easily understood. Those of the Rogers name are numbered consecutively in figures; those of other names, by families, with letters; the Roman capitals denote the generation, as does the small figure with the name; when the surname is given, I use the generation figure with that, as in that manner it is more

Preface.

easily read and understood; in giving the line, in parenthesis, the name Rogers, as a surname, is to be supplied, except when small capitals are used, and they denote another surname.

The sign — denotes that the party died without issue; + denotes that the name is carried forward in its regular order; † denotes that the name is carried down on the same page; and = denotes that the party is unmarried; when names are not marked, nothing further in relation to them is given.

J. H. D.

October 1, 1898.

JOHN ROGERS OF MARSHFIELD.

I. JOHN ROGERS¹ *of Marshfield.*

Neither the date or place of his birth, nor the time when he came to this country has been ascertained.

John Rogers, aged thirty-four, came from London to Barbadoes in the Falcon, in April, 1635; and John Rogers, aged eighteen, came to Barbadoes from London in the same vessel, Dec. 19, 1635. 2 Brown's Gen. p. 1131.

These ages suit John of Marshfield and John of Duxbury, but the former must have been married at that date and no mention is made of his wife.

It has been said that John of Marshfield was a relative of Rev. William Witherell and came to this country with him. In 1635, William Witherell of Maidstone, Schoolmaster, Mary, his wife, three children and one servant came in the Hercules; the certificate is dated March 14, 1634/5. Founders of New England, pp 82, 83.

No Rogers is named in the list; it is possible that John Rogers was the "servant," but his wife and child are not accounted for. There was a tradition that the mother of Mr. Witherell was a daughter of John Rogers the Martyr, and the inference has been drawn that the father of John of Marshfield was a brother of Witherell's mother. But the tradition is, at least, doubtful, for the Martyr suffered in 1555 and William Witherell was born in 1600, when the youngest child of the Martyr was over forty-five years old.

Deane says that John Rogers came to Scituate in 1644, but this is erroneous, for the name of John Rogers is given in the 1643 list of freemen of Scituate, although the date of his admission has not been found.

On September 20, 1699, John Rogers[2], the son of John Rogers[1] of Marshfield, gave a deposition before the Justices of the Court at Plymouth, that, in or about the year 1647, his father, John Rogers, lived in Scituate on a lot of land between the land of Thomas Hicks and the land of John Stockbridge, adjoining Hicks's swamp; and about the year 1647, "my father John Rogers aforesaid, being about to move out of said Scituate" (in effect) sold his house and land to Thomas Simons, "and my father removed out of Scituate about the time aforesaid, and I lived with him many years and never heard him lay any claim to said land after he removed from it." Plym. Deeds, Bk. III, p. 144.

This fixes 1647 as about the date of his father's removal into Marshfield, where he continued to reside till his death in the early part of 1661. He was fined (as appears by the town records) for not attending town meeting, Dec. 11, 1649, May 15, 1651, Aug. 23, 1652, Nov. 8, 1652, and Mar. 28, 1653.

The family name of his wife, Frances, has not been discovered, nor the date of their marriage. Their son, John, was born in 1632 or 1633, in all human probability before they left England.

Miss Thomas, in her history of Marshfield, suggests that Frances Rogers was Frances [Vassal] Adams, daughter of William Vassal and widow of James Adams; but Frances Vassal was not married till July 16, 1646, and did not become a widow till Jan. 6, 1651, when Frances Rogers had grown up children.

DAVIS, in his "Landmarks of Plymouth," under John

Rogers of Marshfield, says "by wife Frances, perhaps daughter of Robert Watson," &c.: also, Robert Watson came to Plymouth early, but finally settled in Connecticut; by wife Elizabeth, he had, born in England, George, 1603, Robert, Samuel, and perhaps Frances, who married John Rogers. No authority for this statement has been found; but if Robert Watson had a daughter, Frances, who married a John Rogers, there can be scarcely a doubt that he was John Rogers[1] of Marshfield.

Frances survived her husband, and married Walter Briggs of Scituate. In his will d. Jan'y 16, 1676/7, p. June 4, 1684, Walter Briggs mentions, among others, his wife, Frances. Deeds, Vol. VI, p. 9.

Administration on the estate of Frances Briggs, widow, of Scituate, was granted Oct. 14, 1687, *to her sons*, John and Joseph Rogers. Probate, Vol. I, p. 11.

John Rogers[1] died about May, 1661, and his widow in 1687.

II. Children, part probably born in England, and the others in Scituate:

+   2.   John[2], b. about 1632.
+   3.   Joseph[2],
+   4.   Timothy[2],
+   5.   Ann[2],
+   6.   Mary[2],
+   7.   Abigail[2],

These are given in the order named in the will d. Feb. 1, 1660 (O. S.) p. June 5, 1661, which mentions wife, Frances; children, John Rogers, Jr.: Joseph Rogers; Timothy Rogers; Ann Hudson; Mary Rogers and Abigail Rogers; his grandchildren, Posy Russell and John Russell.

William Witherell acknowledged June 23, 1665, that he sold "to John Rogers, Sen. of Marshfield, now deceased," "ten acres of upland laying at N. W. side of Nemassakeetpit brook." Dux. Rec. p. 12.

William Brett "of Bridgewater, sometime of Duxbury," made oath June 3, 1665, that some years past he sold to "John Rogers of Marshfield, now deceased," all his lands, meadow and upland "lying in Matakesit which was given to me by the town." Dux. Rec. p. 11.

John, Timothy and Joseph Rogers were Freemen in 1684.

2.

III. JOHN ROGERS² (*John¹*) was born about 1632, probably before his father came to this country: he married, October 8, 1656, Rhoda King, daughter of Elder Thomas King of Scituate, born October 11, 1639; she died about 1662, and he married, about 1663, Elizabeth ——: she died September 13, 1692: he married Elizabeth ——: she died May 9, 1705: he died May 7, 1717, in his eighty-fifth year, according to the church record, which date however is not consistent with the date of his will and the probate of it.

Children, born in Marshfield:

By first wife:

+   8.   John³, bap. Aug. 23, 1657.
+   9.   Thomas³, b. Dec. 25, 1659; bap. Mar. 25, 1660.
—   9a.   Rhoda³, bap. Aug. 3, 1662; died young.

By second wife:

+   10.   Abigail³, b. Nov. 3, 1663.
+   11.   Mary³, b. Mar. 10, 1665; bap. April 16, 1665.
+   12.   Johanna³, b. Oct. 7, 1667.
+   13.   Elizabeth³, b. May 19, 1669.

The dates of births are taken from the Friends' records, in which the months are given as first, second, &c., instead of by name. Transcripts have been made in which the names of the months have been given, but erroneously, for January was taken as the first month, instead of March, and so on.

The baptisms are taken from Rev. Mr. Witherell's records, part of which have been preserved.

John² joined the Quakers in 1660, Deane says, but probably a little earlier, for John³ was baptized in 1657, by Mr. Witherell, while Thomas³ born in 1659, and Rhoda³ born in 1661 or 1662, were baptized on the account of their mother, Rhoda, who had evidently continued to adhere to Mr. Witherell's church.   Apparently his second wife, Elizabeth, was also a member of that church, for the record of the baptism of her daughter is " Mary, ye daughter of Elizabeth Rogers."

The Friends' records commence in 1680, but a large number of births, which occurred before that date, were entered; among them all the children of John², except John³ and Rhoda³.

He took the oath of freeman in 1657, and is often mentioned in the public records for nearly sixty years after that date.

On the Friends' records (Scituate) is the following :

" Sufferings of John Rogers of Marshfield.   27 day of 2 mo. 1681, came the constable Joseph Waterman to my house and brought two men with him and brought a warrant with him which he said came from the magistrate John Alden.   The constable could not read it nor any that were with him, it was so blotted : and the constable demanded of me 01-04-02, which he said was rates to the priest, Samuel Niles of Marshfield, the which I could not pay for conscience sake.   Whereupon the constable seized upon a steare of two years old and took him away from me.   John Rogers of Marshfield."

Those records have many similar entries among them, one by John Rogers¹ of Scituate, dated 26 of 3 mo. 1683, in which he says that the constable took away " two platters and two porringers which they prized at 11 shillings."

On May 16, 1659, John Rogers, Jun., was chosen grand juryman by the town.

In 1692, John² was one of the Selectmen of Marshfield and assisted in running the line between that town and "the Two Miles in Scituate."

On June 16, 1692, he was on a jury " to lay out and remove highways " in Marshfield; in their return they describe a way, which ran near the houses of the three brothers :

" And in the new way which said Rogers [John²] lately made and so on over the cove creek by his house and so along by French's tinnament and Henry Perry's house to the upper end of the field before said Perry's door; and then turning southward along by the land of Thomas King and John Silvester's lot and so till it meet the

Scituate way. And also by the cove creek downward as the old way leadeth by the house of Timothy Rogers and up the hill by his house, and so as the new way now lieth near to Joseph Rogers' fence and so on to the line of Elisha Bisbee."

On August 30, 1692, on the request of her husband it was voted by "The Meeting" to hold meetings once a month at the house of Elizabeth Rogers on account of her illness. She died two weeks later.

He and his third wife, Elizabeth, signed, May 11, 1699. the certificate of the marriage of his daughter, Elizabeth, at Friends' meeting, after their manner.

In a deposition given June 16, 1713, John[2] says that he was seventy-nine years old or thereabouts.

In his will d. May 9, 1718, p. June 24. 1718, he describes himself as "aged"; mentions his son, John, to whom he gives the three hundred pounds "which he hath already received of me in money and three score pounds more"; gives legacies to his daughter, Abigail Chamberling; his daughter, Joanna Butler; his grandson, Samuel Dogged; his granddaughter, Mary White, and his granddaughter, Sarah Allyn; the residue he gives to his son, Thomas.

Thomas King, in his will dated in 1691, gives legacies to his two grandsons, John and Thomas Rogers.

Mr. Witherell has, among records of baptisms, "1657 John, ye son[ne] of John Rogers jun. August 23," "Rhoda, ye daughter of Rhoda Rogers, Aug. 30, 1662."

In 1708, the Friends' "Women's Meetings" were held at the houses of John Rogers of Marshfield, Edward Wanton of Scituate, and Robert Barker and Arthur Howland of Duxborough now Pembroke.

3.

III. JOSEPH ROGERS[2] (*John[1]*). It is not known when or where he was born, but either before his father came to this country or in Scituate; he married Abigail Barker, daughter of Robert and Lucy [Williams] Barker of Hingham (according to the history of that town), but certainly of Duxbury at one time; Joseph[2] lived in Duxbury close to the Marshfield line and in that part which became Pembroke; he died in 1716, about June, and she, in 1718, about May.

Children, born in that part of Duxbury which became Pembroke:

+ 14. Joseph³, b.
+ 15. John³, b.
+ 16. Timothy³, b.
— 17. Thomas³: apparently died without issue.
— 18. Moses³: died unmarried.
— 19. Lydia³: apparently died unmarried.
+ 20. Rebecca³, b.
+ 21. Abigail³, b.
— 22. Francis³: apparently died without issue.

Marshfield, on July 4, 1670, gave to Joseph Rogers, Sen., of Duxbury, its interest in a certain parcel of land (four or five acres) at Mattachesitt. Town Rec. p. 124.

The will of Joseph Rogers of Pembroke, d. Apr. 10, 1716, and p. July 16, 1716, describes him as "aged"; gives to Joseph, his oldest son, his meadow in Marshfield; to his wife, Abigail, land at a place called the cove in Marshfield, his home farm, (except a small lot given to his son, John Rogers), his stock, &c., and other real estate; gives a lot to his son, Thomas, and ten acres to his son, Timothy, lying near that which he already has; to his daughters, Lydiah and Rebecca, twenty pounds apiece; to the children of his daughter, Abigail Parrice, deceased, fifty shillings each; and to his grandson, commonly called Joseph Staples, five pounds. He left the care of his son, Francis, to his wife, and after her death to be maintained by the children to whom his wife should leave the real estate.

He left the bulk of his estate to his wife to be disposed of to his children as she should deem most convenient, but it was his will that if his two sons, John and Thomas "do behave themselves kind and obligeing to their mother during her life, that after her decease all my said housing and lands, meadow and swamp, lying in Pembroke aforesaid shall be left to them." He appointed his wife executrix with his trusty and well-beloved brothers, John Rogers, Francis Barker and Robert Barker, overseers.

Abigail Rogers of Pembroke, "widow and relick" of Joseph Rogers late of said Pembroke, deceased, in her will d. April 19, 1718,

p. June 20, 1718, gives all her lands, &c., in Pembroke, to her son, John Rogers; thirty pounds and her best bed and its furnishings to her daughter, Lydia Rogers; one horse and heifer, to her grandson, commonly called Joseph Staples; one heifer, to her granddaughter, Mercy Parris, to be paid when she becomes of age; and the remainder of her movable estate to be equally divided between her sons, Joseph Rogers, Timothy Rogers, her daughters, Rebecca Andrews and Lydia Rogers, and the children of her daughter, Abigail Parris, deceased. She made John Rogers, executor.

Moses[3] died in 1707, in his father's lifetime. Being about to join the troops at Port Royal in the French and Indian War, he undertook to make a will which is described to be "most peculiarly worded, badly written and awkwardly executed." In a protest against its being probated it is called "a scrool." It is dated April 12, 1707; the witnesses were examined in relation to it September 1, 1707, and October 24, 1707; one was his brother, Timothy, one his sister, Lydia, and the other, James Hunter, understood to be an Indian. He gave legacies to his father, Joseph Rogers, his brother, Joseph Rogers, and to his mother, not naming her. A protest was filed against its allowance by Thomas Parris of Duxbury, and Abigail, his wife, sister of said Moses. The will was recorded, but there is no record showing that it was admitted to probate.

Joseph Rogers of Duxbury conveyed, Jan'y 27, 1706/7, to his son, Moses Rogers of Marshfield, about six acres of land in Marshfield, being same land owned by John Rogers of Marshfield deceased and lying between land of John Rogers deceased, and Samuel Niles and Timothy Rogers and "next to land I sold my son, Joseph Rogers." Deeds B. VII, p. 159.

Francis[3] was evidently laboring under some disability and as neither he nor Thomas, nor any child of either, is named in their mother's will it is quite certain that both died, without issue, between the dates of their father's and their mother's wills.

Robert Barker, whose children were Francis, Isaac, Robert, Rebecca and Abigail, in his will d. Feb'y 18, 1689, mentions his daughter, Abigail Rogers.

We have ascertained nothing in relation to the parentage or history of Joseph Staples.

Joseph and Abigail Rogers conveyed, May 3, 1677, to John Rogers, Sen. of Marshfield, meadow land at Jones's river. Deeds B. I, p. 220.

Joseph Rogers of Duxborough conveyed Sept. 5, 1699, to John Rogers Jr. of Marshfield, twenty acres of land in M. bounded East by the common land, west by land of said Joseph Rogers, south by land of said John Rogers that he had of his father, Timothy Rogers. B. IV, p. 51.

Joseph Rogers of Duxbury conveyed, Jan'y 24, 1706/7, to his son, Timothy Rogers of D., thirty acres of land in D. part of what he bought of James Ford of Marshfield, June 29, 1705, bounded on Hobbamock and Little Ponds; deed witnessed by Rebecca Rogers, his daughter, and Thomas Parris, his son-in-law. B. VIII, p. 87.

Deeds Joseph Rogers of Mattapoisett in Duxbury to Michael Ford, June 19, 1705: Joseph Rogers of Duxbury to John Rogers of Marshfield, Jan'y 15, 1711: and Joseph Rogers of Pembroke to Abram Booth, April 16, 1712. B. IX, pp. 231, 158. 371.

Joseph Rogers[2] and his son, Timothy[3] lived in that part of Duxbury which became part of Pembroke, while his sons, Joseph[3] and John[3] lived in that part of Marshfield which became part of Pembroke, incorporated in 1712.

4.

III. TIMOTHY ROGERS[2], (*John[1]*) was probably born in Scituate; he married Eunice Stetson, daughter of "Cornet" Robert Stetson, born April 23, 1650; he died in 1728, having survived his wife.

Children, born in Marshfield:

+ 23. Timothy[3], b. in 1690, according to age on gravestone.
+ 24. Samuel[3], bap. Sept. 15 [or 18], 1670.
+ 25. John[3],
− 26. Bethiah[3]; probably died unmarried.
+ 27. Honour[3],
+ 28. Eunice[3], bap. Oct. 2, 1677.
+ 29. Mary[3],
+ 30. Hannah[3],

These are the children named in the will, given in the order first therein named. In another part of his will he names his daughters in the following order, probably the order of their births, viz: Eunice, Bethiah, Hannah, Mary and Honour. The baptisms are taken from Rev. Mr. Witherell's records, which show there were two other children :

— 30a. ——¹, a daughter, bap. Aug. 27, 1671 ; d. young.
— 30b. Timothy³, bap. May 31, 1674 ; d. young.

The name of this daughter cannot be deciphered ; it is a name of apparently three or four letters ; at the time it was written Mr. W. was a paralytic.

Cornet Robert Stetson in his will d. Sept. 4, 1702, p. Mar. 5, 1702/3, mentions his daughter, Eunice Rogers, then living.

Timothy Rogers² was admitted a townsman of Marshfield Feb'y 14, 1664/5 ; witnessed a Friend's marriage certificate in 1678 ; was freed from bearing arms on account of lameness in 1681 ; administered upon the estate of Nathaniel Parker in 1690 ; is mentioned in the laying out of a road (apparently near Rogers Brook) in 1692 ; and on March 29, 1699, gave to his son, John Rogers³ of Marshfield, "Land in Marshfield where I now dwell, about 40 acres, bounded by land of my brother, Joseph Rogers," &c. B. IV, p. 50.

Apparently the line between his land and that of his brother, Joseph, was the line between Marshfield and Duxbury.

The will of Timothy Rogers of Marshfield, "Taylor," d. Mar. 24, 1724/5, p. Aug. 5, 1728, mentions sons, Samuel and John ; daughter, Bethiah Rogers, then unmarried and living with him ; and daughters, Hannah Torrey, Eunice Witherel, Mary Carver, and Hannah Lapham ; granddaughter, Judith Rogers, wife of Joseph Rogers ; son-in-law, William Torrey ; and son, Timothy, to whom he gives the bulk of his property, and whom he makes executor of his will.

5.

III. ANN ROGERS² (*John¹*) was probably born in Scituate; she married (1) George Russell, probably son of George Russell; he died before 1659; she married (2) John Hudson, who died about 1688, leaving her surviving him.

Children, born in Marshfield:

By first husband :

    i. George Russell³.
    ii. John Russell³ ; apparently died young.

By second husband :

    iii. Hannah Hudson³, m. Japhet Turner.
    iv.   Rhoda Hudson³, m. —— Palmer.
    v.   Elizabeth Hudson³, m. —— Vickery (Vicory).
    vi.   Abigail Hudson³, m. —— Stetson.

"Posy" and John Russell are mentioned in the will of their grandfather, John Rogers¹.

In an agreement dated July 2, 1673, between John and Ann Hudson, on the one part, and George Russell (the "Posy" of the will)
on the other part, it is recited that Ann had been the "former wife
of George Russell deceased," and George was their eldest son.

John and Ann Hudson, Feb'y 4, 1674, gave to John Rogers a
receipt for the legacies to Ann given to her in the will of her father,
John Rogers, late of Marshfield, deceased ; the receipt is witnessed
by Joseph Rogers and George Russell.

John Hudson's will (Nov. 20, 1683) gives all his property to his
wife, Ann Hudson.

6.

III. MARY ROGERS² (*John¹*). *married Nathaniel Fox 3 m. d 25 t*

Miss Thomas, in her "Memorials of Marshfield," gives
a brief account of John Rouse. She says that John
Rouse, Jr., born in 1643, married Mary Rogers in 1656
and died in 1711; there are errors in some of these
dates, probably clerical; the inscription on his tomb
gives the date of his death as 1717, and his age makes
1643 the date of his birth; he was therefore only thir-
teen in 1656, and that date is erroneous, probably
intended for 1666. So far as I can discover, John
Rouse, Jr., was son of the John Rouse who was a servant
of Gov. Prence, and after completing his term of service
with the one to whom he was transferred with the con-
sent of all interested, married Anna Pabodie, received
grants of land, and is easily traced in the records till his
death in 1684.

The History of Duxbury says that a John Rouse married Mary Rogers in 1659, but this date certainly seems to be erroneous, or the name was "Rane," not "Rouse."

Miss Thomas undoubtedly had authority for her statement that John Rouse, Jr., married Mary Rogers. If so, the Mary Rogers must have been this daughter of John[1]; she was single in 1660; and upon the authority of Miss Thomas, I conclude that she married John Rouse, Jr., in 1666; that she died soon after without issue; and that he married, January 13, 1674/5, Elizabeth Doty, and died October 3, 1717, leaving no issue, his only son having died in 1704.

7.

III. ABIGAIL ROGERS[2] (*John[1]*) was born in Scituate about 1645; she married, January 1, 1678/9, Timothy White, son of Edwin and Elizabeth [Ward] White; he died in 1704, leaving her surviving:

Children, born in Scituate:

    i. Timothy White[3], b. in 1679.
    ii. Abigail White[3], b. in 1682.
    iii. Sarah White[3], b. in 1685; married Joseph Tilden.
    iv. Elizabeth White[3], b. in 1688; m. James Cudworth.

His will d. May 16, 1704, p. Sept. 22, 1704, mentions wife, Abigail; children, Timothy, Abigail White, Sarah White and Elizabeth White; son Timothy, Exr.

He gives to his daughters, land at Drinkwater, "formerly the land of Cornett Robert Stetson, but now in my possession."

8.

IV. JOHN ROGERS[3] (*John[2], John[1]*) was born in Marshfield in 1657, [baptized Aug. 23, 1657]; he was twice married, but neither the name of his first wife nor the date of their marriage, nor the surname of his second wife, is known; the Scituate record of his family says, "John Rogers and Hannah his wife were married September 14, 1701"; he died between March 1 and July 18, 1738, leaving her surviving.

Children, born in Scituate:

By first wife :

+ 31. John⁴, b. Mar. 14, 1682/3.
+ 32. Alice⁴, b. Mar. 26, 1685.
− 33. Daniel⁴, b. Mar. 31, 1688 ; d. young.
  34. Elizabeth⁴, b. Oct. —, 1691.
  35. Thomas⁴, b. Aug. 15, 1695.

By second wife :

  36. Hannah⁴, b. May 26, 1704.
+ 37. Joshua⁴, b. April 22, 1708.
  38. Mary⁴, b. April 15, 1712.
+ 39. Caleb⁴, b. April 14, 1718.

His will d. Mar. 1, 1737/8, p. July 18, 1738, describes himself as of Scituate, a shipwright, "aged and under infirmity of body" ; directs that his wife shall be supported out of his estate by his executor ; gives his son, John, ten shillings, "having given him considerable formerly" ; to his grandchildren, the children of his daughter, "Else," [Alice] who married Thomas Clark, "twenty pounds in bills of credit of ye old Tenor, or silver equivalent thereto, one ounce of silver being reconed equal to twenty-seven shillings of said bills" ; and legacies to his daughter, Hannah Thrift; to the children of his daughter, Elizabeth deceased; to the son of his son, Thomas, deceased; to his daughter, Mary Staples ; to his son, Caleb Rogers ; and to his son, Joshua Rogers, whom he appoints executor and to whom he gives "the farm and land where I now dwell in Scituate" and all his other property, but charging upon it the support of his wife "his [Joshua's] mother" and the payment of the legacies, except Caleb's, which was real estate.

John Rogers of Scituate, shipwright, acknowledges "to have received of Thomas Rogers of Marshfield, Executor of the last will and testament of my then father, John Rogers late of Marshfield, aforesaid, the full and just sum of three hundred pounds in money in

full for ye legacy given me in ye last will and testament of the said
John Rogers." Signed John Rogers, Jr., and acknowledged at
Plymouth, Dec. 23, 1728, before Jona. Cushing, Justice of the Peace.

Elizabeth[4], as appears by the will of her father, married and had
children, but the name of her husband has not been found.

Thomas[4] also married, had one son and died before March 1, 1737,
the date of his father's will.

Hannah[4]. I have had doubts in relation to the name " Hannah
Thrift " in the record of the will, for on Nov. 7, 1726, William *Swift*
of Portsmouth and Hannah Rogers of Scituate lay their intentions of
marriage before " the meeting " and a committee was appointed to
"inquire into their character in this respect." But perhaps the
report was unfavorable, for nothing further is found on the Friends'
records. Moreover there was a William Thrift in Scituate, who had
a daughter, Hannah, (probably named for her mother) born in 1732,
who married John Gaynes of Boston, in 1759, and a daughter, Mary,
who married Jabez Stanley in 1760. The will of Joanna Butler also
has the name of Hannah Thrift.

Mary[4] married Joshua Staples, Oct. 21, 1731.

9.

IV. THOMAS ROGERS[3] (*John*[2], *John*[1]) was born in
Marshfield, December 25, 1659, according to the
Friends' records, but December 2, 1659, according to
the town records; he married, June 6, 1712, Bethiah
Ewell, daughter of Gershom and Mary Ewell, born
March 3, 1682/3; he died March 6, 1745/6, and she,
January 23, 1756.

Children, born in Marshfield.

+   40.   Rhoda[4], b. May 28, 1713.
+   41.   John[4], b. Dec. 19, 1714.
+   42.   Thomas[4], b. Oct. 28, 1716.
+   43.   Bethiah[4], b. Sept. 29, 1718.

They were married in Friends' Meeting after the manner of that
sect; but according to the town records they were also married on
the same day by Joseph Otis.

The will of Gershom Ewell, p. March 19, 1717/18, mentions his daughter, Bethiah Rogers.

Will of Thomas Rogers of Marshfield, d. Sept. 10, 1745, p. Mar. 12, 1745/6, mentions wife, Bethiah; children, Rhoda Wing, Bethiah Wadee and John and Thomas who were Ex'ors. Vol. X, p. 139.

Will of Bethiah Rogers, relict of Thomas Rogers of Marshfield, d. June 10, 1755, p. May 4, 1756, mentions sons, Thomas and John; daughters, Rhoda Wing and Bethiah Wady; granddaughter, Rhoda Wing; and son-in-law, Benjamin Wing, Ex'or. Bristol Co. Vol. XV, p. 28.

Gershom Ewell, born Nov. 14, 1650, was the son of Henry Ewell, who married, Nov. 22, 1638, Sarah, the daughter of Anthony and Sarah Annable. Henry came over in the Hercules in 1635, with Rev. William Witherell; he was a soldier in the Pequod war in 1637.

10.

IV. ABIGAIL ROGERS[3] (*John[2]*, *John[1]*) was born in Marshfield, November 3, 1663; she married, September 9, 1681, Nathaniel Chamberlain, probably son of Henry, born in Hull, September 4, 1659; he died in Pembroke in 1716, leaving her surviving.

Children, born in Marshfield:

    i.   Elizabeth Chamberlain[4], b. June 18, 1682.
    ii. Nathaniel Chamberlain[4], b. Aug. 10 [13], 1683.
    iii. John Chamberlain[4], b. Dec. 26, 1684.
    iv. Mary Chamberlain[4], b. Feb'y 5, 1685/6.
    v.   Johanna Chamberlain[4], b. Jan'y 17, 1686/7.
    vi. Abigail Chamberlain[4], b. Feb'y 28, 1687/8.
— vii. Sarah Chamberlain[4], b. Ap'l 8, 1689; d. Sept. 2, 1689.
    viii. Patience Chamberlain[4], b. Ap'l 28, 1690.

These are taken from the Scituate Friends' records; at a meeting August 31, 1690, the record states, that Nathaniel Chamberlain "being about to remove to Hull," &c.; he did remove there and we find on the Hull records the names of the foregoing children, and of four others, born in Hull, as follows:

    ix. Bathsheba Chamberlain[4], b June 28, 1692.
    x.   Experience Chamberlain[4], b, June 28, 1692.

xi. Ruth Chamberlain[4], b. Dec. 1, 1693.

xii. Thomas Chamberlain[4], b. May 21, 1695.

About 1695 he removed to Scituate and had other children, born there as follows:

xiii. Freedom Chamberlain[4], b. in 1697.

xiv. Eunice Chamberlain[4], b. in 1698.

xv. Joseph Chamberlain[4], b. in 1699.

It also appears from the Probate Records, that there was another son,

xvi. Benjamin Chamberlain[4], probably born in 1700, but possibly in 1696.

In 1712, when Pembroke was incorporated, Nathaniel Chamberlain was one of the " Heads of Families."

Edward Wanton, by his will dated in 1716, gave his wearing apparel to Nathaniel Chamberlain of Pembroke, and to his two daughters, Abigail and Joanna, five pounds each.

Joanna Butler, in her will (1745), gave legacies to her "cousins," Elizabeth and Patience Chamberlain.

Nathaniel[4] was appointed Adm'r in 1716, and dower was set off to the widow, Abigail, in 1721; the rest of the property was assigned to Benjamin[4], "son of the deceased," who gave bond, with Thomas Parris, as surety, to pay at the death of Abigail, the widow, certain sums to the others, or a part of them, among whom were Joseph, Eunice and Patience, "children of Nathaniel Chamberlain of Pembroke, and to the son of Ruth Fletcher, deceased, grandson to said Nathaniel."

March 6, 1723/4, Benjamin Chamberlain[4] made a nuncupative will, not probated, in which he provided that his mother and Eunice, Patience and Joseph should have a living out of his estate, "as long as they live or as long as the property holds out," and as his "cosen," Naomi, had been sick a great while, he gave her ten pounds "to pay ye Doctor"; he also gave to his sisters Abigail, and Joanna, twelve pounds each.

11.

IV. MARY ROGERS[3] (*John*,[2] *John*[1]) was born in Marshfield, March 10, 1665; she married, January 24, 1682, Samuel Doggett [Daggett], son of Thomas; she died April 15, 1690; he married (2) Bathsheba Holmes, January 21, 1691/2.

Children of Mary, born in Marshfield:

i. Samuel Doggett[4], b. Dec. 21, 1683.
ii. Mary Doggett[4], b. April 26, 1687.
iii. Sarah Doggett[4], b. April 7, 1689.

These are the grandchildren of John[2], named in his will as Samuel Dogged, Mary White and Sarah Allyn.

Samuel[4] receipted for his legacy in 1721; he married, Feb'y 2, 1710, Bethiah Waterman, daughter of Joseph and Sarah [Snow] Waterman of Marshfield, born Aug. 20, 1687. 4 Maine Hist. and Gen. Rec., p. 127.

Mary Doggett[4] married Eleazer White and they had, born in Marshfield:

i. Nehemiah White[5], b. Jan'y 14, 1712/3.
ii. Peregrine White[5], b. Sept. 8, 1715.
iii. Eleazer White[5], b. Mar. 8, 1716/7.
iv. Elkanah White[5], b. Dec. 10, 1719.
v. Mary White[5], b. Mar. 23, 1720/21.
vi. Benaiah White[5], b. Sept. 19, 1724.
vii. Penelope White[5], b. June 13, 1727.
viii. Thomas White[5], b. June 29, 1729.
ix. Rebecca White[5], b. Aug. 18, 1731.

12.

IV. JOHANNA ROGERS[3] (*John*[2], *John*[1]) was born in Marshfield, October 7, 1667; she married Judah Butler, son of Daniel and Hannah [Howes] Butler of Falmouth; he died before 1712, and she in 1747.

Child, born probably in Marshfield:

— i. Judah Butler[4], b. in 1702; d. Nov. 10, 1720, in his nineteenth year.

In the old Wanton and Rogers burying-ground in old Scituate, there are (or were recently) one gravestone and a fragment of another still standing; the latter has upon it part of the inscription giving

the year of death and the age the same as that of Judah Butler;
other portions of the inscription agree, so that there is no reasonable
doubt that this fragment marks Judah's grave.

Will of Daniel Butler, Sr., of Falmouth, d. Sept. 10, 1712, p. Jan'y
10, 1717/8 (Barns. Prob. Vol. III, p. 433) gives Judah Butler, only
son of Judah Butler, deceased, land and buildings in Falmouth.

In Plym. Co. records (Vol. XXXIV, p. 87) is a memo. of a suit by
a Marshfield man, against Judah Butler of Falmouth, sailor, in 1698;
the officer's return (Sept. 16, 1699) is "*non est inventus.*"

Joanna Butler in her will, d. Dec. 6, 1745, p. Jan'y 16, 1748/9,
describes herself as of Marshfield, and gives her property to her
"cousins," in which term she includes nephews and nieces. She
mentions (omitting the word "cousin") John Rogers of Hanover
[nephew]; Hannah Thrift, "the daughter of my brother John Rogers,
deceased"; Elizabeth Chamberlain, to whom she gives an annuity for
life and various articles among which is "a silver spoon which used
to be called the boy's spoon"; Mary White and Sarah Allen (children of Samuel and Mary [Rogers] Doggett); Patience Chamberlain; Joanna, daughter of Joseph Rogers of Marshfield; Susanna
Rogers, daughter of Joseph Rogers; Elizabeth Stetson, daughter of
Samuel Stetson of Scituate; "the said Joseph Rogers"; Moses
Rogers, son of Joseph; Jemima Torrey and Kezia Torrey of Scituate
[not identified]; Rhoda Wing, "daughter of my cousin, Rhoda
Wing"; Samuel Russell [son of George Russell who was son of Ann
Rogers[2]]; Bethiah Wady; "Sarah Rogers, wife of John Rogers, son
of my brother, Thomas Rogers"; sons of Rhoda Wing; and gives to
"cousin John Rogers, son of Brother Thomas" all the residue; and
makes him executor. Among the witnesses are Caleb and Mary Torrey.

Abigail Hudson[1], the aunt of Joanna Butler, married a Stetson,
and Elizabeth Stetson was probably her granddaughter; but Barry's
"Stetson Family" gives no such marriage, and no Samuel with a
daughter Elizabeth, who could have been this Elizabeth.

13.

IV. ELIZABETH ROGERS[3] (*John*[2], *John*[1]) was born in
Marshfield, December 19, 1669; she married, May 11,
1699, as his second wife, Hugh Copperthwaite, who
came from England and settled in Flushing, L. I., where

he lived fifty-six years and was a Friends' minister nearly forty years; he died, May 20, 1730, at the age of eighty-two years; his first wife, Elizabeth, died November 25, 1697; his second wife, Elizabeth Rogers[3], died, August 27, 1707; we have found no record of any children.

14.

IV. JOSEPH ROGERS[3] (*Joseph[2], John[1]*) was born in that part of Duxbury which became Pembroke; he married Judith ——, his cousin once removed, daughter of —— Rogers and granddaughter of Timothy Rogers[2]; he died in 1760, leaving her surviving.

Children, born in Marshfield:

    44. Moses[4], b.
    45. Susanna[4], b.
    46. Joanna[4], b.

Judith Rogers, wife of Joseph Rogers, was baptized, Oct. 15, 1727.

Amos Rogers was appointed administrator of his estate, Oct. 18, 1760; the sureties on his bond were Thomas Rogers and Moses Rogers, and one of the appraisers was Timothy Rogers.

His real estate was divided in 1761, among Moses, his only son; the children of Joanna Patrick, deceased, "who was a daughter of said Joseph Rogers"; and Susannah Rogers, only surviving daughter of the deceased; reserving to the widow Judith her dower; payments were made by the administrator to Seth Bryant, guardian of the Patrick children.

In 1745, Joanna Butler left legacies to Joseph Rogers[3], his son Moses[4], and his daughters, Susanna[4] and Joanna[4].

Joseph Rogers[3] of Marshfield conveyed to his uncle, John Rogers[2] of M., Jan'y 27, 1706/7, thirty acres of land which he had purchased of his father Joseph Rogers[2], Jan'y 23, 1706/7; Joanna Butler was a witness to the deed. B. VII, p. 158.

Moses[4]. No mention of him has as yet been found in the town or church records.

Susanna[4]. The only reference to her (save in the Probate record given above) is the following from the record of the Second Church:

"Susanna, daughter of Joseph Rogers and her son, Lemuel, were baptized Sept. 18, 1757."

Joanna[4] married, May 2. 1742, Derby Fitz Patrick; he died before June 16, 1754, as on that day "the widow, Joanna Patrick, and her children" were baptized; she had died before 1761.

Children, born in Marshfield:

    i.   John Patrick[5],   bap. June 16, 1754.
    ii. Lydia Patrick[5],   " " " "
    iii. Eliner Patrick[5],   " " " "
    iv. Edmund Patrick[5], " " " "

15.

IV. JOHN ROGERS[3] (*Joseph,*[2] *John*[1]) was born in that part of Duxbury which became Pembroke: he married, March 6, 1722/3, Leah Lincoln, daughter of Daniel and Sarah [Nichols] Lincoln, of Hingham, born December 9, 1695: she died (at the house of her uncle, Moses Lincoln, of Hingham) March 11, 1728/9: he married, widow Sarah [Wing] Turner, daughter of Elisha and Mehetable [Butler] Wing, of Wareham, born May 4, 1708: she had died before 1752, and apparently he had also.

Children, born in Pembroke:

By first wife:

  —   47.   Leah[4], b. April 27, 1724; d. June 9, 1736.
       48.   Abigail[4], b. Oct. 4, 1725.
       49.   Daniel[4], b. Oct. 2, 1727.

By second wife:

  +   49a. Elizabeth[4], [Betty] b. Feb'y [Ap'l] 5, 1731.
  —   49b. Daughter[4]; probably died young.

We have not traced Abigail[4], nor Daniel[4].

Philip Turner ("son of Sarah Rogers, the wife of John Rogers, of Marshfield, and grandson to Elisha Wing") and Rebecca Jenney, daughter to Nathan Jenney and Priscilla, his wife, were married "7 mo. 7th, 1750" Sandwich Fr. Rec.

Elisha Wing, of Wareham, in his will, (1752) mentioned "Philip Turner, the son of my daughter, Sarah," "and the two children my daughter, Sarah, left by her husband, John Rogers," giving them one-third of his household stuff.

And Elizabeth Wing, daughter of Elisha, in her will (1756) gave a legacy to Philip Turner, son of her sister, Sarah Rogers, and also, to "Betty Hoxie, wife of Silas Hoxie, and daughter to my said sister, Sarah Rogers." Vol. XIV, p. 199, 326.

16.

IV. TIMOTHY ROGERS[3] (*Joseph,*[2] *John*[1]) was born in that part of Duxbury which became Pembroke; he married, April 6, 1710, Sarah, the daughter of Josiah and Hannah [Dingley] Keen; she died and he married, January 31, 1732/3, Damaris Macomber, of Taunton.

Child, born in Pembroke:

    50. Abigail[4], b. Sept. 8, 1712.

The fullest investigation of the history of this family gives very unsatisfactory results.

His first wife had been previously married, but to whom has not been ascertained. The Pembroke record has an entry, made after her second marriage, "Jeannette, second daughter of Sarah Rogers, and daughter-in-law of Timothy Rogers, born in Pembroke, Oct. 9, 1708."

It appears by a deed (B. LXXVI, p. 247), that he had moved to Middleboro before 1717, but the record of that town gives nothing more than the second marriage.

Josiah Keen, of Duxbury, in his will, d. May 28, 1695, p. Sept. 15, 1710, mentions sons, Josiah, John, Ephraim and Matthew, and four daughters, names not given.

Josiah Keen, Sr., John Keen, Matthew Keen, Ephraim Keen, Isaac Oldham, and Hannah, his wife, John Bishop, and Elizabeth, his wife, of Pembroke, Hudson Bishop, and Abigail, his wife, of Scituate, and Timothy Rogers, and Sarah, his wife, of Middleboro, by deed, dated October 30, 1717, sell to Israel Thomas, land in Duxbury, laid out in 1713.

20.

IV. Rebecca Rogers[3] (*Joseph[2] John[1]*) born in that part of Duxbury which became Pembroke, is mentioned in her mother's will as Rebecca Andrews; we do not find her mentioned in any of the Andrews Genealogies, and we have not traced her.

21.

IV. Abigail Rogers[3] (*Joseph[2], John[1]*) was born in that part of Duxbury which became Pembroke: she married, as his second wife, Thomas Parris (son of John, of London), who came to Long Island in 1683, married and moved to Boston, where his wife died, leaving one daughter, an older one having died in infancy: he came to Duxbury, now Pembroke, in 1697, where he spent the rest of his life; he died in 1752: whether his wife survived him or not, has not been ascertained.

Children, by second wife, born in (now) Pembroke:

    i. Samuel Parris[4], d. 1730 : had one son, who died young.
   ii. John Parris[4]: settled in Middleboro.
  iii. Thomas Parris[4], b. May 8, 1701.
— iv. Mercy Parris[4], probably d. young.
   v. Elizabeth Parris[4], m. Eleazer Bonney.
  vi. Anne Parris[4], m. Edward May.
 vii. Moses Parris, settled in Middleboro.

Hon. Albion Keith Parris, Governor of Maine, U. S. Senator, and Judge of the Supreme Court of Maine, descended from this family. He gave a genealogical account of it in 1836, an abstract of which is given (but containing some errors), in the History of Danby, Vt., pp. 222, *et seq.*: that abstract gives the foregoing (except Mercy), as the children "raised" by Thomas. Willis, evidently upon the authority of the same account, says that he had four sons and three daughters by his second wife.

An account of a part of the children of Thomas may be found in the History of Bridgewater, p. 264: see also History of Danby, Vt., pp. 218, *et seq.*

Virgil D. Parris, M. C., of Maine, also descended from this family. See History of Paris, Maine, p. 687.

23.

IV.   TIMOTHY ROGERS[3] (*Timothy[2], John[1]*) was born in Marshfield, about 1690: he married, February 9, 1719/20, Lydia Hatch, daughter of Israel and Elizabeth [Hatch] Hatch, born October 16, 1699: he died December 10, 1763, and she, November 5, 1766.

Children, born in Marshfield:

- \+   51.   Timothy[4], b. in 1720.
- \+   52.   Israel[4], b. Nov. 22, 1722.
- \+   53.   Peleg[4], b. Nov. 26, 1725.
- \+   54.   Lydia[4], b.
- \+   55.   Amos[4], b. about 1728.
- \+   56.   Zaccheus[4], b. July —, 1731: perhaps in 1730.
- \+   57.   Adam[4], b. Feb'y 4, 1732/3.
- \+   58.   Elizabeth[4], b.
- \+   59.   Jane[4], b.
- \+   60.   Eunice[4], b.

These names are not arranged in the order of births: the dates of births given are taken from records in possession of descendants: when only the year is given, that is found from the age given at date of death: if these were all correct, we ought to be able to arrange the order with comparative accuracy: but Lydia was married in 1743, and Elizabeth is mentioned in a will dated Jan'y 3, 1733/4, so they must come nearer the head of the list.

Will d. July 6, 1763, p. Dec. 27, 1763, mentions wife, Lydia, and children, Timothy, Adam, Amos, Israel, Peleg, Zaccheus, Lydia Lewis, Elizabeth Toleman, Jane Oldham and Eunice Ford.   Vol. XVI, p. 543.

Will of Israel Hatch, d. Jan'y 3, 1733/4, p. Nov. 8, 1740, mentions daughter, Lydia, wife of Timothy Rogers, and two granddaughters, Lydia, and Elizabeth Rogers. Vol. VIII, p. 248.

This is the family whose united ages were said, in a letter published in a Bangor (Maine) paper sixty years ago, to have been 988
years — an average of nearly ninety-nine years each; and the statement has been, from time to time, repeated in the newspapers down
to within a year: but the records show that the ages of five of them
are overstated, in the aggregate, fifty-three years, and the ages of the
other five have not been ascertained.

24.

IV. SAMUEL ROGERS[3] (*Timothy,[2] John[1]*) was born in
Marshfield about 1670: he married, December 3, 1697,
Jael Huet, daughter of Ephriam and Elizabeth [Foster]
Huet, born March 15, 1673/4: she was admitted to the
church, October 6, 1706: he died in 1747, having sur-
vived her.

Children, born in Marshfield:

+   61. Ruth[4], bap. in 1699.
+   62. Elizabeth[4], bap. in 1701.
+   63. Samuel[4], bap. June 23, 1706.
+   64. Mary[4], bap. June 23, 1706.
+   65. Jael[4], bap. Aug. 8, 1708.
+   66. Susanna[4], bap. Oct. 8, 1710.
+   67. Ebenezer[4], bap. Oct. 24, 1714.
+   68. Sarah[4], bap. June 16, 1717.

The baptisms are taken from the records of the Rev. Nath. Eels,
which are prefaced with the following entry:

"When the Rev[d]. Mr. Lawson forsook this church, he left no catalogue of them that were baptised by him; neither is there any to be
found of those that have been baptised since the death of Rev. Mr.
Mighil; therefore, I thought fit soon after my ordination, to desire
those that have been, and have had their children, baptised since
that time to give in their names to me, and according to my request
many have done; whom, I have here recorded."

The first two children were baptised before his day, and the others
by him.

Will d. July 16, 1747, p. Oct. 31, 1747, mentions children, Samuel,
Ebenezer, Mary Truant, Elizabeth Turell, Jael Harney, Ruth
Porter, Sarah Holmes, and Susanna Rogers.   Vol. X, p. 518.

25.

IV.   John Rogers[3] (*Timothy[2], John[1]*) born in Marshfield, married, December 11, 1700, Hannah Sprague,
daughter of Samuel and Sarah Sprague: she died, and
he married (2) Sarah ——: he died in 1762, leaving her
surviving.

Children, born in Marshfield:

+   69.   Hannah[4], b. Feb'y 9, 1701/2.
+   70.   Sarah[4], b. Sept. [Dec.] 26, 1705.
   70a.   Stephen[4], b.

It is probable that there were other children, but no others have
been identified.

He died about 1762, and Thomas Stockbridge was appointed
Adm'r: no real estate: the papers describe him as a tailor and mention
widow and heirs, but no names are given: his estate was insolvent.

An indenture, dated Oct. 16, 1710, shows that Hannah Rogers,
wife of John Rogers[3], of Marshfield, was the daughter of Samuel and
Sarah Sprague, and was then living.

Several deeds from John Rogers, of Marshfield, tailor, between
1710 and 1744 have been found, to none of which is his wife, Hannah, a party: among them is a deed in 1732, to his son, Stephen, of
Marshfield. B. XXVII, p. 180.

In 1744, there is a deed in which he mentions the land of his son,
Stephen, and his wife, Sarah, joins, as she does in deeds after that
date. B. XXXVII, p. 77.

In 1748, he conveyed land to Moses Rogers, but the deed was
not acknowledged, and was proved in Court in 1763, after his death:
Sarah's name is not in this deed. B. XLVII, p. 227.

Stephen[4] has not been traced. The only mention of him that has
been found, other than in his father's deeds, is in a deed in which
his wife, Sarah, joins, from him to his father, "John Rogers, of
Marshfield, Tailor." B. XXXVI, p. 166.

27.

IV.   Honour Rogers[3] (*Timothy,[2] John[1]*) was born in
Marshfield. She married, July 12, 1711, as his second

wife, William Torrey, son of Dea. James and Elizabeth [Rawlins] Torrey, born in 1683: the dates of their deaths have not been ascertained.

· Children, born in Scituate:

     i. Honour Torrey⁴, b. Dec. 18, 1711, m. Joshua Pratt, Feb'y 4, 1741/2.

—   ii. William Torrey⁴, b. Dec. 22, 1713, d. in infancy.

     iii. Hannah Torrey⁴, b. Sept. 25, 1715.

     iv. William Torrey⁴, b. April 17, 1718.

     v. Samuel Torrey⁴, b. June 2, 1720.

     vi. Mercy Torrey⁴, b. Aug. 4, 1722.

     vii. Eunice Torrey⁵, b. March 31, 1725.

These are the children shown by the town records of Scituate: but there were certainly others: Joanna Butler mentioned in her will, (1745),

     viii. Jemima Torrey⁴, and

     ix. Kezia Torrey⁴,

and described them as her "cousins," the children of Honour Rogers *were* her "cousins," and they seem to be the only ones by the name of Torrey who could have come within any meaning of that word.

This family lived in that part of Scituate which, in 1727, became Hanover, and in the church records we find the birth of

     x. "————, child of William and Honour Torrey, b. April 5, 1731."

Among the deaths is also recorded:

"Child of William and Honour Torrey, March 27, 1730/1:" also,

     xi. "Japhet, the son of Honour Torrey, and servant of Mr. Recompense Tiffany," was drowned, March 8, 1736/7.

Also, the deaths of William Torrey, Nov. 22, 1746, and William Torrey, June 10, 1768, are recorded, but there is nothing to identify them.

28.

IV. EUNICE ROGERS[3] (*Timothy*[2], *John*[1]) was born in Marshfield; she married, May 26, 1698, Samuel Wither-ell, son of Samuel, and grandson of Rev. William Witherell, born October 10, 1678.

Children, born in Scituate:

— i. Samuel Witherell[4], b. Jan'y 10, 1699/1700: d. young.
ii. Theophilus Witherell[4], b. March 31, 1703.
iii. Isabel Witherell[4], b. Feb'y 20, 1704/5.
iv. Daniel Witherell[4], b. March 20, 1706/7.
v. Joseph Witherell[4], b. June 5, 1709.
vi. Samuel Witherell[4], b. Jan'y 25, 1710/11.
vii. Eunice Witherell[4], b. June 1, 1713.
viii. Timothy Witherell[4], b. Aug. 10, 1715.
ix. Mary Witherell[4], b. Nov. 29, 1716.
x. Hannah Witherell[4], b. July 19, 1720.

29.

IV. MARY ROGERS[3] (*Timothy*,[2] *John*[1]) born in Marsh-field, married, December 22, 1709, John Carver, son of William and Elizabeth [Foster] Carver, born Decem-ber 1, 1683.

Children, born in Marshfield:

i. Mary Carver[4], b. April 12, 1713.
ii. Caleb Carver[4], b. April 5, 1715.
iii. Jemima Carver[4], b. Dec. 8, 1716.
iv. Daughter[4], b. Aug. 28, 1727.

This list is quite certainly incomplete, but no other data have been obtained.

30.

IV. HANNAH ROGERS[3] (*Timothy*[2], *John*[1]) born in Marshfield, married, November 19, 1701, Samuel Lap-ham, son of Thomas and Mary Lapham, born in 1676;

she died before May 19, 1741, and he married Sarah
——, and died in 1757.

Children, born in Marshfield:

    i. David Lapham⁴, m. Rebecca King⁴ (Elder Thomas¹,)
        Dec. 4, 1727.
    ii. Hannah Lapham⁴, m. William Stetson, Nov. 21, 1723.
    iii. Elizabeth Lapham⁴, b.
    iv. Mercy Lapham⁴, b.
    v. Joshua Lapham⁴, b. Dec. 22, 1710.
    vi. Thankful Lapham⁴, m. Joseph King⁴ (Elder Thomas¹).
    vii. Mary Lapham⁴, b.
    viii. Lydia Lapham⁴, b.

These (except Joshua) are given in the order named in the will,
d. Feb'y 10, 1747/8, p. Mar. 24, 1757, which mentions children,
David, Joshua, Hannah Stetson, Elizabeth Sherman, Marcy Ewell,
Thankful King, Mary Lapham and Lydia Lapham. He gives David
the lot which "I had of my father, Timothy Roggers"; also refers to
the marriage settlement with his "present wife, Sarah Lapham, we
made before marriage, bearing date, May 19, 1741."

31.

V. JOHN ROGERS⁴ (*John³, John², John¹*) was born in
Scituate, March 4, 1682/3; he married, April 13, 1707,
Deborah Hatch, daughter of Jeremiah and Mary
[House] Hatch, born March 24, 1678.

Children, born in Scituate:

  + 71. Daniel⁵, b. Oct. 17: 1708.
  + 72. Elizabeth⁵, b. Jan'y 4, 1709/10.
  + 73. John⁵, b. Feb'y 29, 1711/12.
  + 74. Deborah⁵, b. Feb'y 14, 1713/14.
  + 75. James⁵, bap. Feb'y 19, 1726/7.
  + 76. Jeremiah⁵, bap. Feb'y 19, 1726/7.

Mary Hatch of Scituate, widow of Jeremiah Hatch, in her will d.
Oct. 26, 1714, p. Sept. 22, 1716, mentions (with other children) her
daughter, Deborah Rogers.

32.

V. ALICE ROGERS[4] (*John[3], John[2], John[1]*) was born in Scituate, March 26, 1685; she married, September 14, 1705, Thomas Clark, son of Thomas and Martha [Curtis] Clark; she was baptized, March 6, 1718/19, "at her request, being sick and supposed to be near unto death"; she died not long after, and he married Alice Parker and moved to Rochester in 1731.

Children, by first wife:

    i. John Clark[5], bap. May 3, 1719.
    ii. Mary Clark[5], " " " "
    iii. Joseph Clark[5], " " " "
    iv. Seth Clark[5], " " " "
    v. Martha Clark[5], " " " "
    vi. Caleb Clark[5], " " " "

His second wife was baptized, November 12, 1721, but Ezra, a son of Thomas *and Alice*, had been baptized, Sept. 4, 1720; the records make it a little uncertain whether Ezra was not a son of the first wife.

35.

V. THOMAS ROGERS[4] (*John[3], John[2], John[1]*) was born in Scituate, August 15, 1695; he probably married Deliverance Slocum, daughter of Ebenezer and Mary [Thurston] Slocum, born August 15, 1691; he died before 1737 and probably before 1729, and apparently she had also died before 1729.

Child, born in Scituate:

    76a. Thomas[5], b.

John[3], in his will (1737), mentions his grandson, Thomas Rogers, son of his son, Thomas, deceased.

Mary Slocum, widow of Ebenezer, in her will (1729) mentions her grandson, Thomas Rogers.

37.

V. Joshua Rogers[4] (*John*[3], *John*[2], *John*[1]) was born in Scituate, April 22, 1708; he married, November 26, 1729, Mehitable Chittenden, daughter of Stephen and Mehitable [Buck] Chittenden, born June 8, 1686.

Children, born in Scituate:

+ 77.   Hannah[5], b. June 10, 1730.
+ 78.   Joshua[5], b. Mar. 31, 1737.
− 79.   Thomas[5], b. May 4, 1738; d. in infancy.
− 80.   John[5], b. Feb'y 2, 1740/1; d. in infancy.
+ 81.   Thomas[5], b. July 26, 1745.
+ 82.   John[5], b. April 15, 1748.
− 83.   Elisha[5], b. May 3, 1751; d. in infancy.
+ 84.   Elisha[5], b. Dec. 16, 1752.

39.

V. Caleb Rogers[4] (*John*[3], *John*[2], *John*[1]) was born in Scituate, April 14, 1718; he married [pub. Mar. 28, 1741] Mary Harlow, daughter of Samuel and Mary [Barstow] Harlow, born June 21, 1717; he was baptized in Hanover, May 15, 1743; he died, January 16, 1805, aged 88, and she, February 26, 1812, aged 96.

Children, born in Hanover:

+ 85.   Mary[5], bap. May 15, 1743.
+ 86.   Alice[5], bap. Apr. 7, 1745.
+ 87.   Caleb[5], b. Dec. 16, 1747; bap. May 8, 1748.
− 88.   Son[5], b. —— 1751; d. Ap'l 5, 1751.
+ 89.   Susanna[5], bap. June 7, 1752.

40.

V. Rhoda Rogers[4] (*Thomas*[3], *John*[2], *John*[1]) was born in Marshfield, May 28, 1713; she married, October 19,

1738, Benjamin Wing, son of Matthew and Elizabeth [Mott] [Rickertson] Wing, born April 1, 1698; she died April 21, 1758:

Children, born in Dartmouth:

  i. Thomas Wing⁵, b. April 3, 1740.
  ii. Rhoda Wing⁵, b. Dec. 27, 1741.
  iii. David Wing⁵, b. Mar. 2, 1743.
  iv. Jonathan Wing⁵, b. Nov. 18, 1745.
  v. Prince Wing⁵, b. Sept. 27, 1750.

*Rhoda*⁴ was his second wife; he married (1) Content Tucker, Aug. 18, 1722; and married, a third time, Dec. 6, 1764.

41.

V. JOHN ROGERS⁴ (*Thomas³, John², John¹*) was born in Marshfield, December 19, 1714; he married, December 29, 1737, Sarah Wing, daughter of Ebenezer and Elizabeth [Backhouse] Wing, born March 7, 1709/10; he died September 5, 1791, and she, February 16, 1790.

Children, born in Marshfield:

 + 90. John⁵, b. Dec. 21, 1738.
 + 91. Wing⁵, b. June 14, 1740.
 + 92. Joseph⁵, b. Jan. 26, 1742/3.
 + 93. Elizabeth⁵, b. Aug. 11, 1746.
 + 94. Stephen⁵, b. Feb'y 7, 1748/9.

The permit for the marriage, from the Marshfield meeting, was dated Nov. 30, 1737.

Joanna Butler left a legacy (in 1745) to Sarah Rogers, wife of John, the son of her brother Thomas.

Sarah Wing is said to have been a descendant of Rev. Stephen Bachilor, whose daughter married John Wing and had Stephen Wing, who married (2) Sarah Briggs, daughter of John and Catharine Briggs, Nov. [Mar.?] 7, 1753/4; he died Feb'y 24, 1710, and she, Mar. 26, 1689. They had Ebenezer Wing, born Nov. 5, 1671,

who married, Feb'y 29, 1698/9, Elizabeth Backhouse; he died,
Dec. 24, 1738, and she, April 21, 1757; and they were the parents
of Sarah Wing, who married John Rogers.[4]   C. C. W.

   See also 18 Hist. & Gen. Register, p. 267.

42.

V. THOMAS ROGERS[4] (*Thomas[3], John[2], John[1]*) was
born in Marshfield, October 28, 1716; he married, September 8, 1744, Deborah Otis, daughter of Dr. Isaac
and Deborah [Jacobs] Otis, born October 16, 1723; he
died December 6, 1810, and she, December 8, 1807.
   Children, born in Marshfield:

    95. Bethiah[5], b. Feb'y 9, 1745/6.
+ 96. Hannah[5], b. Oct. 4, 1747.
— 97. Thomas[5], b. Feb'y 15, 1748/9 ; d. Sept. 29, 1752.
— 98. Deborah[5], b. Oct. 20, 1751; d. unm. Mar. 16, 1775.
+ 99. Priscilla[5], b. Feb'y 27, 1754.
+ 100. James[5], b. Ap'l 16, 1756.
— 101. Abigail[5], b. Oct. 10, 1758; d. unm. Nov. 29, 1842.
+ 102. Huldah[5], b. Sept. 30, 1760.
— 103. Rhoda[5], b. Feb'y 23, 1762; d. without issue.
— 104. Lucy[5], b. Mar. 21, 1765; d. without issue.

Bethiah[5] married, June 10, 1777, [pub. May 24, 1777] as his
second wife, Jonathan Slocum, son of Peleg and Rebecca [Williams]
Slocum, born Ap'l 3, 1729; he is credited with one son by his first
wife, but is not credited with any by his second wife; he moved to
"Nine Partners," N. Y., and was living there in 1807.

The publisher has a letter to Priscilla [Rogers] Ellis, written in
1829, by her sister, Abigail[5], from Granville, N. Y., showing that she
and her sister, Lucy, both then unmarried, had just moved there
from Marshfield; the letter also mentions her "sister Slocum" and
her "sister Russell."

43.

V. BETHIAH ROGERS[4] (*Thomas,[3] John,[2] John[1]*) was
born in Marshfield, September 29, 1718: she married,
October 1, 1741, John Wady, son of Humphrey and

Sarah [Wing[2]] Wady, born July 14, 1721. It has been supposed that they lived in Sandwich, but in a deed, dated August 10, 1751 (B. XLII, p. 131) they are described as of Dartmouth, and it is quite certain that they lived in Dartmouth in 1756, at the time of the death of Bethiah's mother, for her will was probated in Bristol County; see *ante* p. 19.

The dates of their deaths and names of their children (if any) have not been ascertained.

On July 15, 1801, more than forty-five years after the probate of the will of Bethiah Rogers, her daughter, Bethiah Wady, then nearly eighty-three years old, receipted to John and Rhoda [Wing] Tucker for $490.00, "being in full satisfaction of all and every part of all the legacy that my mother, Bethiah Rogers, has given me in her last will and testament", and discharged them, as well as the Executors of her mother's will, from all further claims.

This receipt is a curiosity, for it is upon officially stamped paper bearing the impression of two stamps; it was given while the Stamp Act of 1797 was in force: the amount of the stamp was fifty cents.

Rhoda [Wing] Tucker was the daughter of Benjamin Wing and his wife, Rhoda Rogers, who was the sister of Bethiah [Rogers] Wady who signed the above described receipt. Why she waited forty-five years for the payment of her legacy is not explained.

Joanna Butler, in her will (1745), mentions her cousin, Bethiah Wady.

49a.

V. ELIZABETH [BETTY] ROGERS[4] (*John[3], Timothy[2], John[1]*) was born in Pembroke, February [April] 5, 1731; she married, June 20, 1750, Silas Hoxie, son of Solomon and Sarah [Robinson] Hoxie, born, October 10, 1725; he died, April 4, 1765, and she, September 9, 1819.

Children, born in East Sandwich:

— i. Barnabas Hoxie[5], b. Apr. 30, 1751; d. July 16, 1758.
ii. Isaac Hoxie[5], b. July 22, 1754; d. Jan'y 20, 1825.
iii. Sarah Hoxie[5], b. July 2, 1765: d. Sept. 1, 1848.

The accidental discovery of the record of a deed, has led to investigations which make it quite certain that Elizabeth's mother did not marry John[3] (*Joseph[2]*), No. 15, but his cousin, John[3] (*Timothy[2]*), No. 25. See pp. 24, 29.

The investigations will be completed and the result given under the head of "Additions and Corrections" at the end of this volume.

51.

V. TIMOTHY ROGERS[4] (*Timothy[3], Timothy[2], John[1]*) was born in Marshfield in 1720; he married, August 28, 1755, Desire Sylvester; he died, December 27, 1798, aged seventy-eight.

His wife's parentage has not been ascertained; there was no administration on his estate; we have not been able to obtain any account of his family, except that deeds have been discovered which show that he had one son:

— 104a.   Prince[5], b. about 1765.

Prince Rogers[5] married, March 21, 1790, Mary Gorham; he died, May 28, 1832, a. 67, and she, June 19, 1835, a. 82; no children.

He witnessed the will of Amos Rogers, Jan'y 21, 1799; he conveyed, April 1, 1826, to David Gorham, "all my homestead farm lying in Marshfield, which came to me from Honor'd father, Timothy Rogers, deceased " * * "excepting the mill and mill privilege which I have heretofore disposed of" * * "reserving to myself and my wife, Mary Rogers, the use" * * * "during our natural lives." B. CLXXVII, p. 238.

David Gorham sold the farm, Sept. 9, 1834, and described it as the homestead farm of Prince Rogers, which came to him from his father, Timothy Rogers, deceased.

His will, d. Jan'y 28, 1832, p. June 5, 1832, mentions wife Mary; David Gorham; Calvin Hatch Rogers, son of Abijah [who was son of Nathaniel[5] (Israel[4])]; Mercy Gorham, daughter of David Gorham; "the widow, Ruth Rogers" [widow of Zaccheus[5]]; Bethia Rogers, Jr. and Eunice Rogers, singlewomen and daughters of Nathaniel Rogers; Elisha Rogers; Prince Rogers 2[d]; Bethia Conant; Hannah Phillips, wife of Jonathan; Elijah Leonard; Lemuel Hall and Hatch Tilden.

52.

V. ISRAEL ROGERS[4] (*Timothy[3], Timothy[2], John[1]*) was born in Marshfield, November 22, 1722; he married, December 31, 1767, Bethiah Thomas, daughter of Samuel and Rebecca [Howland] Thomas, born January 23, 1728/9; he died, November 29, 1811, and she, June 15, 1819.

Children, born in Marshfield:

+ 105. Israel[5], b. Feb'y 12, 1748/9.
+ 106. Nathaniel[5], b. Sept. 7, 1740.
+ 107. Thomas[5], b. June 8, 1752.
+ 108. Asa[5], b. May 25, 1754.
— 109. Abijah[5], b. June 24, 1756; bap. Aug. 15, 1756; probably d. young.
  110. Araunah[5], b. Nov. 5, 1758.
+ 111. Bethiah[5], b. Feb'y 24, 1761; bap. May 10, 1761.
  112. Howland[5], b. Sept. 3, 1763.
+ 113. Rebekah[5], b. Dec. 3, 1766; bap. "on her own account" Sept. 25, 1790.
+ 114. Samuel[5], b. Apr. 27, 1769.
+ 115. Mercy[5], b. Nov. 22, 1772.

Israel Rogers and Bethiah, his wife, and their children, Israel, Nathaniel, Thomas and Asa were baptized, Jan'y 11, 1756.

He and his sons were shipbuilders and gained a high reputation as such. See Briggs' "Shipbuilding on North River."

Four of his children married children of Benjamin and Mercy [Philips] Hatch of Scituate; see deed dated Mar. 3, 1790. B. LXIX, p. 266.

Israel Rogers of Marshfield conveyed, Apr. 29, 1783, to his son, Nathaniel of M., part of a lot "which fell to me in the division of the estate of my Father, Timothy Rogers, deceased".

Abijah[5]. Beyond the record of his birth and baptism, nothing has been found relating to him; while his death is not recorded in the church records, he probably died young.

Araunah[5]. Briggs, in his "Shipbuilding," says that Araunah married Deborah Davis. There is a faint tradition that he went "Down

East". We find no mention of him — even of his marriage — in any record.

Howland⁵. Briggs also says that Howland married Hannah Davis.

But the History of Thomaston, Maine, says that Capt. Howland Rogers, born in 1764, came early from Marshfield to Thomaston as a ship carpenter; married Hannah Bradford; removed to Medford, Mass., where he died, March 1, 1814. His children were:

      1. Capt. Thomas, who moved to Boston.
      2. Mehitable, who married Ephraim Wood of Camden.
      3. Nancy, who married Oakes Perry of Camden.
      4. Hannah, who married Simon Kent of Camden.

53.

V. PELEG ROGERS⁴ (*Timothy³, Timothy², John¹*) was born in Marshfield, November 6, 1725; he married, April 26, 1754, Hannah Stevens; he died, August 13, 1820, and she, April 26, 1806.

Children, born in Marshfield:

    + 116. Peleg⁵, b. in 1755.
    + 117. Nathaniel⁵, b. Aug. 6, 1757.
    + 118. Patience⁵, b. about 1760.
    + 119. Isaac⁵, b.
    + 120. Timothy⁵, b.

No record, public or private, of this family has been found. It is by no means certain that these are all the children, and it is not *absolutely* certain that Patience and Timothy belong here.

Patience⁵ named her oldest son "Peleg" and that son (Peleg Mann) named his oldest son for his *wife's* grandfather, and his second son "Peleg Rogers," presumably for *his* grandfather.

Timothy⁵ died in 1845; and Arthur Rogers⁶ oldest son of Isaac⁵, petitioned, as "next of kin," for the appointment of the administrator. If Timothy was brother of Isaac, he had outlived all his brothers, and Arthur was his oldest nephew, and "next of kin."

54.

V. LYDIA ROGERS[4] (*Timothy[3], Timothy[2], John[1]*) was born in Marshfield; she married, December 1, 1743, James Lewis, son of John and Sarah [Marsh] Lewis, born September 9, 1712; H. C. 1731; he "owned the covenant" and was baptized April 23, 1749; he died in 1785.

Children, born in Marshfield:

 i. Lydia Lewis[5], b. Dec. 8, 1744; bap. Jan'y 13, 1744/5.
 ii. Achsah Lewis[5], b. Jan'y 7, 1746/7; bap. Feb. 22, 1746/7.
 iii. James Lewis[5], b. May 14, 1750; bap. Nov. 4, 1750.
 iv. Calvin Lewis[5], bap. Oct. 15, 1752.
 v. Luther Lewis[5], bap. Aug. 10, 1755.
 vi. Joseph Lewis[5], bap. July 2, 1758.
 vii. Bela Lewis[5], bap. Aug. 2, 1761.

No mention of this family in Marshfield records after 1761, has been found; in the Harvard catalogue, the year only of his death is given.

55.

V. AMOS ROGERS[4] (*Timothy[3], Timothy[2], John[1]*) was born in Marshfield about 1728; he "owned the covenant" and was baptized, December 21, 1755; he married, December 1, 1757, Rachel Wales, daughter of Rev. Atherton and Mary [Niles] Wales, born, February 2, 1734/5; he died, August 26, 1802, and she, January 19, 1798.

Children, born in Marshfield:

 + 121. Rachel[5], bap. Oct. 1758.
 + 122. Persis[5], bap. May 14, 1761.
 + 123. Atherton Wales[5], bap. May 1, 1763.
 — 124. Mary[5], b. Mar. 5, 1765; d. Mar. 6, 1765.
 — 125. Amos[5], bap. June 1, 1766; d. June 28, 1766.
 — 126. Thela[5], d. April 1769, aged three weeks.
 — 127. Mary[5], bap. May 14, 1770; d. May 28, 1770.
 — 128. Amos[5], b. Ap'l 8, 1772; d. same day.

Five gravestones, in a row, mark the graves of the last five children.

Will d. Jan'y 21, 1799, p. Sept. 6, 1802, witnessed by Nathaniel Rogers and Prince Rogers, mentions grandsons, George Little, Edward P. Little and Amos Rogers Little; daughter, Rachel Little; grand-daughters, Persis Oakman, Polly Rogers, Rachel Rogers, Polly Oakman, Rachel Oakman and Rachel, Persis, Polly, Almira and Statira Little: Ex'or, son in law, George Little, whose son, George Little, was appointed Adm'r *de bonis non* in 1810.

56.

V. ZACCHEUS ROGERS⁴ (*Timothy³, Timothy², John¹*) was born in Marshfield, in July, 1731; he was baptized, December 4, 1757; he married, [published April 4, 1756] Rebecca Lapham, daughter of David and Rebecca [King] Lapham, born, September 21, 1732; she died ————; he married, November 27, 1766, Submit Jones, of Hingham, daughter of Benjamin and Mary [Jordan] Jones, born, October 1, 1733; she died, June 19, 1798; he married, December 13, 1802, Naomi Hatch, of Scituate, daughter of Benjamin and Jerusha [Phillips] Hatch, baptized May 6, 1748; he died, September 15, 1817, aged eighty-six years and two months, and she, August 11, 1825, aged seventy-eight.

Children, born in Marshfield:

By first wife:

+ 129. Eggatha⁵, bap. Dec. 4, 1757.
+ 130. Rebecca⁵, bap. July 15, 1759.
+ 131. Zaccheus⁵, bap. Nov. 22, 1761.
  132. Allen⁵, bap. Oct. 2, 1763.
— 133. Lapham⁵, bap. June 2, 1765; d. young.

By second wife:

+ 134. Charles⁵, b. Feb'y 22, 1768.
+ 135. Benjamin⁵, b.————, 1770.
+ 136. Mary⁵, b. May 23, 1772; bap. July 5, 1772.   See No. 114.

Will d. Feb'y 22, 1817, p. Oct. 6, 1817, mentions wife Naomi *King* ers; sons, Allen, Charles and Benjamin; daughters, Aggatha Hart and Rebecca Wright; and children of son, Zaccheus, and of daughter, Mary, both deceased.

Record of administration on Naomi's estate shows that she was sister of Submit, Jane and Joseph, children of Benjamin Hatch.

There is doubt about the date of birth of Zaccheus[4]; his age as given in the record of his third marriage makes him born in 1730.

Zaccheus Rogers, of Marshfield, shipwright, conveyed (his wife, Submit, joining in the deed) Dec. 22, 1767, to Timothy Rogers, yeoman, "all my real estate, both upland and meadow, that fell to me in the division of the real estate of my late honored father, Timothy Rogers, deceased, except the Pine land." B. LIV, p. 17.

57 and 148.

V. ADAM ROGERS[4] (*Timothy[3], Timothy[2], John[1]*) was born in Marshfield, February 4, 1732/3; he married [published October 12, 1757] Lydia Rogers[5], daughter of Samuel[4], and Experience [Thomas] Rogers, born, November 17, 1734; he died, October 24, 1834, aged one hundred and one years and eight months, and she, January 31, 1813.

Children, born in Marshfield:

- — 136a. Adam[5], b. in 1758; d. Sept. 26, 1761, a. 3 years.
- — 137. Lydia[5], b. Mar. 23, 1760; bap. Aug. 4, 1765; d. unm. Aug. 12, 1819, a. 59.
- + 138. Samuel[5], b. in 1761; bap. Aug. 4, 1765.
- + 139. Elizabeth[5], b. Nov. 30, 1763; bap. Aug. 4, 1765.
- — 140. Hannah[5], b. Oct. 9, 1765; bap. Dec. 1, 1765; d. unm. in old age, and blind.
- + 141. Walter[5], b. Aug. 5, 1767; bap. Oct. 4, 1767.
- + 142. Adam[5], b. Jan'y 9, 1769; bap. July 2, 1769.
- + 143. Eunice[5], b. 17, 1771; bap. April 25, 1771.
- + 144. Jane[5], [Jeane] bap. May 16, 1773.
-   145. Abel[5], b.———; bap. May 25, 1775.
- + 146. Elisha[5], b. July 5, 1777; bap. Aug. 17, 1777.

Adam Rogers, Blacksmith, and Lydia, his wife, conveyed, December 16, 1789, land in Middleboro, with dwelling house thereon, to Thomas Rogers, Jr., of Marshfield. B. LXXV, p. 269.

By deed acknowledged Nov. 24, 1832, Adam Rogers conveyed to Elisha Rogers, his farm in Marshfield, he (Adam) and his daughter, Hannah, to have an honorable maintenance out of the same during their lives. B. CLXXVI, p. 107.

The farm is still occupied by a descendent of Elisha, who has the Family Bible of Adam Rogers, and the site of his blacksmith shop is still known.

58.

V. ELIZABETH ROGERS[4] (*Timothy[3], Timothy[2], John[1]*) was born in Marshfield ; she married, April 11, 1754, Lt. Joseph Tolman, probably son of Benjamin and Elizabeth Tolman, of Scituate, baptized, November 6, 1716; no record found.

59.

V. JANE ROGERS[4] (*Timothy[3], Timothy[2], John[1]*) was born in Marshfield ; she married, December 10, 1752, Thomas Oldham, of Scituate; no record found.

60.

V. EUNICE ROGERS[4] (*Timothy[3], Timothy[2], John[1]*) was born in Marshfield; she married, February 12, 1756, Nathaniel Ford, son of Peleg and Alice [Warren] Ford, born July 11, 1731 ; she is said to have died in 1837.

Children, born in Marshfield:

    i. Peleg Ford[5], b. April 19, 1757.
    ii. Nathaniel Ford[5], b. March 20, 1759.
    iii. Charles Ford[5], b. Aug. 5, 1761.
    iv. James Ford[5], b. Oct. 20, 1763.
    v. Eunice Ford[5], b. April 3, 1765.
    vi. Elsie Ford[5], b. Sept. —, 1768.
    vii. Lydia Ford[5], b. Nov. 2, 1770.
    viii. Phebe Ford[5], b. Oct. 7, 1773.

This family is said to have moved to Readfield, Maine.

61.

V. RUTH ROGERS[4] (*Samuel3, Timothy2, John1*) was
born in Marshfield; was baptized in 1699; she married,
November 19, 1722, Nicholas Porter, of Abington, son
of Nicholas and Bostina [Reed] Porter, born in Weymouth, October 26, 1700; she died, (probably) August
31, 1775.

Children, born in Abington:

—   i.   Nicholas Porter5, b. Jan'y 11, 1724; d. Mar. 31, 1724.
    ii.   Nicholas Porter5, bap. May 1, 1726.
    iii.   Ruth Porter5, bap. May 12, 1728; m. Samuel Ames, of
         Marshfield.
    iv.   Job Porter5, b.
    v.   Daniel Porter5, b.
    vi.   Lucy Porter5, b.

Ruth Porter, Elizabeth Tirrell, and Susanna Rogers, without their
husbands, executed a joint release, in 1747, for the legacy left to
each of them in the will of their father, Samuel Rogers. Deeds, B.
XXXIX, p. 42.

62.

V. ELIZABETH ROGERS[4] (*Samuel3, Timothy2, John1*)
was born in Marshfield; was baptized in 1701; she married, (Duxbury record) September 18, 1720, Thomas
Tirrell, (also called Terrill and Turell) son of William
and Abigail [Pratt] Tirrell, of Abington; he died in
1732.

Children, born in Abington:

—   i.   Thomas Tirrell5, b. Feb'y 27, 1721/2; d. in infancy.
    ii.   Thomas Tirrell5, b. July 31, 1723.
    iii.   Jacob Tirrell5, b. April 21, 1727.
    iv.   Mary Tirrell5, b. April 3, 1729.
    v.   Samuel Tirrell5, b. Oct. 16, 1730.

Some of Jacob's children settled in Bridgewater, as stated in
Mitchell's History.

His brother, William, was appointed Admr., July 18, 1732; his estate was insolvent; "necessary utensils" were set out to his widow, Elizabeth. Oct. 6, 1732; he was indebted, under his father's will, to his sisters, six in number, the names of whom and of the husband of each are given in the probate papers.

63.

V. SAMUEL ROGERS[4] (*Samuel[3], Timothy[2], John[1]*) was born in Marshfield, July 27, 1703; he married, November 25, 1731, Experience Thomas, daughter of Daniel and Experience [Tilden] Thomas, born, July 1, 1709; he died, November, 1761, and she, February 9, 1802.

Children, born in Marshfield:

+ 147. Penelope[5], b. June 7, 1733.
+ 148. Lydia[5], b. Nov. 17, 1734; m. Adam Rogers, No. 57.
+ 149. Thomas[5], b. Jan'y 25, 1735/6.
+ 150. Simeon[5], b. May 18, 1737.
— 151. Hannah[5], b. Dec. 19, 1740; bap. Feb'y 22, 1740/1; d. young.
— 152. Samuel[5], bap. April 22, 1744; d. young.
— 153. Experience[5], bap. May 3, 1746; d. young.
+ 154. Mary[5], bap. Feb'y 26, 1748/9.

Will of Samuel Rogers, of Marshfield, housewright, d. Nov. 4, 1761, p. Nov. 24, 1761, mentions wife, Experience; sons, Thomas and Simeon; and daughters, Penelope Foord, Lydia and Mary Rogers., Vol. XVI. p. 237.

64.

V. MARY ROGERS[4] (*Samuel[3], Timothy[2], John[1]*) was born in Marshfield; was baptized, June 23, 1706; she married John Trouant, son of John; he died in May, 1749, leaving her surviving.

Children, born in Marshfield:

i.   Samuel Trouant[5], b.
ii. Mary Trouant[5], b.
iii. Lydia Trouant[5], b.
iv. John Trouant[5], b.

His will, d. May 17, 1749, p. May 29, 1749, mentions wife, Mary, and sons, Samuel and John, and daughters, Mary and Lydia, then minors and probably under fourteen years of age.

John Trouant and Mary, his wife, executed a release of the legacy left her in her father's will, Nov. 6, 1747, at Plymouth.

In the later records the name is Truant.

65.

V. JAEL ROGERS[4] (*Samuel[3], Timothy[2], John[1]*) was born in Marshfield; was baptized, August 8, 1708; she married, January 14, 1739/40, Michael Harney.

Children, born in Marshfield:

    i.   Rebecca Harney[5], bap. May 30, 1742.
    ii.   Susanna Harney[5], bap. June 24, 1744.
    iii. Sarah Harney[5], bap. Dec. 4, 1748.

They seem to have moved to Boston; for the release to Ebenezer Rogers for the legacy left to Jael[4] in the will of her father, Samuel, dated Sept. 28, 1747, was acknowledged by both *in Boston*, Nov. 3, 1747. Deeds, B. XXXIX, p. 41, 42.

66.

V. SUSANNA ROGERS[4] (*Samuel[3], Timothy[2], John[1]*) was born in Marshfield in 1709; baptized October 8, 1710; she married, November 13, 1749, as his second wife, WILLIAM ROGERS; he died in 1764, and she, January 27, 1794, in her eighty-fifth year.

Child, born in Marshfield:

    155.   Jonah[5], bap. May 24, 1752.

The parentage of William Rogers has not been ascertained; he had married January — 1731/2, Margaret Sylvester, daughter of Joseph; she died about 1748.

Children, by first wife, born in Marshfield:

    156.   William, bap. Aug. 10, 1740.
    157.   Sarah, bap. Aug. 10, 1740.
— 158.   Hannah, bap. April 25, 1742; d. young.
    159.   Joseph, bap. May 5, 1745.
— 160.   Malachi, bap. Mar. 29, 1747; d. young.

The record of baptisms, from which the foregoing was taken, begins, in 1739; it is not certain, therefore, that there were not older children; but if so, they must have died young, because none are mentioned in the will; for the same reason, it is assumed that *Hannah* and *Malachi* also died young.

Will of William Rogers of Marshfield, laborer, d. April 13, 1764, p. May 20, 1764, mentions wife, Susanna; sons, Jonah Rogers and Joseph Rogers; daughter, Sarah Rogers and grand-daughter, Lydia Rogers whose parents are not named, but probably the daughter of his son, William, as Malachi, if living, was only about seventeen years old at date of will.

67.

V. EBENEZER ROGERS[4] (*Samuel[3], Timothy[2], John[1]*) was born in Marshfield, about 1713; he married Sarah————, who was baptized, December 20, 1739, after her marriage; she died about 1784, and he married, November 23, 1788, Hannah [Willson] Cole of Scituate, widow of George Cole (whom she married in 1768) and daughter of William and Hannah [Bourn] Willson, born in 1741; he died February 16, 1798, "aged about 85" she survived him, married (3) Caleb Torrey of Scituate and died in 1825.

Children (by first wife) born in Marshfield:

> 161. Ruth[5], bap. Jan'y 6, 1739/40.
> 162. Betty[5], bap. May 31, 1741.
> 163. Jael[5], bap. in 1743, being sick.

These are all the children disclosed by the town or church records, and there was no administration on his estate.

In a deed, given in 1783, his wife Sarah joins (B. LXXXIV, p. 105), but in a deed dated April 18, 1794, given to his grandson, Ebenezer Rogers Lapham, his wife, Hannah, joins to release dower.

Ruth[5] married, Nov. 12, 1761, Stephen Lapham, who died, April 22, 1804, aged about 68.

Betty[5] married, Dec. 17, 1767, Asa Lapham; she died, July 6, 1823, aged 82; the church records give them, born in Marshfield,

    i.   Sarah Stetson Lapham⁶, bap. May 6, 1770.
   ii.   Ebenezer Rogers Lapham⁶, bap. June 23, 1771.
  iii.   Rebecca Lapham⁶, bap. May 23, 1773.

The names of these children indicate that the first wife of Ebenezer Rogers was Sarah Stetson.

Jael⁵ married, June 9, 1766, "Frederic Anderson of London."

68.

V. SARAH ROGERS⁴ (*Samuel³, Timothy², John¹*) was born in Marshfield about 1716; she married Josiah Holmes; she died November 11, 1812, aged 96, having survived her husband.

    Children, born in Marshfield:

      i.   Mercy Holmes⁵, bap. Dec. 9, 1739.
    ii.   Huet Holmes⁵, bap. Jan'y —, 1742.
   iii.   Ruth Holmes⁵, bap. Sept. 29, 1745.
   iv.   Josiah Holmes⁵, bap. Oct. 16, 1748.
    v.   Usla [Ursula?] Holmes⁵, bap. Sept. 8, 1751.
   vi.   Sarah Holmes⁵, b. Sept. 15, 1754.
  vii.   Molly Holmes⁵, b. June 13, 1756.
 viii.   Lydia Holmes⁵, b. July 13, 1756.
   ix.   Betty Holmes⁵, b. July 16, 1758.

There may have been one or more children older than Mercy, as the record of baptisms began in 1739.

In 1747, Josiah Holmes and Sarah, his wife, receipted for the legacy given to her in the will of her father, Samuel Rogers.

She joined in a deed, April 10, 1796, describing herself as a "widow and spinster."

69.

V. HANNAH ROGERS⁴ (*John³, Timothy², John¹*) was born in Marshfield, February 9, 1701/2; she married, July 8, 1724, Thomas Stockbridge, of Scituate, son of Thomas and Sarah [Reed] Stockbridge, born, February 13, 1702/3; he died in 1790, having long survived her.

Children, born in Scituate:

-   i. Thomas Stockbridge⁵, bap. Aug. 6, 1725; he died un-married in the life time of his father.
-   ii. Hannah Stockbridge⁵, bap. Sept. 26, 1728; d. young.
-   iii. Stephen Stockbridge⁵, bap. Mar. 24, 1733/4.

Will of Thomas Stockbridge, of Scituate, d. Jan'y 1, 1787, p. Ap'l 26, 1790; he, "being aged," gives all his property to his son, Stephen Stockbridge.

*Stephen Stockbridge*⁵ died about 1800, leaving a widow but no children. His property was divided between Rachel Stockbridge, his widow, and Bettie Hoxie, his "heir at law." The real estate was sold by Nathaniel Freeman, as attorney for Betty Hoxie, appointed by the judge for that purpose; the money seems to have been paid to him; he settled an account in the Probate Court and paid the balance over to Betty Hoxie, taking a release signed by her, dated Jan'y 7, 1803, and witnessed by Isaac Hoxie and Sarah Hoxie 3ᵈ, her children; see No. 49a, p. 37.

July 7, 1803, the administrator was ordered by the Probate Court, to pay the balance in his hands "to Rachel Stockbridge, widow of said Stephen, and to Betty Hoxie, heir at law of said Stephen." The relationship of Betty Hoxie to Stephen Stockbridge⁵, which made her his heir-at-law" will be stated in the "Additions and Corrections."

70.

V. SARAH ROGERS⁴ (*John³*, *Timothy²*, *John¹*) was born in Marshfield, December 26, 1705; she married, October 16, 1728, Samuel Ford, son of William and Elizabeth [————] Ford, born, May 11, 1701; she died, June 13, 1796, aged 91.

Children, born in Marshfield:

- i. Jemima Ford⁵, b. Oct. 18, 1729.
- ii. Keziah Ford⁵, b. Ap'l 14, 1732.
- iii. Samuel Ford⁵, b. June 16, 1735.
- iv. Sarah Ford⁵, b. July 31, 1739.
- v. Luke Ford⁵, b. July 27, 1741.

    vi.   Peleg Ford⁵, b. Mar. 1, 1746/7 ; probably d. young.
    vii. Lydia Ford⁵, b. Aug. 1, 1748 ; probably d. young.
    viii. Betty Ford⁵, b. May 31, 1749.

The foregoing was taken from the town record; an unpublished genealogy does not give Peleg or Lydia; but gives Elizabeth [Betty] born May 31, 1747.

The mother of *Hannah*⁴ and *Sarah*⁵ was, quite certainly Sarah, daughter of Thomas Chillingworth, Secretary of Massachusetts Colony, 1686-1692.

71 to 75.

VI.   The children of JOHN⁴ (*John³, John², John¹*) seem to have left Scituate, and but little is known of them or is found in the records.

*Daniel*⁵ (71) married Ruth Parker, Nov. 20, 1733, and the Hanover church records show that they had :

    164. Charity⁶, b. Jan'y 14, 1734/5.
    165. Child⁶, b. Nov. —, 1741.
    166. Ruth⁶, bap. Oct. 31, 1742.

*Elizabeth*⁵ (72) is probably the one who married Timothy Macomber of Dartmouth, Jan. 25, 1738/9.

*John*⁵ (73) is not mentioned in town or church records and they have nothing to indicate whether he died young or went away.

*Deborah*⁵ (74) is probably the one who married William Wood of Dartmouth, June 3, 1740; the church records give the death of "Deborah Rogers, July 16, 1752," but she was probably the mother of Deborah⁵.

*James*⁵ (75) married, May 7, 1741, Rachel Bailey. She died Oct. 23, 1744; they had :

  — 167. Bailey⁶, bap. Oct. 27, 1744; d. Dec. 22, 1744.

The record describes Bailey⁶ as "the only son of James Rogers," perhaps indicating that there was a daughter; the record of his baptism states that his mother died, within a few hours after his birth.

As the probate records show no settlement of the estate of either Daniel, John or James, the presumption is very strong that they moved away.

76.

VI. JEREMIAH ROGERS[5] (*John[4]*, *John[3]*, *John[2]*, *John[1]*)
was born in that part of Scituate which became Hanover, about 1717, but not baptized till February 19,
1726/7; he married, August 23, 1738, Deborah Bailey
of Hanover, daughter of John and Abigail Bailey; she
died August 21, 1761; he married again and removed,
about 1773, to Freeport, Maine, where he died, February 24, 1803, and his second wife, June 29, 1795.

Children, all by first wife, born in Hanover:

— 168. Thomas[6], b. Sept. 12, 1739; bap. May 30, 1742; d.
Dec. 7, 1744.
169. Rhoda[6], bap. May 30, 1742; m. Thomas Rose.
170. Mark[6], bap. May 30, 1742; m. Mary Bray.
— 171. Hannah[6], bap. Jan'y 8, 1743/4; d. young.
172. James[6], b. in 1746; m. twice in Maine.
— 173. John[6], bap. May 22, 1748; d. July 9, 1748.
— 174. Infant son[6], b. ——; d. Nov. 19, 1749.
— 175. John[6], bap. Mar. 31, 1751; d. June 2, 1751.
— 176. Jeremiah[6], bap. Oct. 29, 1752; d. Jan'y 15, 1753.
— 177. Seth[6], bap. Mar. 24, 1754; d. young.
— 178. Deborah[6], bap. June 1, 1755; d. Nov. 30, 1755.

His surviving children, with their families, moved with him to
Freeport, Me.; an account of them is given in the Maine Historical
and Genealogical Recorder, Vol. IV, p. 83, Vol. IX, p. 51.

77 to 84.

VI. The children of JOSHUA[4] (*John[3]*, *John[2]*, *John[1]*)
obtained but slight mention in the Scituate records,
church or town, and it is quite certain that they moved
away.

Joshua[5] (78) married, March 15, 1764, Sarah Nash, daughter of
James Nash; they renewed their covenant and had their two children
baptized, May 11, 1766. They had born in Scituate:

179. Joshua[6], b. Dec. 10, 1764.
180. Sarah[6], bap. May 11, 1766.

John[5] (82) married Mary Lambert of Scituate, March 26, 1770.

Neither the estate of *Joshua*[4], nor that of either of his sons, was settled in the Probate Court of Plymouth County.

In the division of the estate of James Nash, one share was assigned to "Sarah Rogers, wife of Joshua Rogers of Chesterfield." Vol. XXXIII, p. 276.

Joshua Rogers (wife Mehitable) conveyed real estate, Sept. 12, 1763. B. XLVIII, p. 253.

85.

VI.   MARY ROGERS[5] (*Caleb*[4], *John*[3], *John*[2], *John*[1]) was born in Hanover, Nov. 7, 1742; she married, April 2, 1767, Samuel Harden of Pembroke; no further record found.

86.

VI.   ALICE ROGERS[5] (*Caleb*[4], *John*[3], *John*[2], *John*[1]) was born in Hanover, Feb. 19, 1745; baptized, April 7, 1745; she married, December 14, 1766, Samuel Stetson, son of Samuel and Rebecca [Turner] Stetson, born about 1725; he died, February 5, 1791, and she, May 29, 1820.

Children, born in Hanover:

    i.   Turner Stetson[6], b. Sept. 8, 1767 ; m. Lydia Rose.
  — ii.   Reuben Stetson[6], b. ——, 1769; d. Sept. 21, 1778.
   iii.   Samuel Stetson[6], b. May —, 1772.
    iv.   Rebecca Stetson[6]. b. Sept. 10, 1776; m. Timothy Church.
     v.   Lydia Stetson[6], b. ——— ; m. Ezekiel Turner.

87.

VI.   CALEB ROGERS[5] (*Caleb*[4], *John*[3], *John*[2], *John*[1]) was born in Hanover, December 16, 1747; he married, December 26, 1779, Hannah [Torrey] Bates, widow of

Thomas Bates (who died, Oct. 22, 1769), and daughter
of Jesse and Mary [Buker] Torrey, baptized, October
14, 1749; she died, May 12, 1807, "aged 59"; he married
[published January 1, 1815,] Sarah Beals [Beal, Beales],
then of Hanover; he died, March 26, 1833, and she, in
1837.

Children, all by first wife, born in Hanover:

+ 181.   Reuben[6], bap. Oct. 24, 1784.
  182.   Mary[6], bap. Oct. 24, 1784; m. Houghton Sumner.
  183.   Hannah[6], bap. Oct. 24, 1784; m. Martin Winsor of
         Duxbury, Sept. 8, 1805.
  184.   Ruth Torrey[6], bap. Nov. 12, 1786.

Ruth Torrey Rogers[6] married Capt. Levi Curtis, son of Snow and
Bathsheba [Hatch] Curtis, born Oct. 29, 1787; no children.

The *printed* record of inscriptions on their gravestones says that
Caleb[5] died in his *eightieth* year, and his first wife in her *sixty-sixth*
year; the former should be *eighty-sixth* year, and the latter *sixtieth*
year.

In the settlement of the estate of Caleb Rogers, his widow, Sarah,
is mentioned; the estate was held in common with Reuben Rogers,
and distribution was made to Reuben, Houghton Sumner as heir in
right of his wife, Martin Winsor as heir in right of his wife, and Levi
Curtis in right of his wife.

Sarah Rogers (wife of Caleb) made her will, June 19, 1837, p. Oct.
—, 1837, in which she mentions Joseph C. Stockbridge; Ruth
Turner, widow; Zadoc Beal; Reuben Rogers; Priscilla Turner,
widow; Lydia Beals; Tryphena Whiting, widow; Harriet N. Rogers;
Ruth Warren; Noah Beals, Jr.; David Beals; Nathan Beals; David
Smith, and Deborah Turner, widow, but the relationships are not
stated; these names indicate that her maiden name was Stockbridge,
and that she was a widow when she married Caleb[5].

89.

VI. Susanna Rogers[5] (*Caleb[4], John[3], John[2], John[1]*)
was born in Hanover, May 3, 1752; she married, Sept.
5, 1771, David Torrey, son of Stephen and Rachel
[Bates] Torrey, baptized, April 21, 1745.

Children, born in Hanover:

—   i.   David Torrey[6], bap. July 18, 1773 ; d. in infancy.

      ii.   Susa Torrey[6], bap. Aug. 4, 1776.

    iii.   David Torrey[6], bap. Oct. 19, 1777.

90.

VI.   JOHN ROGERS[5] (*John[4], Thomas[3], John[2], John[1]*) was born in Marshfield, December 21, 1738; he married, July 18, 1759, Sarah Chapman, daughter of John and Sarah [Booth] Chapman, born, September 5, 1738; he removed to Tinmouth, Vt., where he and his wife died.

Children, born in Pembroke:

     185.   Sarah[6], b. Aug. 7. 1760; m. Isaac Howland, May 5, 1779.

     186.   John[6], b. Feb. 11, 1764.

     187.   Isaac[6], b. June 11, 1767 : m. Olive Barker, Jan. 26, 1792.

+   188.   Abraham Booth[6], b. May [June?] 1, 1769.

     189.   Phebe[6], b. Jan'y 20, 1772.

—   190.   Nicholas[6], b. Feb'y 10, 1775 ; d. unm.

     191.   Elizabeth[6], b. April 13. 1779.

91.

VI.   WING ROGERS[5] (*John[4], Thomas[3], John[2], John[1]*) was born in Marshfield, June 14, 1740; he married, April 4, 1764, Deliverance Chapman, daughter of John and Sarah [Booth] Chapman, born, August 4, 1736; she died, January 27, 1766.

Child, born in Pembroke:

     192.   Deliverance[6], b. Jan'y 1, 1766.

He married (2) Mercy Hatch; (3) Rebecca Sherman, and (4) Hannah Titus. In a deed dated Jan'y 20, 1774, he describes himself as of Hanover; but in 1776, he had moved to Danby, Vt., where he lived till 1800, when he moved to Ferrisburg, Vt., where he died. The History of Danby (pp. 235, 236) gives some account of him, saying that he had other children, viz.:

193. Elizabeth[6], b.
194. Augustus[6], b.
195. Asa[6], b.
196. Rufus[6], b.
197. Ruth[6], b.
198. Wing[6], b.
199. Mary[6], b.
200. Lester[6], b.
201. Lydia[6], b.

92.

VI. JOSEPH ROGERS[5] (*John[4], Thomas[3], John[2], John[1]*)
was born in Marshfield, January 26, 1742/3; he married,
April 23, 1766, Mary [sometimes called Mara] Chapman, daughter of John and Mary [Booth] Chapman,
born, March 2, 1743/4; she died, October 29, 1784; he
married, February 11, 1789, Elizabeth [Allen] Kirby,
widow of Barnabas Kirby and daughter of Prince and
Deborah [Butler] Allen, born November 28, 1751: he
died, January 23, 1816, and she, August 2, 1830.

Children, born in Marshfield:

By first wife:

202. Abraham[6], b. Nov. 25, 1766.
+ 203. Stephen[6], b. Jan'y 23, 1770.
+ 204. Mary[6], b. Nov. 13, 1772.
+ 205. Anna[6], b. Feb'y 2, 1775.
+ 206. Esther[6], b. April 19, 1777.
207. Sarah[6], b. Oct. 19, 1784; m. Edward Gifford, Jan'y
        11, 1804.

By second wife:

+ 208. Edy[6], b. Nov. 19, 1789.
209. Elizabeth[6], b. June 5, 1794; m. Nathaniel Phillips.

Some of these dates differ from those of other authorities; these
are from the Friends' Records.

Will d. Oct. 25, 1815, p. Feb'y 5, 1816, mentions wife Elizabeth;
sons Abraham and Stephen; daughters Mary Kirby, Anna Wing,
Easter Dillingham, Sarah Gifford, Edy Little and Elizabeth Rogers;

and Stephen Rogers, Ex'or. Moses F. Rogers was Ex'or of will of Stephen Rogers and residuary legatee under it; Stephen R. Rogers was Ex'or of will of Moses F. Rogers, and on April 12, 1886, was appointed Adm'r *"de bonis non"* with will annexed," of Joseph Rogers.

Will of Elizabeth Rogers of Marshfield, d. Mar. 22, 1825, p. Mar. 1, 1831, mentions (among others) her son Restcome Kirby; her daughters Edy Little and Elizabeth Phillips; and her sons-in-law, Edward P. Little and Nathaniel Phillips, who are Ex'ors. Vol. XXV, p. 445.

93.

VI. ELIZABETH ROGERS[5] (*John[4], Thomas[3], John[2], John[1]*) was born in Marshfield, August 11, 1746; she married, February 17, 1768, John Wing, son of Edward and Rebecca [Slocum] [Bennett] Wing, born August 16, 1735.

Children, born in Marshfield:

    i.   Aaron Wing[6], b. July 8, 1768.
    ii. Sarah Wing[6], b. Dec. 16, 1769.
    iii. Edward Wing[6], b. May 23, 1772.
    iv. John Wing[6], b. Mar. 9, 1775.
    v.   Sands Wing[6], b. Dec. 9, 1778.

94.

VI. STEPHEN ROGERS[5] (*John[4], Thomas[3], John[2], John[1]*) was born in Marshfield, February 7, 1748/9; he married, June 25, 1772, Lydia Lapham, daughter of Joshua and Hannah [Shearman] Lapham, born, May 28, 1751; he died, March 17, 1826, and she, March 3, 1832.

Children, the first two probably born in Marshfield, and the others in Danby, Vt.:

  210.   Joseph[6], b. April 2, 1773.
— 211.   Asa[6], b. July 4. 1774; d. Aug. 6, 1777.
+ 212.   Aaron[6], b. May 6, 1776.
  213.   Sarah[6], b. July 4, 1779.
  214.   John[6], b. Aug. 17, 1781.

215.   Hannah[6], b. Nov. 7, 1782.
216.   Stephen[6], b. Oct. 9, 1784.
217.   Ruth[6], b. June 29, 1787.
218.   Elizabeth[6], b. Jan'y 18, 1789.
219.   Sylvia[6], b. Dec. 27, 1791.

Joshua Lapham was the son of Samuel and Hannah[3] [Rogers] Lapham.   No. 30-v, p. 32.

96.

VI. HANNAH ROGERS[5] (*Thomas[4]*, *Thomas[3]*, *John[2]*, *John[1]*) was born in Marshfield, October 4, 1747; she married, July 6, 1773, Joshua Dillingham of Hanover, son of Melatiah and Meriah [Gifford] Dillingham, born March 17, 1740/41; they "moved west" [to New York], and died at dates not ascertained.

Children, born in Hanover:

    i.   Stephen Dillingham[6], b. Mar. 6, 1774.
    ii. Deborah Dillingham[6], b. June 11, 1775.
    iii. Otis Dillingham[6], b. Mar. 5, 1777.
—   iv. Joshua Dillingham[6], b. Oct. 12, 1778; d. Oct. 3, 1779.
    v.   Lydia Dillingham[6], b. Nov. 12, 1779.
    vi. Joshua Dillingham[6], b. July 20, 1781.
    vii. Hannah Dillingham[6], b. Mar. 11, 1783.
    viii. Sarah Dillingham[6], b. Sept. 12, 1784.
    ix. Rhoda Dillingham[6], b. Sept. 4, 1787.

99.

VI. PRISCILLA ROGERS[5] (*Thomas[4]*, *Thomas[3]*, *John[2]*, *John[1]*) was born in Marshfield, February 27, 1754; she married, December 3, 1777, Mordecai Ellis, son of Mordecai and Sarah [Otis] Ellis, born, April 8, 1746; he died, August 18, 1829, and she, September 8, 1850, in her ninety-seventh year.

Children, born in Hanover:

+   i.   Huldah Ellis[6], b. Mar. 3, 1779.
+   ii.   Rebecca Ellis[6], b. Mar. 17, 1781.
+   iii.   Abigail Ellis[6], b. Oct. 16, 1782.
−   iv.   Mordecai Ellis[6], b. July 16, 1785; died, Feb. 25, 1796.
+   v.   Priscilla Ellis[6], b. April 30, 1787.
+   vi.   David Ellis[6], b. June 19, 1789.
    vii.   Sarah Ellis[6], b. Mar. 25, 1791.
+   viii.   Otis Ellis[6], b. Nov. 4, 1795.
+   ix.   Elizabeth Ellis[6], b. July 4, 1797.

Sarah Ellis[6] married Simeon Hoxie of Sandwich; he died Jan. 28, 1851, and she, May 23, 1863; no children.

[These will be given at the end of those carried forward in figures.]

100.

VI.   JAMES ROGERS[5] (*Thomas[4], Thomas[3], John[2], John[1]*) was born in Marshfield, April 16, 1756; he married, March 5, 1787, Deborah Smith, daughter of Samuel and Mary [Anthony] Smith, born November 14, 1762; he died November 29, 1832, and she, May 4, 1813.

Children, born in Marshfield:

+   220.   Deborah[6], b. Aug. 28, 1788.
    221.   James[6], b. May 15, 1790.
    222.   Mary[6], b. July 19, 1792.
    223.   Hannah[6], b. June 18, 1794.
    224.   Samuel[6], b. Jan. 27, 1797.
    225.   Rhoda[6], b. June 21, 1799.
    226.   Thomas[6], b. Jan. 9, 1802.

In 1812 he moved to Peru, Clinton Co., N. Y., where he and his wife died.

102.

VI.   HULDAH ROGERS[5] (*Thomas[4], Thomas[3], John[2], John[1]*) was born in Marshfield, September 30, 1760; she married, December 4, 1783, Tristram Russell of Dutchess County, N. Y., son of Benjamin and Rebecca Russell, and they had children:

    i.   Samuel Russell⁶, b.
   ii.   Rhoda Russell⁶, b.

105.

VI. ISRAEL ROGERS⁵ (*Israel⁴, Timothy³, Timothy², John¹*) was born in Marshfield, February 12, 1748/9; he married [published, December 23, 1776,] HANNAH ROGERS, who has not been identified; he died in Charlestown, before 1831, leaving her surviving.

Children, born probably in Charlestown:

  227. Ruth⁶, b.
  228. Hannah⁶, b.

In 1796, Israel Rogers bought two lots of land in Charlestown, one fronting on Water Street; the other he conveyed Oct. 6, 1796, his wife, Hannah, joining in the deed.

On Feb'y 12, 1831, Benjamin Barrell conveyed his interest in the house on Water Street, consideration one dollar, to Ruth Rogers, singlewoman — "it being * * * the house that was the dwelling lately occupied by Israel Rogers, lately deceased."

Hannah Rogers and Benjamin Barrell, both of C., were married, June 10, 1802.

We find no record of the births of any other children of Israel and Hannah Rogers, or of any children of Benjamin and Hannah Barrell: but Benjamin Barrell, single, son of Benjamin and Hannah, died in C., Oct. 27, 1858, aged 55 years, 5 mos. None of the estates were settled in Probate Court.

Mrs. Rogers, a widow, lived at No. 23, Water Street, in 1834, and, according to the Directory, Benjamin Barrell lived there in 1848.

About 1839, the widow, and Ruth and her married sister were living together in Charlestown.

Ruth Rogers, of Orleans, and John H. Twiss of Boston, were married in Charlestown, Nov. 29, 1838; perhaps Ruth⁶, but probably not.

106.

VI. NATHANIEL ROGERS[5] (*Israel[4], Timothy[3], Timothy[2], John[1]*) was born in Marshfield, September 7, 1750; he married, January 7, 1779, Bethia Clift, daughter of William and Bethiah [Hatch] Clift, born, June 18, 1747; baptized, August 4, 1747; he died, March 20, 1833, and she, April 19, 1842.

Children, born in Marshfield:

— 229. Bethiah[6], b. July 2, 1780; bap. Mar. 18, 1781; d. unm. Jan'y 25, 1844.
+ 230. Abijah[6], bap. June 9, 1782.
— 231. William Clift[6], b. Feb'y 28, 1784; bap. June 6, 1784; d. Mar. 17, 1805.
— 232. Eunice[6], bap. July 6, 1788; unm. in 1832; d. without issue.

Prince Rogers, in will, d. Jan'y 28, 1832, p. June 5, 1832, mentions Bethia Rogers, Jr. and Eunice Rogers, singlewomen, and daughters of Nathaniel Rogers.

Nathaniel Rogers conveyed, by deed ack., June 28, 1830, to his daughters, Bethia, Jr. and Eunice Rogers, the land that his father, Israel Rogers, gave him in 1805, being his homestead farm. B. CLXX, p. 187.

Also Prince Rogers, by deed ack., Jan'y 27, 1832, conveyed land to Bethia Rogers, Jr., and Eunice Rogers, daughters of Nathaniel Rogers of Marshfield, singlewomen. B. CLXXVI, p. 110.

Also Stephen Rogers and Abijah Hatch, by deed ack., Dec. 16, 1833, conveyed land to Bethia and Eunice Rogers. B. CLXXXIII, p. 12.

Eunice Rogers was appointed Adm'r of Bethia Rogers, of Marshfield, March 5, 1844.

107.

VI. THOMAS ROGERS[5] (*Israel[4], Timothy[3], Timothy[2], John[1]*) was born in Marshfield, June 8, 1752; he mar-

ried, August 16, 1781, Eggatha* Hatch, daughter of
Benjamin and Mercy [Phillips] Hatch, of Scituate, born,
June 14, 1762; baptized, August 1, 1762; he died,
October 2, 1841, and she, December 4, 1857.

Children, born in Marshfield:

+ 233.   Thomas⁶, b. July 18, 1782 : bap. Oct. 6, 1782.
+ 234.   Martin⁶, b. Ap'l 13, 1784 ; bap. July 24, 1784.
+ 235.   Phillips⁶, b. Mar. 14, 1787 ; bap. July 22, 1787.
+ 236.   Egatha⁶,* b. July 25, 1795 ; bap. Nov. 8, 1795.
+ 237.   Howland⁶, b. June 18, 1797 : bap. Oct. 8, 1797.
+ 238.   Warren⁶, b. Oct. 9, 1804 ; bap. Oct. 20, 1805.

See deed ack. Mar. 3, 1790. B. LXIX, p. 256.

108.

VI.   Asa Rogers⁵ (*Israel⁴, Timothy³, Timothy², John¹*)
was born in Marshfield, May 25, 1754; he married,
December 13, 1781, Abiah Oakman, daughter of
Edward and Sarah [Doggett] Oakman, born, April 26,
1756; he died, September 30, 1836, and she, November
4, 1830, in Boston.

Children, born in Marshfield:

  239.   Abiah⁶, b. Sept. 7, 1783.
  240.   Sarah⁶, b. Nov. 9, 1785.
+ 241.   Asa⁶, b. June 21, 1787.
− 242.   Temperance⁶, b. Oct. 12, 1788 ; d. unm.
+ 243.   Amos⁶, b. Feb'y 24, 1791.
  244.   Bethiah⁶, b. May 25, 1792.
  245.   Alice⁶, b. Sept. 19, 1793.
  246.   Edward⁶, b. Aug. 23, 1796.
+ 247.   Henry⁶, b. Aug. 23, 1796.
  248.   Thomas⁶, b. July 21, 1802 : m. Jane Tilden ; pub.
           Nov. 5, 1826.

111.

VI.   Bethiah Rogers⁵ (*Israel⁴, Timothy³, Timothy²,
John¹*) was born in Marshfield, February 24, 1761; she

* This name is variously written, but is really Agatha.

married, February 28, 1782, Anthony Eames Hatch, son of Benjamin and Mercy [Phillips] Hatch, born, April 18, 1753; he died, September 10, 1842, and she, July 23, 1844.

Children, born in Scituate:

  i. Bethiah Hatch[6], b. Sept. 6, 1783; bap. Nov. 16, 1783.
  ii. Anthony Eames Hatch[6], b. Mar. 4, 1785; bap. May 15, 1785.
  iii. Abijah Hatch[6], b. Feb'y 28, 1787; bap. May 6, 1787.
  iv. Mercy Hatch[6], b. Mar. 7, 1789; bap. May 3, 1789.
  v. Celia Hatch[6], b. June 12, 1791: bap. Aug. 7, 1791.
  vi. Calvin Hatch[6], b. Aug. 14, 1793; bap. Nov. 10, 1793.
  vii. Grace Hatch[6], b. May 21. 1796.
  viii. Elisha Hatch[6], b. Nov. 17, 1798; bap. June 16, 1799.
  ix. Laura Hatch[6], b. Mar. 18, 1801; bap. Sept. 20, 1801.

113.

VI. REBEKAH ROGERS[5] (*Israel*[4], *Timothy*[3], *Timothy*[2], *John*[1]) was born in Marshfield, December 3, 1766; she married, December 9, 1794, Ichabod Hatch, son of Benjamin and Mercy [Phillips] Hatch, born, May 8, 1767; she died in Charlestown on a visit (probably to her daughter, Roxalina) July 9, 1829; he married (2) her sister, Mercy.

Children, born in Marshfield:

 — i. Ichabod Hatch[6], b. Dec. 5, 1795; d. Jan'y 8, 1797.
 +248a. ii. Rebecca Hatch[6], b. Feb'y 20, 1798.
 † iii. Ichabod Hatch[6], b. Dec. 28, 1799.
 + iv. Benjamin Hatch[6], b. Aug. 30, 1802 : See No. 278.
  v. Roxalina Hatch[6], b. Oct. 22. 1804.
 — vi. Deborah Hatch[6], b. May 20, 1807; d. Aug. 31, 1807.

This family lived on the "Two Mile," which was granted to Scituate, Nov. 30, 1640, but set off to Marshfield, March 10, 1787.

Roxalina[6] married, March 1, 1827, Jotham Hatch, and died in Charlestown, January 10, 1832; and he died the second of June following, leaving a son, Frederick, who was baptized, Nov. 4, 1832, at the request of his grandparents.

113—iii.

VII. *Ichabod Hatch*⁶ married, November 20, 1828, Sela Sylvester Palmer, daughter of Elijah and Sarah [Sherman] Palmer, born, February 29, 1804: he died, November 20, 1876, and she, February 1, 1874.

Children, born in Marshfield :

> +   i.   Lucinda Hatch⁷, b. Jan'y 14, 1830; see No. 350.
> ii.   Albion Hatch⁷, b. Oct. 11, 1833.
> iii.   Arethusa Hatch⁷, b. Oct. 11, 1833.
> iv.   George Hatch⁷, b. Feb'y 7, 1836.
> v.   Anson Hatch⁷, b. Feb'y 22, 1838.

*Albion*⁷, m. Mercy Rogers Hatch, Nov. 24, 1860.
*Arethusa*⁷, m. Henry Phillips Oakman⁷, Mar. 8, 1853.
*Anson*⁷, m. Joan Randall, Dec. 2, 1865.

114 and 136.

VI. SAMUEL ROGERS⁵ (*Israel*⁴, *Timothy*³, *Timothy*², *John*¹) was born in Marshfield, April 27, 1769; he was baptized, July 6, 1783, in private, being dangerously sick; he married, January 3, 1796, MARY ROGERS⁵ (*Zaccheus*⁴, *Timothy*³, *Timothy*², *John*¹) born in Marshfield, May 23, 1772; she died, February 20, 1812; he married, November 5, 1812, Rachel Clift, daughter of Wills and Rachel [Tilden] Clift, born, February 8, 1784; baptized, May 15, 1795; he died, August 2, 1832, and she, October 10, 1857.

Children, born in Marshfield:

By first wife :

> + 249.   Maria⁶, b. January 23, 1800; bap. May 3, 1801.
> + 250.   Alfred⁶, b. Sept. 1, 1803; bap. Ap'l 8, 1804.
> − 251.   Zadock⁶, b. Mar. 23, 1810; bap. Aug. 5, 1810; d. Oct. 20, 1811.

By second wife:

— 252. Samuel⁶, b. Feb'y 5, 1814; d. Aug. 12, 1817.
— 253. Rachel Wills⁶, b. June 12, 1818; bap. Sept. 27, 1818; d. unm. Dec. 20, 1853.

115.

VI. MERCY ROGERS⁶ (*Isaiah⁴, Timothy³, Timothy², John¹*) was born in Marshfield, November 11, 1772; she married, June 10, 1830, Ichabod Hatch, who had previously married her sister, Rebecca [No. 113]; he died, July 17, 1845, and she, July 31, 1852; no children.

116.

VI. PELEG ROGERS⁵ (*Peleg⁴, Timothy³, Timothy², John¹*) was born in Marshfield in 1755; he married, December 9, 1784, Jemima Ames, daughter of Jedediah and Bethiah [Tilden] Ames, born, January 18, 1759; he died, September 18, 1805, aged 50, and she, October 9, 1795.

Children, born in Marshfield:

— 254. Peleg⁶, b. Oct. 11, 1785; bap. Oct. 29, 1786; d. Jan'y 16, 1795.
— 255. Jedediah⁶, b. Nov. 18, 1788; bap. Aug. 21, 1789; d. Sept. 14, 1789.
  256. Nancy⁶, bap. April 17, 1796.
  257. Almira⁶, bap. April 17, 1796.

Timothy Rogers was appointed, Dec. 2, 1805, Adm'r of his estate upon petition of creditors representing that Timothy had the most of Peleg's property in his hands and so could do the business at less expense.

117.

VI. NATHANIEL ROGERS⁵ (*Peleg⁴, Timothy³, Timothy², John¹*) was born in Marshfield, August 6, 1757; he married, July 23, 1781, Hannah Ford of Duxbury,

daughter of Amos and Lillis [——] Ford, born about
1757; she died about 1790, and he, January 28. 1834, in
Boston.

Children, born in Marshfield:

    258. Asenath[6], b. about 1782.
    259. Deborah[6], b. about 1784.
+ 260. Patience[6], b. about 1786.
    261. Elizabeth[6], b. about 1789.

She died about 1791, for in that year he was appointed guardian
of these children "by his wife Hannah Rogers, deceased," they then
being under fourteen years of age. Vol. XXVI, p. 246.

Thomas Ford, of Duxbury, Silvina Ford and Sarah Ford of Dux-
bury, seamsters, Asenath Ford of Marshfield, seamster, and Nathaniel
Rogers Jr. of Marshfield, as guardian of his children, by his wife,
Hannah, deceased, conveyed, May 9, 1791, to Robertson Turner and
Lillis, his wife, land that was purchased "by our father, Mr. Amos
Foord, late of Duxbury." B. LXXIV, p. 58.

On Oct. 16, 1807, a levy was made on an execution in favor of
Nathaniel Rogers of Lincolnville, Maine; and the circumstances
indicate with great certainty that he was this Nathaniel[5].

"Nathaniel Rogers, son Peleg Rogers (deceased) died in Boston,
and buried here, Jan. 1834." Records of Second Church in Marshfield.

The Boston record is "Nathaniel Rogers died, Jan'y 28, 1834,
aged 76; buried at Duxbury."

118.

VI. PATIENCE ROGERS[5] (*Peleg[4], Timothy[3], Timothy[2],
John[1]*) was born in Marshfield about 1760; she married.
March 12, 1782, John Mann of Scituate, son of Thomas
and Deborah [Briggs] Mann, born, May 10, 1761; she
died, December 14, 1799, aged 39; he married, June 18,
1803, Rebecca Briggs; he died, June 6, 1841.

Children, born in Scituate:

    i. Patience Mann[6], b. April 5, 1782.
    ii. Peleg Mann[6], b. Feb'y 3, 1784.

iii. John Mann⁶, b. Nov. 1, 1785.
iv. Sarah Mann⁶, b. Dec. 16, 1787.
v. Isaiah Mann⁶, b. Dec. 23, 1789.
— vi. Polly Mann⁶, b. Aug. 12, 1792 ; d. unm. Jan. 8, 1880.
vii. Thomas Mann⁶, b. June 17, 1795.
viii. Mary Mann⁶, b. Nov. 21, 1797.

He had also four children by his second wife.

119.

VI. ISAAC ROGERS⁵ (*Peleg⁴, Timothy³, Timothy², John¹*) was born in Marshfield; he married, April 2, 1792, Hannah Ford of Duxbury, daughter of Levi and Penelope [Rogers⁵, No. 147] Ford.

Children, born in Marshfield:

262. Nathan⁶, b. Feb. 23, 1793 ; d. Nov. 5, 1793.
— 263. Salome⁶, b. Sept. 30, 1794 ; d. unm. in 1882.
264. Arthur⁶, b. Nov. 2, 1796.
265. Nathan⁶, b. Oct. 27, 1798.
266. Isaiah⁶, b. Aug. 17, 1800.
267. Laura⁶, b. Oct. 10, 1802 ; m. Thaddeus Wheeler.
268. Jotham⁶, m. Louise Bowker.
+ 269. Alden⁶, m. Adeline Humphrey, Aug. 14, 1827.
270. Susan D.⁶, m. Isaac Ewell of Medford, Mar. 25, 1832.
271. Amos⁶, b.

Arthur⁶ married Sarah F. Lapham and, in 1848, was appointed guardian of his children, Arthur F. and Sarah C.: the same year he petitioned for leave to sell land which they owned in common with himself, Nathan Rogers and Betsey A. Rogers.

Nathan⁶. Mr. Briggs mentions but one who died young; but it is certain that the second Nathan had a family, although we have not been able to get an account of it. He married Betsey A. Lapham, sister of Arthur⁶'s wife.

Amos⁶ was accidentally killed and is understood to have died without issue.

120.

VI. TIMOTHY ROGERS[5] (*Peleg[4], Timothy[3], Timothy[2], John[1]*) was born in Marshfield; he married [published December 15, 1791,] Lydia Keen, daughter of Simeon and Lydia [Stevens] Keen; he died in 1845, having survived her. No children.

Timothy Rogers, Jr. and Lydia, his wife, executed deed, July 18, 1792, which shows that she was the daughter of Simeon Keen. B. LXXVI, p. 247.

See also deed, Jan'y 8, 1793, B. LXXXI, p. 96, in which the widow and some of the children of Simeon Keen, including Lydia and her husband, join.

Dec. 2, 1805, he was appointed Adm'r on the estate of Peleg Rogers Jr., son of Peleg[4].

July 1, 1845, John Ford was appointed Adm'r of the estate of Timothy Rogers, "*the next of kin,* Arthur Rogers," declining to be appointed, and requesting the appointment of Ford. Arthur Rogers was the oldest son of Isaac[5], son of Peleg[4].

He left no real estate, and his personal property was appraised at $70.00, which was paid over to creditors for expenses of last sickness and funeral; among these creditors were Lydia Lewis, Susanna Keen, and Benjamin Keen.

Oct. 16, 1807, his interest in his wife's real estate and real estate of his own, were levied upon, on an execution in favor of Nathaniel Rogers of Lincolnville, Maine, whose agent, George Little, conveyed, Oct. 15, 1808, to Benjamin Keen, so much of the real estate levied upon as Timothy had purchased of Stephen Keen. B. CIX, p. 186.

121.

VI. RACHEL ROGERS[5] (*Amos[4], Timothy[3], Timothy[2], John[1]*) was born in Marshfield about October, 1758; she married, June 24, 1779, George Little, son of Lemuel and Penelope [Eames] Little, born, April 15, 1754; baptized, July 7, 1754; he died, July 22, 1809, and she, August 8, 1838.

Children, born in Marshfield:

- — i. George Little[6], b. Aug. 12, 1781; d. unm. July 23, 1811.
- — ii. Rachel Wales Little[6], b. Dec. 12, 1783; d. unm. Jan'y 21, 1810.
- iii. Persis Rogers Little[6], b. June 4, 1787; m. Aaron Lummas, May 22, 1814.
- iv. Polly Little[6], b. May 3, 1789; m. John Collamore.
- + v. Edward Preble Little[6], b. April 29, 1792. See No. 208.
- — vi. Amos Rogers Little[6], b. Jan'y 7, 1794; d. Aug. 2, 1815.
- vii. Almira Little[6], b. Mar. 8, 1796; m. Joseph Torrey.
- viii. Statira Little[6], b. April 30, 1798.

"Capt. George Little was a distinguished Naval Officer in the Revolution; and again in 1799 and 1800, in the war with France. He was First Lieut. of the 'Protector' and commanded the 'Wanderer' and 'Boston.' He was discharged from the navy, Oct. 20, 1801. under the Peace Establishment Act."

He named his second son for Commodore Edward Preble of Portland, Maine.

Will of Rachel Little, d. June 21, 1838, mentions son, Edward P. Little; daughter Polly, wife of John Collamore [of Scituate]; daughter Persis R., wife of Aaron Lummas [Poplin, N. H.]; daughter Statira, wife of William Eames; grandsons George Torrey and Joseph Grafton Torrey, children of the late Joseph Torrey, deceased.

Statira Little[6] m. Dec. 5, 1821, William Eames, b. Oct. 9, 1794; he d. Feb. 18, 1874, and she May 21, 1881.

122.

VI. PERSIS ROGERS[5] (*Amos[4], Timothy[3], Timothy[2], John[1]*) was born in Marshfield, May 14, 1761; she married, Dec. 2, 1779, Melzar Turner Oakman, son of Samuel and Deborah [Turner] Oakman, born, June 29, 1750; H. C., 1771; she died, December 9, 1785; he married again, and died December 3, [23], 1795, [1797.]

Children, born in Marshfield:

- i. Persis Rogers Oakman[6], b. May 13, 1782.
- + ii. Polly Oakman[6], b. Sept. 7, 1783. See No. 146.
- iii. Rachel Oakman[6], b. Nov. 23, 1785.

123.

VI. ATHERTON WALES ROGERS⁵ (*Amos⁴, Timothy³, Timothy², John¹*) was born in Marshfield; was baptized, May 1, 1763; he married, November 24, 1789, Mary Little, daughter of Lemuel and Penelope [Eames] Little, born, April 1, 1767; he died, June 12, 1792; and she married, October 26, 1797, Joseph Clift, and died in August, 1834.

Children, born in Marshfield:

— 272.   Polly Little⁶, bap. Mar. 20, 1791; d. unm. June 15, 1825.
+ 273.   Rachel Wales⁶, bap. April 29, 1792.

129.

VI. EGGATHA ROGERS⁵ (*Zaccheus⁴, Timothy³, Timothy², John¹*) was born in Marshfield, December 4, 1757; she married, November 12, 1782, John Hatch; no record of family found; undoubtedly they moved away from Scituate.

130.

VI. REBECCA ROGERS⁵ (*Zaccheus⁴, Timothy³, Timothy², John¹*) was born in Marshfield; baptized, July 15, 1759; she married, October 24, 1781, James Wright, son of Abner and Mary [Whittemore] Wright, born March 21, 1760; he died, September 23, 1789, and she, February 28, 1823.

Children, born in Marshfield:

† i.   Christopher Wright⁶, b. Apr. 7, 1782.
  ii.   Child⁶, died unmarried,

130—i.

VII. *Christopher Wright⁶*, married, November 10, 1805, Abigail

Baker of Portland, Me.; he died in Portland, July 6, 1859, and she, March 22, 1866.

Children, born in Portland:

—   i.   Harriet Sumner Wright[7], b. May 16, 1806; d. Sept. 18, 1807.
     ii.   Frances Baker Wright[7], b. Nov. 10, 1807.
     iii.   Franklin Wright[7], b. May 10, 1809.
     iv.   Henry Baker Wright[7], b. Dec. 1, 1810.
     v.   Harriet Sumner Wright[7], b. July 10, 1812.
—   vi.   Christopher Wright[7], b. May 20,1814; d. Nov. 23, 1842.
     vii.   Andrew Jackson Wright[7], b. Sept. 15, 1816.
     viii.   George Augustus Wright[7], b. Ap'l 20, 1819.
     ix.   Susan Sumner Wright[7], b. Feb'y 16, 1821.
     xi.   James Rackleff Wright[7], b. May 17, 1823; d. Nov. 30, 1863.
     xii.   Elizabeth Greely Wright[7], b. Aug. 23, 1825.
     xiii.   Frances Louisa Wright[7], b. June 19, 1830.

Frances Baker Wright[7], married, Dec. 14, 1826, Charles Clement Collins, born, Dec. 18, 1801. She died May 4, 1828, leaving

     i.   Charles Francis Collins[8], b. Ap'l 2, 1828.

Harriet Sumner Wright[7], married, Nov. 26, 1839, Francis Orville Libby. See "Libby Family" p. 493.

131.

VI.   Z ACCHEUS ROGERS[5] (*Zaccheus*[4], *Timothy*[3], *Timothy*[2], *John*[1]) was born in Marshfield; baptized, November 21, 1761; he married, May 9, 1785, Ruth Oakman, daughter of Tobias and Ruth [Little] Oakman, born, December 27, 1761; he died, August 17, 1816.

Children, born in Marshfield:

    274.   Zaccheus[6], b.
+   275.   Ruth[6], b. Sept. 16, 1790. See No. 241.
    276.   Charles[6], b.
—   277.   Fobes[6], b. in 1795; drowned Sept. 10, 1802.
+   278.   Louisa[6], b. June 10, 1801.

The will of Zaccheus[4] gives a legacy to the children of his deceased son, Zaccheus[5].

Zaccheus[6] went to sea young and is said to have settled on an island in the Pacific Ocean.

Charles[6] went to Castine, Me., where he was Postmaster; he married and had children :

    —   1. Mehitable[7], d. unmarried.
    —   2. Louisa[7], d. unmarried.
    —   3. Bethia[7], d. unmarried.
         4. Austress[7], m. twice and lived in Lynn.

134.

VI. CHARLES ROGERS[5] (*Zaccheus*[4], *Timothy*[3], *Timothy*[2], *John*[1]) was born in Marshfield, February 22, 1768; he settled in Portland, Maine; he married, October 17, 1794, Hannah Thomas, daughter of Peter and Karenhappuch [Cox] Thomas, born, December 8, 1775; he died July 20, 1840, and she September 29, 1860.

Children, born in Portland:

  + 279. Charles[6], b. Sept. 1, 1797.
  — 280. Cornelia[6], b. Aug. 14, 1799 ; d. June 10, 1801.
      281. Cornelia[6], b. Dec. 7, 1801.
  + 282. Francis Henry[6], b. Jan'y 6, 1804.
      283. Sally Thomas[6], b. Feb'y 17,1806 ; m. Stephen Emmons.
      284. Almira Lord[6], b. June 1, 1808 ; m. Edward L. Grueby.
  + 285. Martha Caroline[6], b. Sept. 3, 1810.
  — 286. Mary Hobart[6], b. Mar. 23, 1813 ; died young.
  + 287. John Thomas[6], b. Ap'l 7, 1815.
  — 288. Eleanor[6], b. Mar. 27, 1818 ; d. Nov. 13, 1818.

Cornelia[6], married, June 19, 1837, Charles H. Brandt ; no children.

135.

VI. BENJAMIN ROGERS[5] (*Zaccheus*[4], *Timothy*[3], *Timothy*[2], *John*[1]) was born in Marshfield in 1770; he married, July 21, 1799, Rachel Jones, born, December 16, 1777; he died, April 2, 1846, aged seventy-six, and she, Feb'y 17, 1864, aged eighty-seven.

Children, born in Pembroke:

+ 289.   Benjamin⁶, b. May 27, 1800.
+ 290.   Alvan⁶, b. July 31, 1802.
+ 291.   Rachel⁶, b.
+ 292.   Mary⁶, b.
+ 293.   Prince⁶, b. ——, 1808.
+ 294.   Harvey⁶, b. Oct. 3, 1811.

138.

VI.   SAMUEL ROGERS⁵ (*Adam⁴, Timothy³, Timothy²,
John¹*) was born in Marshfield in 1761; baptized, August
4, 1765; he married, January 12, 1786, Patience Little,
daughter of Ephraim and Anna [Baker] Little, born in
Marshfield, August 31, 1761; they settled in Castine,
Me., but about 1807 moved to Lincolnville, Me.; she
died ——, and he married, October 17, 1818, Sarah
Nash; he died, March 31, 1850.

Children, all by first wife, born in Castine:

+ 295.   Anna Little⁶, b. Feb'y 17, 1787.
+ 296.   Lydia⁶, b. Oct. 14, 1788.
+ 297.   Samuel⁶, b. June 30, 1790.
— 298.   Ephraim⁶, b. Mar. 3, 1792; d. unm.; lost at sea.
+ 299.   Atherton Wales⁶, b. Nov. 13, 1793.
+ 300.   Patience Little⁶, b. Aug. 25, 1795.
+ 301.   Alice⁶, b. Ap'l 4, 1797.
+ 302.   Sally⁶, b. Jan'y 15, 1799.
+ 303.   Adam⁶, b. Ap'l 23, 1801.
— 304.   Celia⁶, b. ——, 1803; d. in infancy.
+ 305.   Elisha⁶, b. Dec. 22, 1805.

Patience Little was cousin to George Little who married Rachel
Rogers.

139.

VI.   ELIZABETH ROGERS⁵ (*Adam⁴, Timothy³, Timothy², John¹*) was born in Marshfield, November 30, 1763;
baptized, August 4, 1765; she married, December 26,

1785 (as the second of his four wives), John Pendleton of Long Island in Penobscot Bay, now Islesborough, son of William and Judith [Carr] Pendleton, born in 1752; he died, October 13, 1845, and she, September 24, 1813.

Children, born in Islesborough, Maine:

—   i.   Adam Pendleton[6], b. 1787; d. unm.

     ii. Henry Pendleton[6], b. Feb'y 22, 1790.

    iii. Lydia Jane Pendleton[6], b.

+ 305a iv. Eliza Pendleton[6], b. May —, 1796.

     v. Elisha Pendleton[6], b. 1798.

+ 305b vi. George Pendleton[6], b. Feb'y 22, 1800.

These may not be given in the exact order of births; and there were probably others who died in childhood.

Henry and *Elisha* both settled in Virginia, married and had families; Henry had two sons, both of whom died, unmarried, in the yellow fever epedemic before the war; and Elisha's only son died, unmarried, during the war; Henry died in September, 1876, and Elisha, December 25, 1873.

141.

VI. WALTER ROGERS[5] (*Adam[4], Timothy[3], Timothy[2], John[1]*) was born at Marshfield, August 6, 1767; baptized, October 4, 1767; he married, October 21, 1794, Betsey Barstow, daughter of Daniel and Betty [Tilden] Barstow, born, August 1, 1772; baptized, May 4, 1773; they lived in Marshfield, later in Braintree, and after 1805, in Sudbury, except two years spent in Waltham during the erection of a factory; he died in Sudbury, June 11, 1860, and she, March 10, 1861.

Children, the first three born in Marshfield; the next three in Braintree; the next two in Sudbury and the other in Waltham:

306. Betsey[6], b. Sept. 24, 1795; bap. at M. May 25, 1796.

307. Lydia[6], b. Nov. 16, 1797.

+ 308. Lucy Barstow[6], b. Jan'y 20, 1800.

+ 309. Nabby[6], [Abigail] b. Nov. 21, 1801.
+ 310. Mary[6], b. Feb'y 26, 1803.
+ 311. Jane[6], b. Mar. 4, 1805.
+ 312. Walter[6], b. Nov. 23, 1807.
— 313. Nancy[6], b. May 9, 1810; d. May 31, 1818.
+ 314. Samuel Barstow[6], b. Oct. 15, 1813.

He was taxed in Braintree, in 1802 to 1805, inclusive.

Betsey[6], married, Gardner Hunt; no children.

Lydia[6], married, April 13, 1823, Loring Eaton; she died, August 5, 1826; no children.

142.

VI. ADAM ROGERS[5] (*Adam[4]*, *Timothy[3]*, *Timothy[2]*, *John[1]*) was born in Marshfield, January 9, 1769, according to the record in his father's Bible, but April 17, 1769, according to the record in his own Bible, the record of his marriage and the inscription on his gravestone; baptized, July 2, 1769; he married, September 7, 1801, Olive Gay, daughter of Ephraim (according to the family Bible, but David according to the record of the marriage) and Thankful [Howard] Gay, born January 20, 1777, in Nova Scotia, according to the record of the marriage, but in St. John, N. B., according to the family Bible; he died, April 4, 1857, and she, January 28, 1859.

Children, born in Lincolnville, Maine;

+ 315. Thankful[6], b. July 11, 1802.
+ 316. Celia[6], b. May 13, 1804. See No. 299.
+ 317. Jane[6], b. June 18, 1807.
— 317a. Olive Gay[6], b. Oct. 23, 1809; d. Aug. 19, 1815.
+ 317b. Lydia[6], b. Mar. 13, 1814.
— 317c. Olive[6], b. June 24, 1817; d. Ap'l 28, 1829.
— 317d. Son[6], b. Feb'y 18, 1820; d. same day.
+ 317e. Mary Bradford[6], b. Ap'l 13, 1822.

These names and dates are from the family Bible, and the first three are found on the town record.

He settled at first in Lincolnville, but afterwards moved to Bangor; at what date is not known, but as early as 1838; in 1843 and 1846, Adam Rogers was a carpenter, on Charles Street, and in 1851, a blacksmith boarding with David McCoy and in 1855, with J. Decrow; McCoy was a farmer living on the "Levant Road" in Bangor, now Ohio Street.

Adam Rogers was adjudged insane, Oct. 13, 1856, on the petition of Thankful Decrow, Jane R. McCoy and David McCoy, and a guardian appointed, who settled an account in June, 1857, in which he credits himself with "cash paid A. Rogers to Lowell," Oct. 18, 1856, and with cash paid, Ap'l 8, 1857, for "bringing the body of A. Rogers from Lowell" and expenses of burial.

His wife had evidently remained in Bangor, for the guardian was allowed for bills paid, during that time, to Noah McKusick for her board, and for rent to Thomas Boynton; he also paid a bill for her board after her husband's death, to Jane McCoy.

On settlement of the guardian's account there was about $200 in his hands, but the court record does not show any further proceedings.

In Mt. Hope Cemetery, in Bangor, in the McCoy lot, is a head-stone with the inscription, "Adam Rogers, Born April 17, 1769. Died April 4, 1859. Olive G., his wife, Born June 20, 1777. Died Jan'y 28, 1859." The "1859" in the date of his death on the grave-stone is evidently an error for "1857."

Much time and labor were expended in efforts to trace this family, the only clew at starting being the fact that an Adam Rogers was in Bangor in 1838; and it was not until the manuscript was in the printer's hands that the family Bible was located.

The following, except the figures in brackets is taken from the *Monthly Chronicle*, p. 345, published in 1838 :

"Marshfield, (Mass.) vs. Scarborough (Me.)

"We find in the *Bangor Whig* the following letter from Mr. Adam Rogers, whose family pride appears to have been aroused by the publication of the case he refers to.

"*To the Editors of the Whig and Courier:*

"GENTS : — Having seen in the *Weslyan Journal* of the 25th ult., a notice of a case of remarkable longevity, in a family that originated in Scarborough in this State, the children of which were eleven in number, two of whom are still living, eight having died at the age of eighty years, I take the liberty to send you a notice of another case, which though not exactly of the kind, is in my belief more remarkable.

"My father's family were all born and brought up in Marshfield, Massachusetts, and consisted of six brothers and four sisters. The following died at the ages set against their names.

Timothy Rogers,	100 years.	[78]
Israel Rogers,	105 "	[89]
Peleg Rogers,	107 "	[95]
Amos Rogers,	85 "	[85]
Zacheus Rogers,	97 "	[86]
Adam Rogers, (my father)	104 "	[102]
Lydia Lewis,	90 "	
Betsey Tolman, if living, is about	100 "	
I have not heard of her death.		
Eunice Ford died last year,	100 "	
Jane Oldham, if living, upwards of	100 "	

Making their aggregate ages, 988 "

"It is probable that Betsey Tolman and Jane Oldham died a few years since. If so it will reduce the amount somewhat. Will some one in Massachussetts, who may know the fact, inform me if they are dead, when they died, by letter addressed, Bangor, Maine, directed to me."

ADAM ROGERS.

The figures in brackets are the ages as shown by the records; the ages of the four sisters are known only approximately; while the average age of the ten does not come up to the statement, it is certain that it was over *ninety*—a remarkable longevity.

143.

VI. EUNICE ROGERS[5] (*Adam*[4], *Timothy*[3], *Timothy*[2], *John*[1]) was born in Marshfield, February 17, 1771; baptized April 25, 1771; she married, April 23, 1797, Hezekiah French of "Ducktrap," now Lincolnville, Maine, son of Ebenezer and Rebecca [Kidder] French, born in Billerica, January 18, 1773; he died, May 14, 1843, and she, March 29, 1844.

Children, born in Lincolnville.

    i. Lydia French[6], b. Jan'y 17, 1800.
    ii. Ebenezer French[6], b. July 16, 1801.
—   iii. Eliza French[6], b. Ap'l 9, 1803; d. Nov. 13, 1817.
    iv. Hezekiah French[6], b. Jan'y 8, 1805.

v.   Francis Henry French[6], b. Sept. 3, 1806.
. † vi.   Abel French[6], b. Ap'l 23, 1808.
vii.   Philander French[6], b. Ap'l 27, 1810.
viii.   Beulah French[6], b. Jan'y 14, 1813.
— ix.   Eunice French[6], b. May 4, 1814; d. Jan'y 14, 1816.
x.   Zadock Joshua Heywood French[6], b. Oct. 2, 1817.

The record of the marriage of *Eunice Rogers[5]* states that she was born, Jan'y 4, 1771.

Lydia French[6], married Minot Crehore; she died Aug. 18, 1866: no children.

143—vi.

VII. *Abel French[6]*, married, July 10, 1832, Jane Drinkwater, daughter of Micajah and Amy [Wyman] Drinkwater, born, December 24, 1810; she died February 24, 1844; he married, ——, Eliza Ann Phipps, born, May 27, 1815; she died, October 29, 1850; he married, May 30, 1852, Lucy Ann Pendleton, born, December 29, 1821; he died, April 21, 1889, leaving her surviving.

Children, born in Lincolnville:

By first wife:
† i.   Oscar Wyman French[7], b. Dec. 21, 1834.
— ii.   Louisa French[7], b. Nov. 18, 1836; d. Nov. 26, 1837.
— iii.   Charles French[7], b. Sept. 22, 1838; d. Mar. 5, 1841.
† iv.   Allen Drinkwater French[7], b. Aug. 16, 1840.
v.   Evander LeRoy French[7]. b. Aug. 24, 1842.

By second wife:
— vi.   Edward French[7], b. Ap'l 27, 1847; d. Sept. 18, 1850.

143—vi—i.

VIII. *Oscar Wyman French[7]*, married, Sept. 6, 1856, Angelia Furbish Perry, daughter of Wilder and Hannah [Young] Perry, born Jannary 23, 1836.

Children, born in Lincolnville:
† i.   Jane Isabel French[8], b. Oct. 6, 1859.
† ii.   Mary Perry French[8], b. July 5, 1862.
— iii.   Leon Howard French[8], b. Jan'y 14, 1868.
— vi.   Robert Allen French[8], b. May 28, 1871.

143—vi—i—i.

IX. *Jane Isabel French*[8], married, April 5, 1883, Fred Nathaniel Fletcher, son of Abisha Benson and Miriam [Spratt] Fletcher, born, September 15, 1856.

Children, born in China, Maine:

—   i.   Robert French Fletcher[9], b. Feb'y 12. 1884; d. Jan'y 25, 1885.

     ii.   Ethel Louise Fletcher[9], b. Jan'y 22, 1886.

     iii.   Harold Augustus Fletcher[9], b. Dec. 10, 1888.

     iv.   Howard French Fletcher[9], b. Sept. 12, 1893.

143—vi—i—ii.

IX. *Mary Perry French*[8], married, June 19, 1886, John Frank Rich, son of John and Sarah [Daggett] Rich, born, April 17, 1855.

Children, born in Hope, Maine:

     i.   Perry Frank Rich[9], b. Feb'y 19, 1887.

—   ii.   Raymond Rich[9], b. Dec. 23, 1895; d. July 5, 1896.

143—vi—iv.

VIII. *Allen Drinkwater French*[7], married November 14, 1863, Mary Elizabeth Yates, daughter of Freeman and Mary Lowell [Hall] Yates, born December 11, 1842, at South Berwich, Maine.

Children, born in Belfast, Maine:

†   i.   Clarence Freeman French[8], b. Aug. 2, 1864.

†   ii.   Herbert Allen French[8], b. May 8, 1866.

     iii.   Erminnie Angelia French[8], b. Feb'y 9, 1868.

—   iv.   Oscar Leroy French[8], b. May 8, 1871; d. July 11, 1872.

     v.   Allen Evander French[8], b. Mar. 12, 1873.

143—vi—iv—i.

IX. *Clarence Freeman French*[8], married, July 25, 1891, at Waltham, Mass., Alice Lydia Bates, daughter of Joseph Curtis and Charlotte Elizabeth [Moulton] Bates, born, September 17, 1866.

Children, born in Waltham:

     i.   Joseph Allen French[9], b. Aug. 2, 1892.

     ii.   Herbert Moulton French[9], b. July 19, 1894.

     iii.   George Lowell French[9], b. Ap'l 26, 1896.

     iv.   Clarence Bates[9], b. Ap'l 12, 1898.

143—vi—iv—ii.

IX.   *Herbert Allen French*⁹, married, June 22, 1892, at Waltham, Clara Adelia Comstock, daughter of John Newton and Sarah Ann [Baxter] Comstock, born, June 26, 1867.

Child, born in Worcester:

   i.   Winslow Hall French⁹, b. Oct. 16, 1897.

144.

VI.   JANE [JEANE] ROGERS⁵ (*Adam*⁴, *Timothy*³, *Timothy*², *John*¹) was born in Marshfield, February 17, 1773; baptized, May 16, 1773; she married [published, December 8, 1794] Joshua Palmer of Camden, Me., born, October 30, 1769; she died, October 5, 1803, and he married again.

Children, born in Camden:

   i.   Jane Palmer⁶, b. Dec. 2, 1796.
   ii.   Joshua Palmer⁶, b. Feb'y 17, 1799.
   iii.   Hezekiah Palmer⁶, b. Jan'y 3, 1802.
   iv.   Sophia Palmer⁶. b. Sept. 23, 1803.

By his second wife, Hannah, Joshua Palmer had five children, born in Camden.   See Town Records.

146 and 122—ii.

VI.   ELISHA ROGERS⁵ (*Adam*⁴, *Timothy*³, *Timothy*², *John*¹) was born in Marshfield, July 5, 1777; baptized August 17, 1777; he married [published, March 30, 1806] POLLY OAKMAN⁶, daughter of Melzar Turner and Persis [Rogers⁵] Oakman, born, September 7, 1783; he died June 24, 1832, and she, June 16, 1860.

Child, born in Marshfield:

+   318.   Elisha⁶, b. Ap'l 16, 1807.

147.

VI.   PENELOPE ROGERS[5] (*Samuel[4], Samuel[3], Timothy[2], John[1]*) was born in Marshfield, June 7, 1733; she married, November 29, 1759, Levi Ford, son of William and Hannah [Trouant] Ford, born, May 18, 1739; he died January 9, 1813, and she, April 30, 1830, in her ninety-seventh year.

Children, born in Marshfield:

      i.   William Ford[6], b. ——; died at sea.
      ii.   Asa Ford[6], b.
      iii.   Hannah Ford[6], b. ——. See No. 119.
      iv.   Charles Ford[6], b.
      v.   Samuel Ford[6], b.
      vi.   Lydia Ford[6], b.

Samuel Rogers[4], in his will, mentions his daughter, Penelope Foord.   See No. 63.

149.

VI.   THOMAS ROGERS[5] (*Samuel[4], Samuel[3], Timothy[2], John[1]*) was born in Marshfield, January 25, 1735/6; he married, November 19, 1761, [published, April 14, 1761] Submit Hatch of Scituate, daughter of Benjamin and Jerusha [Phillips] Hatch, baptized, July 15, 1744; he died, December 13, 1813, and she, January 2, 1829.

Children, born in Marshfield:

    319.   Charles[6], bap. Sept. 11, 1763.
—   320.   Jerusha[6], bap. Feb'y 24, 1765; d. unm. Oct. 9, 1850.
    321.   Samuel[6], bap. July 27, 1766.
+   322.   Jennie[6], [Jena] bap. Oct. 3, 1768.
—   323.   Mary Phillips[6], bap. May 1, 1772; d. young.
+   324.   Isaac[6], b. June 15, 1784; bap. Sept. 19, 1784.

His will d. Nov. 4, 1813, p. Jan'y 1, 1814, mentions wife, Submit; sons, Samuel and Isaac; daughters, Jerusha Rogers and Jena Rogers; and children of son, Charles, deceased, Polly, Sally and Mary.

Charles[6], married, May 5, 1788, Lydia Healey; he died at sea, Aug. 4, 1798, leaving the three children named in his father's will.

Samuel[6], (a clockmaker) settled in East Bridgewater, where he married and had a family. See Mitchell's History, p. 288.

150.

VI. SIMEON ROGERS[5] (*Samuel*[4], *Samuel*[3], *Timothy*[2], *John*[1]) was born in Marshfield, May 18, 1737; he married, June 29, 1767, Sarah Clift, daughter of William and Judith [——] Clift, born March 26, 1739; he died, November 16, 1820, and she, February 24. 1814.

Children, born in Marshfield:

— 325. Clift[6], b. July 22, 1768; bap. July 2, 1769; d. 1785.
+ 326. Sarah[6], b. July 29, 1771; bap. May 10, 1772.
+ 327. Luther[6], b. Aug. 21, 1778; bap. Oct. 17, 1778.

His will, d. Ap'l 23, 1812, gives a legacy to his daughter, Sarah Eames (now Ames) and the rest of his property to son, Luther; the payment of legacy to Sarah was acknowledged, May 25, 1823, by John T. Ames and Sarah Ames, his wife.

Deed, dated March 21, 1768, between Thomas Rogers, Jr., and Simeon Rogers, divided the "real estate of our father, the late Samuel Rogers."

154.

VI. MARY ROGERS[5] (*Samuel*[4], *Timothy*[3], *Timothy*[2], *John*[1]) was born in Marshfield, February 26, 1748/9; she married, June 16, 1768, Ezekiel Reed of Abington, son of Ezekiel and Hannah [Beal] Reed, born March 3, 1744; he died, April 12, 1830, and she ——.

Children, born in Abington:

i. Polly Reed[6], b. Sept. 7, 1769.
ii. Zelotes Reed[6], b. Ap'l 9, 1771.
iii. Ezekiel Reed[6], b. Sept. 16, 1772.
iv. Zebulon Reed[6], b. May 30, 1774.
v. Hannah Reed[6], b. Jan'y 22, 1776.

    vi.   Olive Reed[6], b. Ap'l 9, 1777.
    vii. Jesse Reed[6], b. Aug. 29, 1778.
    viii. Charles Reed[6], b. Ap'l 5, 1780.
    ix.   Abraham Reed[6], b. Ap'l 25, 1782.
    x.   Briggs Rogers Reed[6], b. May 2, 1784.
    xi.   Samuel Licander Reed[6]. b. July 24, 1786.

Ap'l 2, 1768, has been given as the date of the marriage, but the Marshfield record gives June 16, 1768; the other is probably the date of the "Intentions."

181.

VII. REUBEN ROGERS[6] (*Caleb*[5], *Caleb*[4], *John*[3], *John*[2], *John*[1]) was born in Hanover, in 1780; baptized, October 24, 1784; he married [published, March 16, 1806,] Abigail Stoddard of Scituate; he died, April 12, 1867, and she, June 11, 1867.

Children, born in Hanover:

    328. Reuben Harlow[7], b. Mar. 21,1807 ; moved to Michigan.
    329. Zenas[7], b. May 10, 1809 ; settled in Braintree.
    330. Edwin[7], b. Dec. 2, 1812.
 — 331. Bela[7], b. July 10, 1816 ; d. in childhood.
    332. Abigail Jane[7], b. July 10, 1816 ; m. Melvin Stoddard of Abington.
 — 333. Harriet Newell[7] ; d. unm. at age 22 ; mentioned in will of Sarah Rogers, widow of Caleb[5].
    334. Andrew[7], b. ——; settled in Chelsea.
    335. Sophronia Mead[7] ; m. Henry Hobel of Pembroke.

Reuben Harlow, Zenas, Edwin, Abigail Jane, "Hariot Newel" and Andrew, children of Reuben and Abigail Rogers, baptized, Aug. 20,1826.

"Sophronia Meed, child of Abigail, wife of Reuben Rogers," "baptized April 27, 1828."

Melzar Sprague was appointed Adm'r, May 13, 1867, upon the petition of Abigail Rogers, widow ; sons, Reuben H. Rogers of Michigan, Zenas Rogers of Braintree, Edwin Rogers of Hanover, and Andrew Rogers of Chelsea ; and daughters, Abigail Stoddard, wife of Melvin Stoddard of Abington and Sophronia R. Hobel [signing "Hobill"] wife of Henry Hobel of Pembroke.

188.

VII. ABRAHAM BOOTH ROGERS[6] (*John*[5], *John*[4], *Thomas*[3], *John*[2], *John*[1]) was born in Pembroke, May [June ?] 1, 1769; he married, December 1, 1791, Mary Keen, daughter of Joseph and Rebecca Keen; they moved to Tinmouth, Vt., where she died in 1835; he married Orpha Harvey, in 1837, and died in 1843.

Children, the first three born in Marshfield, and the others probably in Tinmouth:

    336. Abraham Chapman[7], b. Sept. 2, 1793.
— 337. Rebecca Howland[7], b. Aug. 1, 1795; d. Sept. 17, 1796.
    338. Sarah Chapman[7], b. Aug. 11, 1797.
    339. Joseph[7], b. 1799.
    340. Mary[7], b. 1804.
    341. Isaac[7], b. 1807.
    342. Mercy[7], b. 1812.

The History of Danby, Vt., has a brief account of the families of some of the children.

203.

VII. STEPHEN ROGERS[6] (*Joseph*[5], *John*[4], *Thomas*[3], *John*[2], *John*[1]) was born in Marshfield, May 25, 1770; he married, February 22, 1792, Alice Estes of Hanover, daughter of Robert and Beulah [Wing] Estes, born, March 27, 1772; he died, August 6, 1835, and she, May 25, 1851.

No children.

Will of Stephen Rogers of Marshfield, d. June 13, 1835, p. Nov. 24, 1835, mentions wife, Alice; brother, Abraham Rogers; sisters, Mary Kirby, Anna Wing, Esther Dillingham, Edy Little and Elizabeth Phillips; nephews, Stephen Dillingham and Abraham R. Wing; Stephen R. Rogers, son of Moses F. and Alice R. Rogers, daughter of Moses F.; also his brother-in-law, Estes, and several others not on the Rogers' side of the family.

Apparently his will was not found at first, for on August 26, 1835, administration was granted to Moses F. Rogers; but no further proceedings were had and Nov. 24, 1835, his will was admitted to probate.

204.

VII. MARY ROGERS[6] (*Joseph5, John4, Thomas3, John2, John1*) was born in Marshfield, November 13, 1772; she married, March 14, 1791, her step-brother Restcome Kirby, son of Barnabas and Elizabeth [Allen] Kirby, born, March 30, 1770.

Children, born in Dartmouth:

    i.   Silas Kirby[7], b. July 13, 1792.
    ii. Barnabas Kirby[7], b. Nov. 9, 1793.
    iii. Joseph Kirby[7], b. Mar. 23, 1796.
    iv. Isaac Kirby[7], b. Oct. 29, 1798.
— v. Child[7] b. Jan'y 15, 1801; d. Mar. 20, 1801.
    vi. Elizabeth Kirby[7], b. Mar. 17, 1802.
    vii. Stephen Kirby[7], b. Dec. 23, 1804.
    viii. Abraham Kirby[7], b. June 3, 1807.

205.

VII. ANNA ROGERS[6] (*Joseph5, John4, Thomas3, John2, John1*) was born in Marshfield, February 2, 1775; she married, May 8, 1799, Samuel Wing, son of Paul and Abigail [Wing] Wing of Sandwich, born, October 12, 1774; he died, February 24, 1854, and she, October 1, 1863.

Children, born in Sandwich:

— i. Mary Rogers Wing[7], b. Sept. 15, 1800; d. unm. Sept. 19, 1873.
+ ii. Beulah Wing[7], b. Feb'y 2, 1803. See No. 335.
    iii. Abraham [Abram] Rogers Wing[7], b. July 4, 1805.
    iv. Lindley Murray Wing[7], b. July 9, 1807.
    v. Joseph Rogers Wing[7], b. Aug. 31, 1809.

—   vi.   Hepzibah [Hepsey] Wing[7], b. Jan'y 3, 1812; d. unm.
            May 15, 1836.
     vii.   Stephen Rogers Wing[7], b. July 10, 1814.

206.

VII.   ESTHER ROGERS[6] (*Joseph*[5], *John*[4], *Thomas*[3], *John*[2], *John*[1]) was born in Marshfield, April 19, 1777; she married, July 19, 1798, Joseph Dillingham of Falmouth, son of Ignatius and Deborah [———] Dillingham, born, November 1, 1776; he died, April 20, 1845, and she, July 21, 1856.

Children, born in West Falmouth:

+   i.   Stephen Dillingham[7], b. Oct. 26, 1799. See 99—v—i.
     ii.   Reuben Dillingham[7], b. Feb'y 26, 1802; d. Nov.
            20, 1858.
†   iii. Deborah Dillingham[7], b. Sept. 20, 1804.
     iv.   Mary Dillingham[7], b. Mar. 5, 1807; d. July 16, 1830.
—   v.   Elizabeth Dillingham[7], b. Oct. 23, 1809; d. unm. Ap'l
            20, 1830.
     vi.   Abram Dillingham[7], b. Sept. 4, 1812; d. July 7, 1879.
†   vii. Edward Gifford Dillingham[7], b. Oct. 9, 1814.

206—iii.

VIII.   *Deborah Dillingham*[7], married, June 12, 1823, Jonathan Boyce, son of Jonathan and Anna [Breed] Boyce, born, August 1, 1799; he died, January 10, 1889, and she, April 26, 1891.

Children, born in West Falmouth:

     i.   Gilbert Russell Boyce[8], b. Oct. 2, 1824.
†   ii.   Mary Elizabeth Boyce[8], b. June 30, 1830.

206—iii—ii.

IX.   *Mary Elizabeth Boyce*[8], married, October 23, 1856, William O. Newhall, son of John and Delia [Breed] Newhall, born, November 9, 1828.

Children, born in Lynn.

     i.   William Boyce Newhall[9], b. Jan'y 13, 1860.
†   ii.   Mary Alice Newhall[9], b. Oct. 19, 1861.

206—iii—ii—ii.

X. *Mary Alice Newhall⁹*, married, November 20, 1889, Edmund Francis Buffinton, son of Samuel K. and Mary S. Buffinton of Fall River, born, November 2, 1860.

Child, born in Fall River :

      i. Gertrude Elizabeth Buffinton¹⁰, b. July 10, 1892.

206—vii.

VIII. *Edward Gifford Dillingham⁷*, married, June 16, 1836, Nancy Bassett Sanford, daughter of Ephraim and Rachel [Swift] Sanford, born, February 23, 1815 ; she died, March 24, 1879 ; he resides (1898) in Providence, R. I.

Children, born in Falmouth :

—   i. William Sanford Dillingham⁸, b. Nov. 1, 1837 ; d. Sept. 3, 1854.
    ii. Charles Henry Dillingham⁸, b. May 22, 1840.
   iii. Mary Sanford Dillingham⁸, b. June 15, 1843.
   iv. Joseph Dillingham⁸, b. Nov. 2, 1845.
    v. Betsey Lewis Dillingham⁸, b. May 22, 1848.
   vi. Esther Rogers Dillingham⁸, b. Oct. 18, 1851.

208 and 121—v.

VII. EDY ROGERS⁶ (*Joseph⁵, John⁴, Thomas³, John², John¹*) was born in Marshfield, November 19, 1789; she married, March 13, 1811, EDWARD PREBLE LITTLE⁶, (*Rachel⁵, Amos⁴, Timothy³, Timothy², John¹,*) born in Marshfield, November 7, 1791; he died in Lynn, February 6, 1875, and she in Marshfield, September 16, 1852.

Children, born in Marshfield :

     i. Rachel Wales Little⁷, b. Jan'y 7, 1812.
    ii. George Little⁷, b. May 7, 1814.
   iii. Elizabeth Rogers Little⁷, b. Sept. 6, 1816.
† iv. Sarah Gifford Little⁷, b. Ap'l 23, 1819.
†   v. Almira Little⁷, b. July 2, 1822.
   vi. Amos Rogers Little⁷, b. July 27, 1825.
  vii. Mary James Little⁷, b. Nov. 15, 1827.

Rachel Wales Little[7], married, Ap'l 12, 1832, Joseph Healey, son of Daniel and Lucy.

208—iv.

VIII. *Sarah Gifford Little*[7], married, December 9, 1841, Elisha James Sherman of Marshfield, son of Aaron and Lydia [Mitchell] Sherman, born, April 16, 1813, at Marshfield: he died, April 1, 1849; she married, July 14, 1853, Howard Yarnall, son of Enoch and Hannah [Howard] Yarnall, born, August 29, 1808; he died, November 27, 1875, leaving her surviving.

Children, by first husband, the first born in Marshfield, and the other in Tecumseh, Mich.:

† i. Edy Rogers Sherman[8], b. Oct. 22, 1842.
— ii. Lydia Sherman[8], b. Mar. 1, 1846; d. Mar. 15, 1846.

By second husband, born in Philadelphia:

 iii. Howard Edward Yarnall[8], b. July 11, 1854.
 iv. David Gould Yarnall[8], b. Sept. 26, 1857.

208—iv—i.

IX. *Edy Rogers Sherman*[8], married, at Philadelphia, October 3, 1866, Theodore Ashmead Mehl, son of Jacob and Harriet [McCalla] Mehl, born, February 14, 1833, at Germantown, Philadelphia; she died, August 8, 1886, in Philadelphia.

Children, born at Germantown, Philadelphia:

† i. Alfred Sherman Mehl[9], b. Ap'l 18, 1868.
 ii. Frederic Howard Mehl[9], b. July 8, 1870.
 iii. Theodore Ashmead Mehl[9], b. Oct. 10, 1871.

208—iv—i—i.

X. *Alfred Sherman Mehl*[9], married, November 19, 1896, Anna Sutterley, daughter of George Hamilton and Cordelia [Fuller] Sutterley, born, August 4, 1874.

Child, born in Philadelphia:

 i. Alfred Sherman Mehl[10], b. Jan'y 29, 1898.

208—v.

VIII. *Almira Little*[7], married, at Pembroke Meeting, February 15, 1844, Richard Peterson, son of George and Jane [Evans] Peterson, born in Philadelphia, March 8, 1823; he died at Haverford, Pa., December 12, 1893.

Children, born in Philadelphia :

- —   i.   Eliza Gould Peterson[8], b. Jan'y 17, 1845.
- †   ii.   Jane Peterson[8], b. Aug. 31, 1850.
-      iii.   Esther Evans Peterson[8], b. Oct. 16, 1853.
- =   iv.   George Peterson[8], b. Sept. 27, 1856.
- †   v.   Almira Little Peterson[8], b. Dec. 27, 1859.
- †   vi.   Rosalie Berens Peterson[8], b. July 22, 1861.
- —   vii.   Florence Peterson[8], b. Ap'l 14, 1864 ; d. Aug. 27, 1866.

According to the family tradition, the table, upon which the wedding dinner was spread, came over in the Mayflower.

Esther Evans Peterson[8], married, Jan'y 27, 1876, Walter Thomas Baird, son of Matthew and Anne Eliza [Monroe] Baird, born, August 29, 1851 ; he died, August 3, 1881 ; no children.

208—v—ii.

IX.   *Jane Peterson*[8], married, December 12, 1872, Robert Knox McNeely, son of William Tennent and Ann [Wilson] McNeely, born, October 2, 1842.

Children, born in Philadelphia :

-    i.   Florence McNeely[9], b. Feb'y 6, 1875.
-    ii.   Almira Peterson McNeely[9], b. July 17, 1876.
-    iii.   Eleanor McNeely[9], b. Nov. 30, 1878.
-    iv.   Richard Peterson McNeely[9], b. Jan'y 28, 1880.
-    v.   Jane Peterson McNeely[9], b. Jan'y 18, 1881.

208—v—v.

IX.   *Almira Little Peterson*[8], married, April 12, 1887, Charles Howard Colket, son of Coffin and Mary Pennypacker [Walker] Colket, born, July 2, 1859,

Children, born in Philadelphia :

- —   i.   Daughter[9], b. Nov. 19, 1891 ; d. same day.
-    ii.   Tristram Coffin Colket[9], b. May 31, 1896.

208—v—vi.

IX.   *Rosalie Berens Peterson*[8], married, November 12, 1885, Edwin Vernon Dougherty, son of Charles Ashton and Catherine Ann [Arnold] Dougherty, born, October 12, 1860.

Children, born in Philadelphia :

-    i.   Edwin Vernon Dougherty[9], b. Aug. 13, 1886.
-    ii.   Eleanor Dougherty[9], b. Dec. 23, 1893.

212.

VII. Aaron Rogers[6] (*Stephen*[5], *John*[4] *Thomas*[3], *John*[2], *John*[1]) was born in Danby, Vt., May 6, 1776; he married, March 22, 1798, Dinah Folger, daughter of Daniel and Judith [Worth] Folger, born, January 5, 1782; he died, December 30, 1866, at Lynn, Mass., and she, January 16, 1860, at Worcester, Mass.

Children, born in Danby, Vt.:

- — 343. Sarah[7], b. July 2, 1799; d. Sept. 3, 1803.
- 344. Joseph[7], b. Mar. 21, 1801.
- + 345. Moses Folger[7], b. Mar. 25, 1803.
- 346. Aaron[7], b. Jan'y 1, 1805.
- 347. Lydia[7], b. June 28, 1807.
- — 348. Judith[7], b. Sept. 20, 1809; d. unm. Mar. 28, 1883.
- 349. George Dillwyn[7], b. July 8, 1811.
- + 350. Elisha Folger[7], b. June 20, 1813.
- — 351. Hepsibah Folger[7], b. May 19, 1815; d. May 14, 1821.
- — 352. Anson[7], b. Aug. 9, 1817; d. May 18, 1819.
- 353. Eunice Vail[7], b. Aug. 13, 1819.
- 354. Seth[7], b. Feb'y 13, 1823.

Daniel Folger was in the sixth generation from John Folger[1] and grandson of Eleazer[4], whose sister, Abiah Folger, was the wife of Benjamin Franklin.

220.

VII. Deborah Rogers[6] (*James*[5], *Thomas*[4], *Thomas*[3], *John*[2], *John*[1]) was born in Pembroke, August 28, 1788; she married, October 29, 1812, Jacob Willetts, son of James and Joanna [Titus] Willetts, born, January 16, 1785; he died, September 12, 1860, and she, January 11, 1880.

Children, born in Washington, N. Y.:

- — i. Eliza Willetts[7], b. July 10, 1817; d. Nov. 30, 1831.
- † ii. Jane Willetts[7], b. July 25, 1830.

220.—ii.

VIII. *Jane Willetts7*, m. January 15, 1857, Franklin Tompkins Carpenter, son of Isaac and Abby [Sutton] Carpenter and they have :

      i. Willetts Carpenter8, b. Mar. 24, 1859, in Brooklyn, N. Y.

      ii. Frederic Walton Carpenter8, b. May 12, 1876, in Millbrook, N. Y.

230 and 111—iv.

VII. ABIJAH ROGERS6 (*Nathaniel5, Israel4, Timothy3, Timothy2, John1*) was born in Marshfield, January 21, 1782; baptized June 9, 1782; he married, December 5, 1811, Mercy Hatch, daughter of Anthony Eames and Bethiah [Rogers] Hatch, born, March 7, 1789 (see No. 111—iv); he died, September 22, 1867, and she, March 24, 1863.

Children, born in Marshfield:

    355. Mary Williams7, b. Nov. 14, 1815.

  — 356. Calvin Hatch7, b. Aug. 3, 1820; d. unm. Dec. 8, 1849.

  + 357. Eunice Ann7, b. Aug. 27, 1826. (See No. 375.)

Abijah Rogers, his wife, Mercy, releasing dower, by deed ack. June 15, 1830, conveyed land adjoining that belonging to his father, Nathaniel Rogers. B. CLXX, p. 147.

Mary Williams7 m. John Phillips Tilden of Marshfield; they moved to Illinois.

233.

VII. THOMAS ROGERS6 (*Thomas5, Israel4, Timothy3, Timothy2, John1*) was born in Marshfield, July 13, 1782: he married, August 15, 1803, Lavina Soule, daughter of Simeon and Jane [Weston] Soule, born, June 21, 1784; she died, May 19, 1805, and he married, November 28, 1805, Mary [Polly] Clift, daughter of William and Mary [Eames] Clift, born, November 14, 1787; he died, November 21, 1864, and she, September 17, 1875.

Children, born in Marshfield:

By first wife:

+ 358.   Jane Soule[7], b. Aug. 31, 1803.

By second wife:

+ 359.   Judith Clift[7], b. Feb'y 23, 1820.
— 360.   Mary Ames[7], b. July 17, 1822 ; d. unm.
   361.   Lavinia Thomas[7], b. Aug. 9, 1825 ; m. John Clapp.
— 362.   Bethiah Oakman[7], b. April 29, 1827 ; d. unm.

His first wife was in the seventh generation from George Soule of the Mayflower.

Lavinia Thomas[7] married John Clapp and had :

   i.   Elton Bradford Clapp[8], b. Sept. 30, 1847 ; d. unm. May 10, 1897.

234.

VII.   MARTIN ROGERS[6] (*Thomas*[5], *Israel*[4], *Timothy*[3], *Timothy*[2], *John*[1]) was born in Marshfield, April 13, 1784; he married, January 16, 1812, Sally Grinnell, daughter of William and Experience [Dodge] Grinnell, born, September 5, 1792; he died, October 20, 1848, and she, January 30, 1874.

Children, the first six born in Marshfield, and the other two in Belfast, Maine:

+ 363.   Phebe Grinnell[7], b. July 22, 1813.
+ 364.   Sarah Phillips[7], b. May 29, 1815.
+ 365.   Mary Ann[7], b. Mar. 24, 1818.
+ 366.   Martin Crosby[7], b. Aug. 28, 1819.
+ 367.   William Thomas[7], b. Oct. 26, 1821.
+ 368.   Almira Eleanor[7], b. Mar. 12, 1824.
+ 369.   Caroline Jane[7], b. Dec. 17, 1826.
+ 370.   Maria Experience[7], b. Feb'y 18, 1829.

235.

VII.   PHILLIPS ROGERS[6] (*Thomas*[5], *Israel*[4], *Timothy*[3], *Timothy*[2], *John*[1]) was born in Marshfield, March 14,

1787: he married Judith Smith; he died in 1848, and she in 1852.

Children, the first born in Marshfield, and the others in Medford:

† 371. Sarah Peterson[7], b. Dec. 15, 1812.
372. Mary Thomas[7].
373. Henry Phillips[7].
374. Martha Brooks[7].

VIII. *Sarah Peterson Rogers[7]* married Ebenezer Waterman, born, November 4, 1811; he died, Jan'y 23, 1885, and she, April 7, 1884.

Children, born in Medford:

i. Arabella Waterman[8], b. June 3, 1840.
ii. Josephine Waterman[8], b. July 8, 1842,
iii. George Henry Waterman[8], b. Mar. 15, 1849.

236.

VII. AGATHA ROGERS[6] (*Thomas[5], Israel[4], Timothy[3], Timothy[2], John[1]*) was born in Marshfield, July 25, 1795; she married, May 28, 1822, as his second wife, Nathan Williamson, son of Nathan, born, March 23, 1791: he died, October 4, 1877, and she, November 20, 1878.

Children, born in Marshfield:

i. Lavinia Williamson[7].
ii. Mercy Williamson[7].
iii. Warren Williamson[7].
iv. George Washington Williamson[7].
v. Martha Brooks Williamson[7].
vi. Andrew Jackson Williamson[7].
vii. Caroline Cushing Williamson[7].

237.

VII. HOWLAND ROGERS[6] (*Thomas[5], Israel[4], Timothy[3], Timothy[2], John[1]*) was born in Marshfield, January 18, 1798; he married, January 1, 1824, Philenda Clift, daughter of Nathaniel and Mary [Clift] Clift, born, May 23, 1802; he died, October 18, 1875, and she, July 5, 1890.

Children, born in Marshfield:

+ 375.   George Howland[7], b. Feb'y 1, 1825.
+ 376.   Wales Allen[7], b. Aug. 4, 1826.
+ 377.   Nathaniel Clift[7], b. May 18, 1833.
+ 378.   Philenda Adeline[7], b. May 28, 1835.

238.

VII. WARREN ROGERS[6] (*Thomas[5], Israel[4], Timothy[3], Timothy[2], John[1]*) was born in Marshfield, October 9, 1804; he married, June 8, 1828, Elizabeth Potter, daughter of John and Elizabeth Potter, born, April 25, 1806; she died, December 14, 1833; he married, May 22, 1836, Jerusha Green Cloon, born, March 15, 1809; he died, October 14, 1849, and she, August —, 1857.

Children, born in Lynn:

By first wife :

— 379.   Zelotis Warren[7], b. May 18, 1830; d. June 12, 1830.
+ 380.   Henry Warren[7], b. Nov. 20, 1831.
— 380a. Martha Elizabeth, b. Aug. 16, 1833; d. Sept. 17, 1833.

By second wife :

— 381.   Susan Elizabeth[7], b. Feb'y 6, 1837.
+ 382.   Lucy Ann[7], b. April 20, 1842.

241 and 275.

VII. ASA ROGERS[6] (*Asa[5], Israel[4], Timothy[3], Timothy[2], John[1]*) was born in Marshfield, June 21, 1787; he married, November 29, 1812, RUTH ROGERS[6], daughter of Zaccheus Rogers[5], born, September 16, 1790; he died in 1851, and she, May 27, 1884, in her ninety-fourth year.

Children, born in Marshfield:

— 383. Ruth Little[7], b. Aug. 5, 1813; d. Jan'y 2, 1818.
   384. Martha[7], b. Nov. 22, 1815; m. James L. Studley,
      Aug. 13, 1837.
   385. Bethiah[7], b. Aug. 25, 1817.
— 386. Ruth Little[7], b. Dec. 6, 1818.
   387. Augusta[7],b. Sept. 28, 1820.
— 388. Louisa Forbes[7], b. May 18, 1823.
— 389. William[7], b. Jan'y 21, 1825.
   390. Edwin Thomas[7], b. Oct. 1, 1826.
   391. Ann Caroline[7], b. July 27, 1829.
— 392. Mercy[7], b. Feb'y 3, 1834; d. Feb'y 20, 1834.

His widow, Ruth, was appointed Adm'x Sept. 29, 1851; her dower was set off, March, 1852, the heirs at law assenting to the same, viz: Ruth L. Rogers; Edwin Curtis, husband of Augusta; Nathaniel J. Damon, husband of Bethiah; Edwin T. Rogers; Ann C. Rogers; Louisa F. Rogers; Martha Day (she had then married a second time), and William Rogers.

243.

VII. AMOS ROGERS[6] (*Asa[5], Israel[4], Timothy[3], Timothy[2], John[1]*) was born in Marshfield, February 24, 1791.

Mr. BRIGGS says (pp. 204, 205) that this Amos married and had sons, "John, who went to Warren, Me., and Josephus, a ship-builder of Bath, Me., where his children and grandchildren have succeeded to the business."

But the very full history of Warren (with genealogies) makes no mention of John; and it is certain that Josephus and his children have not carried on ship-building in Bath. Hon. William Rogers of Bath succeeded his father in that business in Bath, and they are the only persons of the name who have carried on ship-building there. They are not of the Marshfield family, but probably descendants of the Ipswich family.

I have not been able to find any traces of this Josephus in any of our ship-building towns in Maine, but the records are so incomplete that the question is by no means settled.

On the other hand, the historian of the Oakman family says that this Amos "died at sea; probably unmarried."

Maine Historical and Genealogical Recorder, Vol. IV, p. 128.

247.

VII. HENRY ROGERS[6] (*Asa[5], Israel[4], Timothy[3], Timothy[2], John[1]*) was born in Marshfield, August 23, 1796; he married, July 29, 1822, Harriet Greenleaf, daughter of Isaac and Sally [Rhoades] Greenleaf, born, November 17, 1794; he died, October 30, 1852, and she, March 5, 1874.

Children, the sixth and ninth born in South Boston, and the others in Medford:

- — 393.   Harriet[7], b. Mar. 13, 1823; d. same day.
- + 394.   Edward Henry[7], b. Sept. 10, 1824.
- + 395.   James Burdett[7], b. Sept. 3, 1826.
- = 396.   Harriet Abiah[7], b. Feb'y 8, 1828.
- + 397.   Charles Emery[7], b. Dec. 10, 1829.
- + 398.   Sidney Greenleaf[7], b. Mar. 24, 1832.
- + 399.   Andrew Jackson[7], b. Nov. 10, 1833.
- — 400.   Jacob Rhoades[7], b. Sept. 2, 1835; d. Mar. 29, 1836.
- — 401.   Asa Rhoades[7], b. Mar. 18, 1837; d. June 18, 1837.

248a.

VII. REBEKAH HATCH[6] (*Rebekah[5], Israel[4], Timothy[3], Timothy[2], John[1]*) was born in Marshfield, February 20, 1798; she married, May 27, 1828, as his second wife, Joel Hatch, son of Israel and Mary [Hatch] Hatch, born, April 3, 1771; he died, April 4, 1849, and she, November 26, 1882.

Children, born in Marshfield:

- †   i.   Rebekah Rogers Hatch[7], b. Mar. 31, 1830.
-     ii.   Walter Hatch[7], b. Mar. 12, 1832.
- †   iii.   Israel Hatch Hatch[7], b. Dec. 8, 1837.

Joel Hatch married (1) Huldah Trouant, April 21, 1796.

Walter Hatch[7] married Emeline Hall of Marshfield, and died in Chicago, April 25, 1878, without issue.

248a—i, and 358—ii.

VIII. *Rebekah Rogers Hatch[7]* married, August 31, 1851, *Thomas Rogers Oakman[8]*, son of Hiram and Jane Soule [Rogers[7], No. 358], born March 9, 1829; he died, December 26, 1867, leaving her surviving.

Children, born in Marshfield :

†   i.   Louisa Rebecca Oakman[8], b. Aug. 18, 1852.
—   ii.   Lizzie Agnes Oakman[8], b. April 7, 1857 ; d. Aug. 27, 1863.
—   iii.   Ellen Richmond Oakman[8], b. Dec., 1859 ; d. Aug. 21, 1863.

248a—iii.

VIII. *Israel Hatch Hatch[7]* married, August 1, 1859, Caroline Blanchard Oakman, daughter of William Clift and Caroline [Ford] Oakman.

Children, born in Marshfield :

—   i.   Israel Ellis Hatch[8], b. Feb'y 16, 1863 ; d. Nov. 7, 1863.
=   ii.   Alice Soule Hatch[8], b. July 14, 1864.
     iii.   Harris Blanchard Hatch[8], b. May 9, 1866 ; m. Susan M. Jones.
     iv.   Tracy Weston Hatch[8], b. May 27, 1871 ; m. Esther C. Glidden.

248a—ii—i.

IX. *Louisa Rebecca Oakman[8]* married, December 27, 1887, Evan F. Jones, son of Thomas Price and Phebe Maria Jones, born, October 5, 1864.

Children, born in La Grange, Illinois :

     i.   Ethel Louise Jones[9], b. Jan'y 28, 1889.
     ii.   Edna Lillian Jones[9], b. June 22, 1891.

249.

VII. MARIA ROGERS[6] (*Samuel[5], Israel[4], Timothy[3], Timothy[2], John[1]*) was born in Marshfield, January 23, 1800; she married, December 5, 1822, Nathaniel Clift, son of Nathaniel Clift, born in 1799; he died, September 8, 1833, and she, March 6, 1834.

No further account obtained.

250.

VII. ALFRED ROGERS[6] (*Samuel[5], Israel[4], Timothy[3], Timothy[2], John[1]*) was born in Marshfield, September 1, 1803; only a partial account of his family has been obtained.

Children, born in Marshfield:

403. Samuel[7].
403. William A[7].

260.

VII. PATIENCE ROGERS[6] (*Nathaniel[5], Peleg[4], Timothy[3], Timothy[2], John[1]*) was born in Marshfield, about 1786; she married William Sprague, son of Hon. Seth and Deborah [Sampson] Sprague, born, December 28, 1780; she died, Nov. 18, 1833, aged forty-eight; he married (2) Priscilla [Barker] Pierce, and died, October 17, 1840.

Children, born in Duxbury:

    i. Susan Rogers Sprague[7]; m. Charles Copeland.
    ii. Charity Sprague[7]; m. James Gooding.
   iii. Almira Sprague[7]; m. Samuel G. West.
   iv. William Sprague[7].
    v. Harriet Sprague[7]; m. Edward Winsor.
   vi. Eliza Sprague[7]; m. Henry Tolman.
  vii. Seth Sprague[7]; d. at sea in 1843.
 viii. Julia Sprague[7].
   ix. Francis Sprague[7].

269.

VII. ALDEN ROGERS[6] (*Isaac[5], Peleg[4], Timothy[3], Timothy[2], John[1]*) was born in Marshfield in 1807; he married, August 14, 1827, Adeline Humphrey, daughter of

George and Nancy [Ford] Humphrey, born in 1809; he died, July 26, 1891, and she July 2, 1873.

Children, born in Marshfield.

— 404. Amos Alden[7], b. 1828; d. June 4, 1828.
405. Adeline Alden[7], b. 1830.
406. Salome Humphrey[7], b. 1832.
407. Susan Frances[7], b. 1836.

Adeline Alden[7] m. Elbridge Gardner; no children.
Salome Humphrey[7] married, but had no children.
Susan Frances[7] m. Amos Freeman Damon, as his second wife.

273.

VII. RACHEL WALES ROGERS[6] (*Atherton Wales[5], Amos[4], Timothy[3], Timothy[2], John[1]*) was born in Marshfield; baptized April 29, 1792; she married, October 30, 1815, Calvin Stockbridge, son of William and Ruth [Bailey] Stockbridge, born, Sept. 19, 1784; he died, May —, 1833, and she, ——.

Children, born in North Yarmouth, Me.:

— i. William Calvin Stockbridge[7], b. April 6, 1817; d. Feb. 22, 1826.
ii. John Calvin Stockbridge[7], b. June 14, 1818.
† iii. Wales Rogers Stockbridge[7], b. May 18, 1821.
iv. Edward A   Stockbridge[7], b. Sept. —, 1831, in Boston.

John Calvin Stockbridge[7] graduated B. U., 1838; D.D., H. U., 1859; was pastor in Waterville, Me., Woburn, Mass., Bath, Me., Portland, Me., Boston, and Providence, R. I.

273—iii.

VIII. *Wales Rogers Stockbridge[7]* married, August 15, 1850, Margaret Tappan Southwick of Vassalboro, Me., daughter of Jacob and Mary [Wayne] Southwick, born, January 26, 1829; she died, September 1, 1853, and he married, September 19, 1855, Caroline A. Gregg; he died, March 20, 1895.

Children :

By first wife, the first born in Somerville and the other in Cambridge :

    i. Arthur Beauvais Stockbridge[8], b. Nov. 25, 1851.
    ii. Margaret Wales Stockbridge[8], b. Aug. 30, 1853.

By second wife, born in Brookline :

—   iii. Samuel Gregg Stockbridge[8], b. May 13, 1856; d. Aug. 26, 1856.
—   iv. Wadsworth Gregg Stockbridge[8], b. July 4, 1858; d. Sept. 19, 1858.
    v. Wales Rogers Stockbridge[8], b. Aug. 26, 1865.

Arthur Beauvais Stockbridge[8] married, July 2, 1879, Amalia Leontine Aberg, and they have

    i. Arthur Fabian[9].
    ii. Hedvig Caroline[9].
    iii. Carl Wales[9].

Margaret Wales Stockbridge[8] married, September 27, 1883, George Alonzo Mitchell, and they have :

    i. Marjorie Stockbridge Mitchell[9].

Wales Rogers Stockbridge[8] married Harriet Sawyer.

278 and 113—iv.

VII. LOUISA ROGERS[6] (*Zaccheus[5], Zaccheus[4], Timothy[3], Timothy[2], John[1]*) was born in Marshfield, June 30, 1801; she married, February 19, 1826, BENJAMIN HATCH[6], son of Ichabod and Rebekah [Rogers] Hatch, born, August 30, 1802; he died, October 29, 1877, and she, October 17, 1865.

Children, born in Marshfield:

—   i. Benjamin Fobes Hatch[7], b. Sept. 7, 1827; d. unm. May 25, 1848.
—   ii. Louisa Elizabeth Hatch[7], b. Nov. 17, 1828; d. unm. July 28, 1848.
—   iii. Roxalina Hatch[7], b. Jan'y 1, 1831.
    iv. Jotham Hatch[7], b. Dec. 11, 1832.
    v. Mercy Rogers Hatch[7], b. Aug. 22, 1835.

— vi. Marcia Ellen Hatch[7], b. April 25, 1837.
— vii. Mary Ann Hatch[7], b. Sept. 8, 1838 ; d. April 16, 1856.
viii. Ruth Augusta Hatch[7], b. May 11, 1841.
ix. Charles Rogers Hatch[7], b. Oct. 25, 1843.

Jotham Hatch[7] married, Jan'y 10, 1858, Abigail B. Paine.

Mercy Rogers Hatch[7] married, Nov. 24, 1860, Albion Hatch [No. 113—iii—ii]; this date is from the family Bible, but the record has Nov. 20, 1859, which is undoubtedly correct.

Ruth Augusta Hatch[7] married, July 14, 1861, Nathan Sanders Ford.

Charles Rogers Hatch[7] married (1) Isabel White, June 10, 1866 ; and (2) Myra Faunce of Hingham.

279.

VII. CHARLES ROGERS[6] (*Charles[5], Zaccheus[4], Timothy[3], Timothy[2], John[1]*) was born in Portland, Me., September 1, 1797; he married, June 25, 1826, Maria Caroline Adams, daughter of Bartlett and Charlotte [Neal] Adams, born May 15, 1804; she died, May 29, 1827; he married [published, March 29, 1828,] Caroline Gore of Boston; she died, September 26, 1853; he married [published, June 7, 1865,] Eliza W. B. Chapman; he died, September 26, 1863.

Child, by first wife, born in Portland:

+ 408. Charles Bartlett[7], b. May 14, 1827.

282.

VII. FRANCIS HENRY ROGERS[6] (*Charles[5], Zaccheus[4], Timothy[3], Timothy[2], John[1]*) was born in Portland, Me., January 6, 1804; he married, November 6, 1834, Ann H. Meacom of Beverly; he was a shipmaster; he died in Singapore in 1844.

Children, born in Beverly:

— 409. Francis Henry[7], b. Feb'y 22, 1840; d. Aug. 7, 1861.
410. Sarah Emmons[7], b. 1842.

Sarah Emmons[7] married October 5, 1865, George Morrill of Boston, and they have:

    i.   George Morrill[8], b. Sept. 10, 1869.
    ii.   Emeline Frances Morrill[8], b. Aug. 28, 1871.
    iii.   Joseph Morrill[8], b. June 6, 1875; Har. Univ., 1896.

285.

VII. MARTHA CAROLINE ROGERS[6] (*Charles*[5], *Zaccheus*[4], *Timothy*[3], *Timothy*[2], *John*[1]) was born in Portland, September 3, 1810; she married [published, September 4, 1830,] Joseph Robinson Thompson, son of Cyrus and Rebecca [Robinson] Thompson, born, November 21, 1804, in Hartford, Me.; he died in Portland, November 21, 1883, and she, April 16, 1870.

Children, born in Portland:

 †   i.   Henry Francis Thompson[7], b. Aug. 28, 1831.
   ii.   Maria Caroline Thompson[7], b. Jan'y 28, 1833; m. Cornelius D. Maynard.
 —   iii.   Ann Meacom Thompson[7], b. Oct. 12, 1835.
 —   iv.   John Edward Thompson[7], b. May 4, 1837; d. April 28, 1840.
 —   v.   Joseph A. Thompson[7], b. Feb'y 25, 1839; d. May 8, 1840.
 —   vi.   Mary Ellen Thompson[7], b. April 11, 1841.
 —   vii.   Enoch Morse Thompson[7], b. Jan'y 19, 1843.
 —   viii.   Charles Rogers Thompson[7], b. Jan'y 17, 1845; d. Oct. 18, 1849.
 †   ix.   William Drake Thompson[7], b. Dec. 21, 1846.
 †   x.   Sumner Cummings Thompson[7], b. Nov. 13, 1848.
   xi.   Fred Irving Thompson[7], b. Dec. 4, 1850.
 †   xii.   Stephen Emmons Thompson[7], b. June 23, 1853.
 †   xiii.   George Herbert Thompson[7], b. July 28, 1855.

285—i.

VIII. *Henry Francis Thompson*[7] married Luella A. Gilman of Laconia, N. H., in 1875; he died, October 18, 1894, leaving her surviving; they had:

    i.   Lyman Rogers Thompson[8], b. Mar. 3, 1876.

285—ix.

VIII. *William Drake Thompson*[7] married, October 21, 1873, Alice Turner, daughter of George W. and Eliza K. [Springer] Turner, b. Jan'y 20, 1850; he died, June 12, 1896, and she, May 9, 1892.

Children, born in Portland:

    i.   Lizzie Wallace Thompson[8], b. Dec. 18, 1874.

    ii. Charles Harris Thompson[8], b. Aug. 25, 1876.

    iii. Ruth W. Thompson[8], b. Mar. 12, 1881.

285—x.

VIII. *Sumner Cummings Thompson*[7] married, March 3, 1881, Kate M. Connelly; they have:

    i.   Martha Rogers Thompson[8], b. Dec. 10, 1881.

285—xii.

VIII. *Stephen Emmons Thompson*[7] married, September 25, 1879, Addie E. Jordan.

Children, born in Portland:

    i.   Jessie Louise Thompson[8], b. Mar. 9, 1884.

    ii. Lillian Thompson[8], b. Dec. 3, 1885.

285—xiii.

VIII. *George Herbert Thompson*[7] married, October 13, 1884, Hattie M. Hicks, daughter of Nathaniel O. and Janet Hicks, born in Portland, October 12, 1856.

Children, born in Portland:

    i.   Ella Almira Thompson[8], b. Nov. 16, 1885.

    ii. Bertha May Thompson[8], b. May 1, 1887.

287.

VII. JOHN THOMAS ROGERS[6] (*Charles*[5], *Zaccheus*[4], *Timothy*[3], *Timothy*[2], *John*[1]) was born in Portland, April 7, 1815; he married, June 8, 1847, Frances Elizabeth Mountfort, daughter of Daniel and Mary [Mussey] Mountfort, born, January 25, 1826; he died in Farmington, November 6, 1892; his widow and son are living in Florida.

Children, born in Portland:

— 411. Caroline Gore[7], b. June 26, 1849 ; d. July 9, 1853.
— 412. John Thomas[7], Aug. 5, 1850.

289.

VII. BENJAMIN ROGERS[6] (*Benjamin[5], Zaccheus[4], Timothy[3], Timothy[2], John[1]*) was born in Pembroke, May 27, 1800; he married, March 6, 1825, Caroline Clift, daughter of Joseph and Mary [Little] [Rogers] Clift, born, December 15, 1802; he died in Cambridge, December 23, 1875, and she, July 12, 1893.

Children, the first two born in Marshfield, and the others in Boston:

+ 413. Caroline Amanda[7], b. Sept. 14, 1826.
+ 414. Isabel Anne[7], b. Mar. 22, 1828.
+ 415. Benjamin Franklin[7], b. Aug. 16, 1830.
+ 416. Fannie Elvira[7], b. Aug. 25, 1832.
+ 417. Lysander Waldo[7], b. July 25, 1838.

290.

VII. ALVAN ROGERS[6] (*Benjamin[5], Zaccheus[4], Timothy[3], Timothy[2], John[1]*) was born in Pembroke, July 31, 1802 ; he married, June 9, 1835, Mary Dilloway Foster, daughter of Thomas and Betsey [Davidson] Foster, born in Boston, March 30, 1812; he died, March 30, 1885, and she, June 4, 1877.

Children, born in Boston:

+ 418. Charles Alvan[7], b. June 7, 1836.
— 419. Mary Emily[7], b. April 17, 1838 ; d. April 22, 1838.
— 420. George Augustus[7], b. May 23, 1840; d. Sept. 26, 1840.
+ 421. George Edwin[7], b. June 15, 1843.
+ 422. Mary Augusta[7], b. Aug. 28, 1845.

291 and 111—viii.

VII. RACHEL ROGERS[6] (*Benjamin[5], Zaccheus[4], Timothy[3], Timothy[2], John[1]*) was born in Pembroke in 1805;

she married, November 17, 1825, ELISHA HATCH[6] of Marshfield, son of Anthony Eames and Bethiah [Rogers[5]] Hatch, born, November 17, 1798; he died, September 10, 1883, and she, December 31, 1840, "in her thirty-sixth year."

Children, born in Marshfield:

— i. Rachel Maria Hatch[7], b. Dec. 18, 1826.
ii. Melinda Ann Hatch[7], b. Nov. 1, 1829; m. Elias Pratt.
iii. Mary Agnes Hatch[7], b. July 17, 1831; m. Charles Tilden Hatch.
iv. Elisha Cushing Hatch[7], b. Mar. 2, 1839; m. Mary E. Bonney.
v. Calvin Otis Hatch[7], b. Oct. 15, 1840; m. Adelaide Baker.

292.

VII. MARY ROGERS[6] (*Benjamin[5], Zaccheus[4], Timothy[3], Timothy[2], John[1]*) was born in Pembroke, December 19, 1814; she married, December 3, 1835, John Church, son of Cornelius Briggs and Hulda [Magoun] Church, born, June 14, 1809; he died, April 28, 1878, and she, October 10, 1865.

Children, born in Pembroke:

— i. John Harvey Church[7], b. Nov. 5, 1836; d. Nov. 28, 1836.
ii. Edward Rogers Church[7], b. May 8, 1838.
iii. Mary Ann Church[7], b. Mar. 18, 1841; m. Luther White of Marshfield; no children.

293.

VII. PRINCE ROGERS[6] (*Benjamin[5], Zaccheus[4], Timothy[3], Timothy[2], John[1]*) was born in Marshfield, in 1808; he married, Lavinia Parsons, daughter of Dr. Thomas and Joanna [McCrairy] Parsons, born, March 3, 1815; he died, April 14, 1844, and she, February 11, 1890.

Children, born in East Boston:

423. Prince William⁷, b. Aug. 8, 1833.
— 424. Edwin Sidney⁷, b. March 21, 1837; d. June 11, 1843.
+ 425. Isadore Clifford⁷, b. Jan'y 23, 1839.
426. Florence⁷, b. Oct. 9, 1841.

Prince William was called later, William Prince; Isadore Clifford, Clifford Irving; and Florence, Florence Virginia.

Prince William⁷ married, in 1859, Sarah Bennett; he was drowned in California the next year; his widow started for home at once, and she had, born on the passage to New York:

— i. Jessie Fremont⁸, b. in 1860; d. at the age of six months.

Florence⁷ married, in December, 1870, Augustus Sewall Browne, son of Dr. Sewall Browne; she married, May 24, 1884, Dr. John Ordway French; he died, September 28, 1887, leaving her surviving; no children.

The History of East Boston, purporting to quote from the record, gives to Prince Rogers, "a daughter," born, March, 1837, and "a son," born, May 20, 1840.

294.

VII. HARVEY ROGERS⁶ (*Benjamin⁵, Zaccheus⁴, Timothy³, Timothy², John¹*) was born in Pembroke, October 3, 1811; he married, June 12, 1836, in Boston, Helen Johnston, daughter of James and Elizabeth Johnston, born in Edinburgh, Scotland, in 1810; he died in Chelsea, June 9, 1888, and she, December 5, 1888.

Children, the first two born in Boston, and the other in Chelsea:

427. Francis Harvey⁷, b. May 17, 1840.
428. Henry Bateman⁷, b. Mar. 27, 1846.
429. Helena Agnes⁷, b. April 22, 1855.

Francis Harvey⁷ married, May 31, 1869, Jeannette Rathill of Chelsea, daughter of Edward and Catharine Rathill, born in Gardiner, Me., in 1850; he died in Malden, September 14, 1857; no children.

Henry Bateman⁷ married, April 10, 1875, Eunice Holmes of New York city; she died, June 15, 1894; no children; he married, Janu-

ary 26, 1897, Louisa [Mitchell] Thomas, widow of Col. James H.
Thomas of Dayton, Ohio; no children; he is in the U. S. Navy.

Helena Agnes[7] married, June 24, 1873, Charles L. V. Bliss, son of
Elec C. and Adaline Bliss, born in 1851; she died, October 28,
1888; they had:

> i. Florence Rogers Bliss[8], b. Oct. 24, 1874; m. in 1893,
> Alfred M. Little of Chelsea.

295.

VII. ANNA LITTLE ROGERS[6] (*Samuel*[5], *Adam*[4], *Timothy*[3], *Timothy*[2], *John*[1]) was born in Castine, Me., February 17, 1787; she married, in 1805, Francis Evans Bakeman, son of John and Christiana [Smart] Bakeman, born, August 7, 1773; he died, February 14, 1826, and she, August 6, 1880.

Children, born in Brooksville, Me.:

	i.	Christiana Bakeman[7], b. Mar. 27, 1806.
	ii.	John Bakeman[7], b. June 6, 1808.
—	iii.	Francis Bakeman[7], b. Dec. 16, 1810; d. unm.
†	iv.	Atherton Wales Bakeman[7], b. Mar. 9, 1813.
	v.	Celia Anna Bakeman[7], b. Mar. 3, 1815.
—	vi.	Samuel Rogers Bakeman[7], b. May 29, 1817; d. unm.
	vii.	Lavinia Bakeman[7], b. May 13, 1819.
—	viii.	Sarah Maria Bakeman,[7] b. April 10, 1821; d. unm. Feb'y 21, 1897.
	ix.	Hannah Morgan Bakeman[7], b. Mar. 5, 1823.
	x.	Elsy Rogers Bakeman[7], b. April 16, 1824.
—	xi.	Adaline Augusta Bakeman[7], b. April 23, 1826; d. July, 1895.

295—iv.

VIII. *Atherton Wales Bakeman*[7] married (1) Amanda Woodbridge; (2) in 1840, Susan Hall Gardner, daughter of Israel and Rhoda [Willey] Gardner, born, March 4, 1821; he died in March, 1846, and she, May 23, 1889.

Children, the first three born in Brooksville, and the other in Castine, Me.:

108   *John Rogers of Marshfield.*

By first wife :

    i. Amanda Ann Bakeman[8], b. June 14, 1834.

By second wife :

    ii. Francis Wales Bakeman[8], b. April 14, 1841 ; Colby Univ., A. B., 1866, D. D., 1885.

    iii. Lavinia Susan Bakeman[8], b. Feb'y 1, 1843.

— iv. George Albert Bakeman[8], b. Nov. 13, 1844 ; d. Aug. 16, 1864.

296.

VII. LYDIA ROGERS[6] (*Samuel[5], Adam[4], Timothy[3], Timothy[2], John[1]*) was born in Castine, Maine, October 14, 1789.

We have been unable to get a full account of her family. She married (1) ——— Eades ; (2) Israel Richardson, who was a soldier in the British Army in the war of 1812, but left the army and settled in Castine, Maine.

Children, born in Castine :

By first husband :

    i. Patience Eades[7].

By second husband :

    ii. Ann Richardson[7].

    iii. Lydia Jane Richardson[7].

    iv. Isaiah Bradshaw Richardson[7].

    v. ——— Richardson[7].

297.

VII. SAMUEL ROGERS[6] (*Samuel[5], Adam[4], Timothy[3], Timothy[2], John[1]*) was born in Castine, Me., June 30, 1790; he married Lucy Gay and moved to Ohio.

299 and 316.

VII. ATHERTON WALES ROGERS[6] (*Samuel[5], Adam[4], Timothy[3], Timothy[2], John[1]*) was born in Castine, Maine,

November 13, 1793; he married, July 18, 1822, CELIA ROGERS[6], daughter of Adam and Olive [Gay] Rogers, born, May 13, 1804; she died, June 22, 1831; he married, in 1833, Susan Mariner Miller, daughter of Ephraim and Mary [Heal] Miller, born, May 24, 1804; he was lost at sea about December, 1845, and she died, September 30, 1880.

Children, born in Lincolnville:

By first wife:

— 430. Rachel[7], b. in 1823 ; d. in infancy.
+ 431. Patience Jane[7], b. Jan'y 14, 1825.

By second wife:

+ 432. George Atherton[7], b. Oct. 25, 1834.
— 432a. Mary Roxana[7], died in infancy.
 432b. Mary Roxana[7], died in childhood.
+ 433. Lucius Henry Chandler[7], b. Sept. 14, 1840.
— 433a. Ephraim Wales[7], b. May 29, 1843 ; d. unm. Aug. 13, 1864.
— 433b. Josephine Hamilton[7], died in childhood.

300.

VII. PATIENCE LITTLE ROGERS[6] (*Samuel[5], Adam[4], Timothy[3], Timothy[2], John[1]*) was born in Castine, Me., August 25, 1795; she married, Peleg Pendleton, son of Job and Lydia [Decrow] Pendleton, born, February 7, 1793; he died, February 12, 1874, and she, February 11, 1873.

Children, born in Lincolnville, Maine:

 i. Job Pendleton[7], b. Sept. 29, 1815.
 ii. Atherton Wales Pendleton[7], b. May 19, 1817.
 iii. Samuel Rogers Pendleton[7], b. Nov. 25, 1818.
— iv. Lydia Jane Pendleton[7], b. Oct. 7, 1820 ; d. unm.
 v. Lucy Ann Pendleton[7], b. Dec. 19, 1821.
— vi. John Wade Pendleton[7], b. Aug. 15, 1823 ; d. unm.
— vii. William Henry Pendleton[7], b. July 15, 1825 ; d. unm.

viii.   Francis Bakeman Pendleton[7], b. April 26, 1827.
—   ix.   George Edward Pendleton[7], b. Sept. 10, 1829.
x.   Charles Carroll Pendleton[7], b. April 30, 1831.
xi.   Sabrina Dodge Pendleton[7], b. June 29, 1833.
xii.   Oliver Milton Pendleton[7], b. Oct. 7, 1835.
—   xiii.   Albert Reed Pendleton[7], b. October 18, 1837 ; d. unm.
—   xiv.   Reed Wade Pendleton[7], b. Nov. 29, 1839 ; d. unm.

301.

VII.   ALICE ROGERS[6] (*Samuel[5], Adam[4], Timothy[3], Timothy[2], John[1]*) was born in Castine, Maine, April 4, 1797; she married, May 2, 1820, Israel Studley, son of John and Dorcas [Smith] Studley, born, January 13, 1799; he died, August 19, 1822, and she married, March 14, 1825, Jacob Smith Adams, son of Joel and Jemima [Robbins] Adams, born, January 14, 1786; he died, January 23, 1874, and she, August 28, 1882.

Children, born in Lincolnville, Maine:

By first husband :

†   i.   Mary Ann Studley[7], b. Aug. 15, 1820.
ii.   Abigail Studley[7], b. April 22, 1822.

By second husband :

iii.   Israel Studley Adams[7], b. Nov. 4, 1825.
iv.   Eliza Jane French Adams[7], b. Sept. 11, 1828.
—   v.   Elisha Rogers Adams[7], b. Nov. 22, 1830 ; d. Oct. 5, 1835.
—   vi.   Joel Adams[7], b. Mar. 30, 1834 ; d. Oct. 12, 1835.
vii.   Amanda Malvina Adams[7], b. Mar. 3, 1837.
viii.   Clara Maria Adams[7], b. Nov. 23, 1839.

301—i.

VIII.   *Mary Ann Studley[7]* married, December 23, 1848, Henry Crehore, son of Henry and Susan [Tarbell] Crehore, born, January 8, 1821, and they have, born in Lincolnville:

i.   Julia Eliza Crehore[8], b. Nov. 1, 1849.
ii.   Alice Jane Crehore[8], b. Sept. 17, 1851.

    iii.   Joseph Shuttleworth Crehore⁸, b. July 10, 1853.
    iv.   Minot Crehore⁸, b. Aug. 28, 1855.
    v.   Harry Crehore⁸, b. Sept. 22, 1858.
    vi.   Frank Atherton Crehore⁸, b. May 1, 1864; d. May 30, 1867.

302.

VII. SARAH [SALLY] ROGERS⁶ (*Samuel⁵, Adam⁴, Timothy³, Timothy², John¹*) was born in Castine, Maine, January 15, 1799; she married, July 31, 1818, Israel Redman, son of Israel and Abigail [Byard] Redman, born, October 17, 1796; he died, October, 1846, and she, November 26, 1890.

Children, born in Brooksville, Maine:

†   i.   Sarah Ann Redman⁷, b. Mar. 10, 1819.
    ii.   Robert Everett Redman⁷, b. April 21, 1820.
    iii.   Abby Patience Redman⁷, b. Sept. 4, 1821.
—   iv.   Israel Redman⁷, b. Mar. 3, 1823; d. Mar. 5, 1823.
    v.   Emily Somes Redman⁷, b. July 29, 1824.
    vi.   Lydia Maria Redman⁷, b. Jan'y 3, 1826.
    vii.   Lavinia Redman⁷, b. Nov. 10, 1827.
    viii.   Celia Celestia Redman⁷, b. Oct. 16, 1829.
    ix.   Israel Augustus Redman⁷, b. Jan'y 24, 1831.
—   x.   Charles Francis Redman⁷, b. July 23, 1832; d. in Jan'y, 1833.
    xi.   Berenthia Davis Redman⁷, b. Oct. 15, 1833.
    xii.   Mary Jane Redman⁷, b. Mar. 26, 1836.
—   xiii.   Everett Alden Redman⁷, b. June 16, 1838; d. June 5, 1842.
    xiv.   Samuel Bakeman Redman⁷, b. Oct. 17, 1840.
—   xv.   Adelia Viola Redman⁷, b. Aug. 22, 1844; d. March, 1846.

302—i.

VIII. *Sarah Ann Redman⁷* married, December 17, 1840, Erastus Redman, son of John Randall and Abigail [Orcutt] Redman, born, July 2, 1818; he died, August 22, 1894, and she, July 19, 1892.

Children, the first five born in Brooksville, Me., and the others in Ellsworth, Maine :

      i.   Arletta Viola Redman[8], b. Nov. 5, 1841.
      ii.   Abby Sarah Redman[8], b. Dec. 3, 1843.
— iii. Eda Celia Redman[8], b. Nov. 2, 1845 ; d. Feb'y 23, 1847.
■ iv. John Bakeman Redman[8], b. June 11, 1848.
      v.   Erastus Fulton Redman[8], b. June 10, 1849.
      vi. Margaret Randall Redman[8], b. April 7, 1853.
— vii. George Henry Redman[8], b. Oct. 25, 1854; d. Mar. 1, 1855.
     viii. Frances Berenthia Redman[8], b. Aug. 29, 1857.

Arletta Viola Redman[8] married Nathaniel W. Littlefield, Dart. Col.
Abby Sarah Redman[8] married Edward Francis Robinson.
John Bakeman Redman[8] has been the candidate of his party for Governor of Maine.
Erastus Fulton Redman[8], Bowd. Col., 1870; married Julia Jarvis, and they have :

      i.   Fulton Jarvis Redman[9].

Margaret Randall Redman[8] married Prof. Charles A. Cole, Bowd. Col. 1869.
Frances Berenthia Redman[8] married Dr. Charles A. Keene, B. U. and Supt. of Rhode Island Insane Asylum.

303.

VII. ADAM ROGERS[6] (*Samuel*[5], *Adam*[4], *Timothy*[3], *Timothy*[2], *John*[1]) was born in Lincolnville, Maine, April 23, 1801; he married Sarah [Sally] Decrow, daughter of Isaac and Lydia [Gay] Decrow, born, June 6, 1802; the family moved West, first to Ohio, and then to Iowa; he died in July, 1884, and she, in July, 1874.

Children, the first five born in Lincolnville, the next three in Sunbury, Ohio, and the other in Charleston, Iowa:

— 434. Ibry[7], b. July 8, 1822 ; d. in infancy.
     435. Lydia Gay[7], b. June 29, 1825.

436. Sarah Decrow[7], b. April 27, 1828.
436a. Ephraim Buker[7], b. July 29, 1830.
436b. George Henry[7], b. May 20, 1834.
+ 436c. Alice Annie[7], b. Mar. 20, 1837.
436d. Patience Jane[7], b. July 11, 1841.
— 436e. Adam Andrew[7], b. May 23, 1843; d. unm. in 1871.
— 436f. Washington[7], b. in 1845; d. same year.

305.

VII. ELISHA ROGERS[6] (*Samuel[5], Adam[4], Timothy[3], Timothy[2], John[1]*) was born in Castine, Maine, December 22, 1805; he married, in 1832, Olive Jane Decrow, daughter of Israel and Jane [Batchelder] Decrow, born, October 4, 1811; he died, June 19, 1887, and she, August 27, 1877.

Children, born in Lincolnville, Maine:

+ 437. Samuel Walter[7], b. Dec. 9, 1833.
438. Phebe Jane[7], b. May 4, 1835.
— 439. Huldah Maria[7], b. Jan'y 26, 1837.
— 440. Golopha[7], b. Jan'y 26, 1839.
441. Alice[7], b. Jan'y 31, 1841.
442. Delilah[7], b. Feb'y 14, 1843.
— 443. Atherton Wales[7], b. Aug. 27, 1847; d. unm.

Phebe Jane[7] married Thomas Black and has one child:

i. Alice Jane Black[8], b. —— in Rockland, Me.

Alice[7] married Frank Prescott, son of Joel; no children.

Delilah[7] married, June 29, 1868, Oscar Foss; he died in 1870, and she married in 1872, William Blackman; no children.

305a.

VII. ELIZA PENDLETON[6] (*Elizabeth[5], Adam[4], Timothy[3], Timothy[2], John[1]*) was born in Islesboro, Me., May —, 1796; she married Frye Hall, son of Farnham and Sarah [Bailey] Hall, born, October 21, 1788, in Methuen; he settled in Camden, Me., in 1806, but moved to Hope in 1826; being elected Register of Deeds in March, 1828, he moved to Belfast; he was Register of Deeds till 1848 and most of the time was County Treasurer; he died, August 3, 1849, and she, November 29, 1882.

Children, the first six born in Belfast; the next in Hope, and the others in Belfast:

†   i.   Eliza Jane Hall[7], b. August 18, 1815 [1816.]
    ii.   Joseph Frye Hall[7], b. Jan'y 28, 1818.
—   iii.   Sarah Emeline Hall[7], b. Oct. 24, 1820; d. Jan'y 25, 1821.
    iv.   John Farnham Hall[7], b. Sept. 5, 1822.
    v.   Elisha Henry Hall[7], b. Feb'y 22, 1825.
—   vi.   George Dana Hall[7], b. ———; d. in infancy.
▬   vii.   Sarah Boardman Hall[7], b.
†   viii.   Julia Amelia Hall[7], b. May 4, 1833.
▬   ix.   George Clancy Hall[7], b.
▬   x.   Henry King Hall[7], b.
    xi.   William Milson Hall[7], b.

305a—i.

VIII.   *Elisa Jane Hall[7]* married, September 9, 1834, Dr. Richard Moody, son of Col. William Pepperell and Pamelia [Milliken] Moody, born, March 8, 1803, in Saco, Me.; he died, October 3 [4], 1884, and she, January 20, 1887.

Children, born in Belfast, Me.:

†   i.   Augusta Jane Moody[8], b. June 4, 1836.
    ii.   Sarah Elizabeth Moody[8], b. Feb'y 26, 1839.
   iii.   Josephine Moody[8], b. Nov. 1, 1840.
   iv.   William Hall Moody[8], b. Dec. 8, 1842.
   v.   Richard Henry Moody[8], b. July 8, 1847.

305a—i—i.

IX.   *Augusta Jane Moody[8]* married, June 14, 1860, Asa Abbott Howes, son of Samuel and Sarah Hayward [Abbott] Howes, born in Strong, Me., September 21, 1831; she died, March 9, 1890, leaving him surviving.

Children, born in Belfast:

†   i.   James Howard Howes[9], b. June 9, 1861.
†   ii.   Ralph Henry Howes[9], b. Mar. 23, 1864.

305a—i—i—i.

X. *James Howard Howes*[9] married, December 25, 1880, Mary Hazeltine, daughter of Charles Bellows and Frances Louise [Jones] Hazeltine, born in Belfast, July 9, 1861.

Child, born in Belfast:

    i.   Frances Augusta Howes[10], b. Feb'y 2, 1890.

305a—i—i—ii.

X. *Ralph Henry Howes*[9] married, February 15, 1888, Isabelle Maria Conant, daughter of Isaac Adelbert and Damaretta Havilla [Orcutt] Conant, born, July 3, 1864:

Child, born in Belfast:

    i.   Allan Moody Howes[10], b. Jan'y 8, 1896.

305a—viii.

VIII. *Julia Amelia Hall*[7] married, December 8, 1856, in Bangor, Me., John T. Hall; she died, September 26, 1873, at Norfolk, Va.

Children:

—   i.   Walter Frye Hall[8], b. Aug. 25, 1858; d. Sept. 12, 1859.
—   ii.   Julian Pendleton Hall[8], b. Jan'y 11, 1860; d. June 15, 1860.
—   iii.   Ann Eliza Hall[8], b. Feb'y 6, 1862; d. Jan'y 16, 1890.
†   iv.   Marian Boardman Hall[8], b. May 24, 1865.
—   v.   Mary Augusta Hall[8], b. May 24, 1865; d. May 9, 1884.
—   vi.   Waldo Latimer Hall[8], b. Feb'y 10, 1870; d. June 24, 1870.

305a—viii—iv.

IX. *Marian Boardman Hall*[8] married, February 8, 1892, Robert Harwood Barrett, and they have, born in Virginia:

    i.   Sadie Elizabeth Barrett[9], b. May 3, 1893.
    ii.   John Harwood Barrett[9], b. Mar. 31, 1898.

NOTE.

Too late for its insertion in the proper place, the following account is received:

139—v.

VII. *Elisha Pendleton*[6], born in 1798, married at Norfolk, Va., November 24, 1831, Eliza A. H. Wilson; he died, December 25, 1873.

Child, born at Norfolk:

†   i.   William Willson Pendleton[7], b. Nov. 28, 1832.

139—v—i.

VII. *William Willson Pendleton⁷* married, May —, 1858, at St. Paul's Church, Norfolk, Elizabeth Edwards Frisby.

Children, born in Norfolk:

—   i.   Blanche Pendleton⁸, b. May 29, 1859; d. in infancy.
—   ii.   William Pendleton⁸, b. Dec. 14, 1860; d. in infancy.
†   iii.   Wilhelmina Elizabeth Pendleton⁸, b. Dec. 23, 1861.

139—v—i—iii.

IX. *Wilhelmina Elizabeth Pendleton⁸* married, June 25, 1885, at Washington, D. C., Anman Honor Payne, Jr.

Children:

—   i.   Wilhelmina Elizabeth Payne⁹, b. April 23, 1886; d. Feb'y 26, 1890.
   ii.   Mary Singleton Payne⁹, b. March 12, 1888.
   iii.   Elizabeth Edwards Payne⁹, b. July 12, 1891.

305b.

VII. GEORGE PENDLETON⁶ (*Elizabeth⁵, Adam⁴, Timothy³, Timothy², John¹*) was born in Islesboro, Me., February 22, 1800; he married, September 28, 1831, Susan Wealthan Johnson, daughter of Aaron and Huldah [Huntingdon] Johnson, born, December 15, 1810; he died, August 27, 1875, leaving her surviving.

Children, born in Camden, Me.:

†   i.   Ralph Cross Johnson Pendleton⁷, b. July 6, 1832.
†   ii.   George Henry Pendleton⁷, b. July 8, 1834.
†   iii.   Virginia Dare Pendleton⁷, b. Mar. 22, 1837.
—   iv.   Caroline Elizabeth Pendleton⁷, b. Mar. 21, 1840.
†   v.   Susan Johnson Pendleton⁷, b. May 25, 1842.
†   vi.   Lewis Warrington Pendleton⁷, b. Mar. 8, 1844.
†   vii.   Ann Frances Pendleton⁷, b. Mar. 27, 1846.
†   viii.   Edward Waldo Pendleton⁷, b. May 22, 1848.

305b—i.

VIII. *Ralph Cross Johnson Pendleton⁷* married, October 19, 1856, Hannah Davis, daughter of John and Sarah [Davis] Davis, born, September 19, 1834.

Children, the first three born in Yarmouth, Me., and the others in Indianapolis :

      i.   Albert Drinkwater Pendleton[8], b. Dec. 15, 1857.
      ii. John Davis Pendleton[8], b. May 27, 1861.
      iii. Ralph Johnson Pendleton[8], b. May 20, 1865.
—   iv. Hannah Huntingdon Pendleton[8], b. April 23, 1868.
      v. George Henry Pendleton[8], b. Jan'y 21, 1871.
—   vi. Charles Sheldon Pendleton[8], b. Sept. 9, 1874.

305b—ii.

VIII. *George Henry Pendleton*[7] married, January 18, 1859, Harriet Pratt Baker, daughter of Joseph Mason and Sally Pratt [York] Baker, born, August 4, 1835; he died, June 8, 1866, leaving her surviving.

Children, the first born in Gorham, and the others in Yarmouth, Maine :

      i.   Walter Baker Pendleton[8], b. May 11, 1861.
      ii. Carolyn Josephine Pendleton[8], b. April 29, 1863.
—   iii. George Standish Pendleton[8], b. Sept. 15, 1865; d. May 25, 1868.

305b—iii.

VIII. *Virginia Dare Pendleton*[7] married, September 21, 1859, Thomas Sargent Robie, son of Thomas Sargeant and Clarissa [Adams] Robie, born, September 21, 1834, and they had :

      i.   Thomas Sargent Robie[8], b. April 20, 1861, in Waldoboro, Me.
—   ii. Lewis Pendleton Robie[8], b. Jan'y 24, 1863, in Waldoboro, Me.
—   iii. Virginia Huntingdon Robie[8], b. Oct. 18, 1863, in Salmon Falls, N. H.
—   iv. George Pendleton Robie[8], b. Oct. 12, 1870, in Scituate; d. Aug. 10, 1895.

305b—v.

VIII. *Susan Johnson Pendleton*[7] married, December 12, 1867, Charles Henry Sheldon, son of Charles and Janet [Reid] Sheldon, born in 1841.

Children, the first four born in West Rutland, Vt., and the other in Rutland, Vt. :

<ul>
<li>i. James Reid Sheldon[8], b. Sept. 24, 1868.</li>
<li>— ii. Susan Huntingdon Sheldon[8], b. Jan'y 24, 1872.</li>
<li>— iii. Lewis Pendleton Sheldon[8], b. June 9, 1874.</li>
<li>— iv. Richard Sheldon[8], b. July 9, 1878.</li>
<li>— v. Elizabeth Somerville Sheldon[8], b. Sept. 23, 1882.</li>
</ul>

305b—vi.

VIII. *Lewis Warrington Pendleton[7]* married, October 9, 1867, Carrie Sophia Conner, daughter of William H. and Caroline R. [Porter] Conner, born, March 14, 1844; he attained a high degree of eminence in the medical profession at Belfast, Me.; but, desiring a more extensive field, he moved to Portland, where his success continued till his sudden death, January 12, 1898, leaving his wife surviving.

Children, born in Belfast:

<ul>
<li>— i. Katharine Pendleton[8], b. Feb'y 1, 1870; d. Aug. 9, 1870.</li>
<li>— ii. William Lewis Pendleton[8], b. Dec. 22, 1874; d. Aug. 24, 1875.</li>
<li>— iii. Dana Pendleton[8], b. Aug. 17, 1878; d. Sept. 23, 1896.</li>
</ul>

305b—vii.

VIII. *Ann Frances Pendleton[7]* married, July 2, 1872, George Preston Sheldon, son of Charles and Janet [Reid] Sheldon, born, January 17, 1847; she died, September 5, 1885, leaving him surviving.

Children, the first two born in Brooklyn, the next two in Somers, and the other in White Plains, N. Y.:

<ul>
<li>i. Harriet Haskell Sheldon[8], b. April 14, 1873.</li>
<li>ii. George Preston Sheldon[8], b. Nov. 19, 1876.</li>
<li>iii. Frances Sheldon[8], b. Aug. 19, 1878.</li>
<li>iv. Janet Somerville Sheldon[8], b. Aug. 26, 1880.</li>
<li>v. Waldo Sheldon[8], b. Jan'y 11, 1884.</li>
</ul>

305b—viii.

VIII. *Edward Waldo Pendleton[7]* married, November 26, 1895, Mary Elizabeth Porter, daughter of Robert David and Sarah Ann [McManus] Porter, born, October 29, 1849; she died, March 9, 1897; no children.

308.

VII. LUCY BARSTOW ROGERS[6] (*Walter[5], Adam[4], Timothy[3], Timothy[2], John[1]*) was born in Marshfield, January 30, 1800; she married, November 29, 1827, as his second wife (his first having been her sister, Lydia[6]) Loring Eaton, son of Reuben and Elizabeth Eaton, born, February 2, 1797; he died, December 13, 1866, and she, March 3, 1897.

Children, born in Sudbury:

    i. Lydia Jane Eaton[7], b. Dec. 3, 1828; m. John C. Stevens.

    ii. Lucy Ann Eaton[7], b. June 2, 1830; m. William Wilson.

    iii. Marshall Loring Eaton[7], b. April 9, 1832; m. Sarah Sawyer.

    iv. Mary Elizabeth Eaton[7], b. Sept. 13, 1835; m. Alden Appleton Fuller.

    v. Emily Rogers Eaton[7], b. June 27, 1838; m. George C. H. Fuller.

309.

VII. ABIGAIL ROGERS[6] (*Walter[5], Adam[4], Timothy[3], Timothy[2], John[1]*) was born in Braintree, November 21, 1801; she married, April 19, 1827, Edward Brown, son of John and Alice [Howe] Brown, born September 7, 1802; he died, September 19, 1853, and she, November 4, 1889.

Children, born in Sudbury:

    i. Abigail Amelia Brown[7], b. May 1, 1828.

    ii. Edward Everett Brown[7], b. June 10, 1830; d. Feb'y 20, 1891.

—   iii. Francis Frederick Brown[7], b. May 19, 1832; d. June 12, 1833.

    iv. Francis Frederick Brown[7], b. Aug. 12, 1834; d. Jan'y 13, 1890.

    v. Ellen Elizabeth Brown[7], b. Nov. 22, 1836.

    vi. Hubbard Howe Brown[7], b. July 5, 1839.

    vii. Mary Melinda Brown[7], b. April 22, 1842.

310.

VII. MARY ROGERS[6] (*Walter[5], Adam[4], Timothy[3], Timothy[2], John[1]*) was born in Braintree, February 26, 1803; she married, May 8, 1828, Ephraim Moore, son of Ephraim and Ann [Knight] Moore, born, October 2, 1803; he died, March 30, 1861, and she, August 13, 1863.

Children, born in Sudbury:

- ·i. Hobart Moore[7], b. Jan'y 26, 1830.
- ii. Stephen Moore[7], b. Feb'y 9, 1835.
- — iii. Ellen Augusta Moore[7], b. May 29, 1845; d. Nov. 1, 1863.

311.

VII. JANE ROGERS[6] (*Walter[5], Adam[4], Timothy[3], Timothy[2], John[1]*) was born in Braintree, March 4, 1805; she married, December 1, 1831, Thomas Lee Dakin, son of Levi and Lucretia [Wheeler] Dakin, born January 8, 1805, at Cambridge; he died, June 4, 1874, and she, November 3, 1882.

Children, born in Sudbury:

- i. George Thomas Dakin[7], b. Oct. 20, 1832; m. Ellen M. French.
- ii. Nancy Jane Dakin[7], b. May 6, 1836; m. Hiram G. Burr.
- iii. Mary Lucretia Dakin[7], b. Sept. 22, 1838; m. Luther G. Hunt.
- iv. Arthur Dakin[7], b. June 25, 1840; m. Abbie A. Parmenter.
- v. Ann Hasseltine Dakin[7], b. Mar. 20, 1843; m. George W. French.

312.

VII. WALTER ROGERS[6] (*Walter[5], Adam[4], Timothy[3], Timothy[2], John[1]*) was born in Sudbury, November 23, 1807; he married, December 1, 1831, Emily Mariah

Hayden, daughter of William and Hepsibeth [Harrington] Hayden, born, June 20, 1811; she died in Sudbury, November 19, 1854; he married, July 10, 1855, Emeline Susan Stone, daughter of William and Sukey [Cutter] Stone, born, October 16, 1808; he died, April 3, 1896, and she, July 14, 1897.

Children, all by first wife, born in Sudbury:

— 444. Bradley[7], b. Dec. 21, 1832; d. Dec. 27, 1846.
+ 445. Edwin[7], b. Oct. 1, 1834.
+ 446. Albert Dana[7], b. Sept 2, 1838.
+ 447. Homer[7], b. Oct. 11, 1840.
+ 448. Elizabeth Hunt[7], b. Aug. 7, 1842.

314.

VII. Samuel Barstow Rogers[6] (*Walter[5], Adam[4], Timothy[3], Timothy[2], John[1]*) was born in Waltham, October 15, 1813; he married, Nov. 30, 1837, Eliza Jones Parmenter, daughter of Noah and Lydia [Jones] Parmenter, born, September 18, 1818; she died, March 10, 1892, and he April 29, 1898.

Children, born in Sudbury:

+ 449. Melvina Amanda[7], b. Feb'y 15, 1840.
— 450. Alfred Seymour[7], b. Feb'y 11, 1846; d. Sept. 14, 1846.
— 451. Bradley Seymour[7], b. Aug. 25, 1847; d. Aug. 15, 1848.
+ 452. Atherton Wales[7], b. Aug. 10, 1848.

We are greatly grieved to learn, just as this sheet is going to press, of the death of *Samuel Barstow Rogers[6]*, at South Sudbury.

315.

VII. Thankful Rogers[6] (*Adam[5], Adam[4], Timothy[3], Timothy[2], John[1]*) was born in Lincolnville, Maine, July 11, 1802; she married, September 8, 1822, John Decrow, born, August 31, 1793; he died, June 6, 1856, and she, January 6, 1859.

Children, the first five born in Lincolnville, and the other in Bangor, Maine:

† i. Adam Rogers Decrow[7], b. Jan'y 26, 1824.
† ii. Achsa Kidder Decrow[7], b. Aug. 21, 1825.
† iii. Anson Walter Decrow[7], b. Feb'y 18, 1828.
† iv. James Kelley Decrow[7], b. Aug. 4, 1831.
— v. Erastus John Decrow[7], b. June 11, 1834; d. unm. Nov. 1, 1864.
— vi. David Mandell Decrow[7], b. Aug. 13, 1838; lost at sea, 1853.

Erastus John Decrow[7] was a soldier in the civil war, Co. B, 9th Minn. Vols., and died a prisoner of war, at Millen, Georgia.

315—i.

VIII. *Adam Rogers Decrow[7]*, married, October 19, 1847, Sophronia L. Holman, daughter of Levi Holman; she died, October 12, 1859; he married (2) Orissa P. Lobdell of Richfield, Minn., in 1861; she died in 1863 and he in 1864; was in the Union service at Vicksburg and was killed in a Confederate raid.

Children, all by first wife; the first born in Bangor, Me., and the others in Richfield, Minn.:

— i. Alice Eureka Decrow[8], died in infancy.
† ii. Lillie Belle Decrow[8], b. Nov. 26, 1854.
† iii. Frank Rogers Decrow[8], b. Jan'y 28, 1856.

315—i—ii.

IX. *Lillie Belle Decrow[8]*, married January 1, 1878, William Edward Sargent, son of William Becket and Mary Ann [Levery] Sargent, born May 2, 1851.

Children, the first born in Malden, and the other in Bridgeport, Conn.:

— i. Edward Rogers Sargent[9], b. Jan'y 15, 1879.
— ii. Edith Belle Sargent[9], b. Dec. 3, 1890; d. Aug. 9, 1891.

315—i—iii.

IX. *Frank Rogers Decrow[8]*, married October 30, 1880, Eleanor Medcalf, daughter of William and Emerilla [Marsh] Medcalf, born October 25, 1859; she died April 21, 1889; he married, May 12, 1892, Nancy Adeline Oakes, daughter of Daniel Proctor and Maria [Rosenbaum] Oakes, born, June 9, 1863.

Children, the first born in Cheney and the others in Grayling, Michigan:

By first wife :

—   i.   Lillie Belle Decrow⁹, b. June 1, 1882 ; d. Aug. 10, 1883.

    ii.   Thean Ranlett Decrow⁹, b. Ap'l 1, 1886.

—   iii.   Eleanor Decrow⁹, b. Ap'l 12, 1889 ; d. Ap'l 29, 1889.

By second wife :

    iv.   Frank Oscar Decrow⁹, b. Dec. 15, 1893.

    v.   John Erastus Decrow⁹, b. Aug. 2, 1896.

    vi.   Daughter⁹, b. May 5, 1898.

315—ii.

VIII.   *Achsa Kidder Decrow⁷*, married, May 14, 1846, Simeon Otis Pierce, son of Simeon and Sarah [Dean] Pierce, born, July 8, 1823 ; he died October 25, 1886, and she, December 27, 1851 ; no children.

315—iii.

VIII.   *Anson Walter Decrow⁷*, married, June 21, 1850, Rachel Stevens Davis, daughter of John Bunyan and Nancy Royce [Farrington] Davis, born, October 6, 1823 ; he died, November 29, 1886, leaving her surviving.

Children, the first born in Charlestown, and the others in Bangor, Maine :

—   i.   Euna Gertrude Decrow⁸, b. March 23, 1851.

†   ii.   William Emery Decrow⁸, b. Dec. 26, 1853 ; Yale, 1880.

†   iii.   David Augustus Decrow⁸, b. Ap'l 8, 1859 ; Univ. of Me., 1879.

—   iv.   Walter Rogers Decrow⁸, b. June 17, 1863 ; d. June 27, 1863.

Anson Walter Decrow⁷ was for many years in the stove and foundry business in Bangor, but at the outbreak of the civil war, under contracts with the government, he manufactured the equipments for several of the Maine regiments. In 1864, he went to Vicksburg, to engage in raising and shipping cotton to the North, and was enrolled in the Union forces. The war closing, he resumed his old business in Bangor and continued it until his death.

He was an inventor and took out one of the first patents for the keyless combination lock.

315—iii—ii.

IX.   *William Emery Decrow⁸*, married, January 7, 1875, Lottie

Ann Emery, daughter of John Elwell and Hannah Mead [Hobbs] Emery, born, February 12, 1853; and they have

    i. John Walter Decrow[9], b. Feb'y 20, 1876, in Bangor, Me., Yale, 1900.

    ii. Mary Wood Decrow[9], b. Sept. 3, 1883, in Boston; Girl's Latin School.

He was city editor of *Bangor Commercial*; then on editorial staff of *Boston Globe*; and since, General Manager of the New England business of the Gamewell Fire Alarm Telegraph Company.

315—iii—iii.

IX. *David Augustus Decrow[8]*, married, March 22, 1882, Cora Inez Adams, daughter of Damon T. and Jean [McDermott] Adams, born, April 22, 1859; and they have

    i. Vere Royce Decrow[9], b. Jan'y 15, 1886, in Lockport, N. Y.

    ii. Rogers Franklyn[9], b. Feb'y 13, 1888, in Lockport, N. Y.

He is Designing Engineer of the Holly Manufacturing Company, at Lockport, N. Y.

315—iv.

VIII. *James Kelley Decrow[7]*, married, April, 13, 1861, Sarah Jane Glenn, daughter of James Umphais and Wilmonth [Johnston] Glenn, born, January 9, 1833; he died, September 24, 1861, leaving her still (1898) surviving.

No children.

Prior to the civil war, he settled in Columbus, Georgia; when the war commenced, he enlisted in the Confederate service and was commissioned as Lieutenant in Co. E., 12 Reg't Georgia Volunteers ("Muscogee Rifles"); he was wounded in the second battle of Manassas, Aug. 27, 1861, died at Middlebury, Va., Sept. 24, 1861, and was buried in the Confederate cemetery in Middlebury.

It will be noted that his oldest brother, *Adam Rogers Decrow[7]*, was in the Federal service and was killed near Vicksburg in 1864; and that his younger brother, *Erastus John Decrow[7]*, was also in the Federal service and died in a Confederate prison, November 1, 1864.

317.

VII. Jane Rogers[6], (*Adam[5], Adam[4], Timothy[3],*

Timothy², *John¹*) was born in Lincolnville, Maine, June 18, 1807; she May 25, 1828 [published, May 6, 1828] James Auld Kelley, born in Boothbay, April 22, 1805; he died —— and she married, October 14, 1832, David McKoy, son of Robert and Anna McKoy, born, April 7, 1805. He died August [September] 28, 1869, and she, December 7, 1875.

Children, the first four born in Lincolnville, and the others in Bangor, where the family moved in 1839:

By first husband:

—   i.   James Emrie Kelley⁷, b. Dec. 6, 1828; d. May 13, 1829.

By second husband:

     ii.   Olive Ann McKoy⁷, b. July 10, 1833.

†   iii.   Celia Rogers McKoy⁷, b. July 15, 1835.

     iv.   Ellen McKoy⁷, b. Sept. 19, 1837.

—   v.   James Wilmot McKoy⁷, b. Oct. 5, 1841; d. Feb'y 16, 1843.

     vi.   Ada Jane McKoy⁷, b. Sept. 8, 1843.

     vii.   Charles Edward McKoy⁷, b. Dec. 9, 1847.

Olive Ann McKoy⁷, married Ansel C. Hallett.

Ellen McKoy⁷, married Albert Bean.

317—iii.

VIII.   *Celia Rogers McKoy⁷*, married, January 13, 1859, Henry Tweed, son of James and Sarah [Harnden] Tweed, born, November 9, 1833; he died, February 20, 1893; she resides in Boston.

Children, born in Boston:

—   i.   Mary Tweed⁸, b. June 10, 1862; d. May 15, 1864.

     ii.   Jane Rogers Tweed⁸, b. July 31, 1867.

317b.

VII.   LYDIA ROGERS⁶(*Adam⁵*, *Adam⁴*, *Timothy³*, *Timothy²*, *John¹*) was born in Lincolnville, Maine, March 13, 1814; she married, February 23, 1837, at Bangor, Rev. John Studley Springer. He died at Medford, leaving her surviving.

Children:

    i.   Olive Elizabeth Springer[7], b. Mar. 22, 1838.
   ii.   Samuel Babcock Springer[7], b. Nov. 16, 1839.
  iii.   Augusta Adelaide Springer[7], b. Feb'y 23, 1842.
   iv.   Frederick Barnes Springer[7], b.
    v.   Lydia Ashton Springer[7], b.
   vi.   Stephen Emerson Springer[7], b.

317c.

VII. MARY BRADFORD ROGERS[6] (*Adam[5], Adam[4], Timothy[3], Timothy[2], John[1]*) was born in Lincolnville, Maine, April 13, 1822; she married November 17, 1842, Thomas Boynton, son of William and Mary [Huckins] Boynton, born at Effingham, N. H., June 4, 1815; he died in Malden, April 22, 1896.

Children, born in Bangor, Maine:

—   i.   Arthur Livermore Boynton[7], b. Sept. 27, 1843 ; d. unm. Jan'y 25, 1867.
   ii.   Mary Frances Boynton[7], b. Aug. 4, 1845.
— iii.   Daughter[7], b. July 3, 1847 ; d. same day.
   iv.   Annie Smith Boynton[7], b. Aug. 14, 1853.
    v.   George Boynton[7], b. Mar. 10, 1856.
— vi.   Clara Olive Boynton[7], b. May 28, 1861.

Mrs. Boynton resides in Linden (Malden) and has her father's Bible, containing the Family Record.

318.

VII. ELISHA ROGERS[6] (*Elisha[5], Adam[4], Timothy[3], Timothy[2], John[1]*) was born in Marshfield, April 16, 1807; he married, July 26, 1829, Sophia Clapp White, daughter of James and Sally [Lapham] White, of Marshfield, born, November 18, 1806; he died, July 11, 1893, and she, February 18, 1879.

Children, born in Marshfield:

453.   James Adam[7], b. Ap'l 29, 1830.
454.   Amos Sumner[7], b. Aug. 12, 1831.

455. Maria Gilbert[7], b. Ap'l 24, 1833.
+ 456. George Warren[7], b. Sept. 3, 1835.
457. Charles Everett[7], b. Nov. 25, 1837.
458. Mary Frances[7], b. Dec. 10, 1839.
459. Emeline Howard[7], b. Oct. 10, 1841.

322.

JANE [JEANE] ROGERS[6] (*Thomas[5]*, *Samuel[4]*, *Samuel[3]*, *Timothy[2]*, *John[1]*) was born in Marshfield; baptized, October 3, 1768; she married, February 21, 1814, Joshua Vinal; he disappeared, February 28, 1822, and was found dead in a ditch in the marsh, March 10, 1822; she married, August 1, 1824, Asa Lapham, as his second wife; she died, November 17, 1840.

No children.

324.

VII. ISAAC ROGERS[6] (*Thomas[5]*, *Samuel[4]*, *Samuel[3]*, *Timothy[2]*, *John[1]*) was born in Marshfield, June 15, 1784; baptized, September 19, 1784; he married, July 25, 1808, Lucy Little Vinal; he died, May 28, 1853, and she, October 9, 1847.

Children, the first born in Plymouth and the others in Marshfield:

460. Isaac Thomas[7], b. Aug. 5, 1811; married, Huldah Lewis, June 2, 1844; died, Ap'l 17, 1897.
461. Lucy Little[7], b. Jan'y 31, 1818.
462. Eliza[7], b. July 19, 1820; m. Samuel Keene; died leaving no surviving issue.
463. Charles[7], b. Nov. 22, 1823; m. Mary Keene Carver, Sept. 15, 1850.

His will, p. June 7, 1853, mentions sons Isaac T. and Charles, and daughter Lucy Litchfield, wife of Lewis Litchfield of Hanover.

A stone in Hanover cemetery has inscription "LEWIS LITCHFIELD, died March 8, 1890, aged 78 yrs., 5 mos., 13 days; LUCY L., wife of Lewis Litchfield, died Mch 4, 1864, aged 46 yrs., 2 mos., 4 days, & *Infant dau.* LAURA E."

326.

VII. SARAH ROGERS[6] (*Samuel[5], Samuel[4], Samuel[3], Timothy[2], John[1]*) was born in Marshfield, July 29, 1771; baptized, May 10, 1772; she married, July 20, 1792, John Tilden Ames, son of Jedediah and Bethiah [Tilden] Ames, born, June 15, 1764; he died, February 19, 1847, and she, January 1, 1846.

Children, born in Marshfield:

—   i.   Son[7], unnamed, b. Jan'y 13, 1793; d. Jan'y 25, 1793.
     ii. Sarah Tilden Ames[7], b. May 15, 1794; m. Dr. Grilley Thaxter, of Abington, May 2, 1827.
     iii. Tilden Ames[7], b. Dec. 11, 1795; m. Betsey Hatch, Dec. 6, 1818.
     iv. Mary Ames[7], b. Ap'l 4, 1798; m. Charles Hatch, Jan'y 27, 1820.
     v.   Betsey Ames[7], b. July 18, 1800; m. John Damon, Dec. 6, 1821.
     vi. Edward Ames[7], b. Oct. 26, 1803; m. Rhoda C. Hatch, Jan'y —, 1831.
     vii. Almira Little Ames[7], b. Feb'y 3, 1806; m. Calvin Damon, May 16, 1827.
     viii. Susan C. Ames[7], b. June 7, 1811; m. Ira Carver, Jan'y 1, 1833.

327.

VII. LUTHER ROGERS[6] (*Simeon[5], Samuel[4], Samuel[3], Timothy[2], John[1]*) was born in Marshfield, August 21, 1778; baptized, Oct. 18, 1778; he married January 17, 1802, Abigail Little Tilden, daughter of Wales and Abigail [Little] Tilden, born October 4, 1784; he died, March 3, 1860, and she, January 28, 1858.

Children, born in Marshfield:

+ 464. Luther[7], b. July 2, 1803.
+ 465. Wales[7], b. June 20, 1805.
+ 466. Clift[7], b. Dec. 4, 1806.
— 467. Abigail Little[7], b. Ap'l 1, 1809; d. Feb'y 15, 1817.

+ 468. Sarah Little⁷, b. Oct. 7, 1811.
+ 469. Avery⁷, b. June 7, 1814.
— 470. Betsey⁷, b. Jan'y 13, 1817 ; d. Feb'y 11, 1817.
+ 471. Alvin⁷, b. Feb'y 16, 1818.
— 472. Sophia Tilden⁷, b. Mar. 31, 1821.
— 473. William Tilden⁷, b. June 21, 1824 ; d. July 10, 1824.
+ 474. Abigail Frances⁷, b. Sept. 2, 1825.
— 475. Daughter, unnamed⁷, b. 1826 ; d. in infancy.
— 476. Ann Maria⁷, b. July 28, 1830 ; d. Ap'l 2, 1832.

Luther⁷ and *Clift⁷* spelled their surname "Rodgers."

345 and 205—ii.

VIII. MOSES FOLGER ROGERS⁷ (*Aaron⁶, Stephen⁵, John⁴, Thomas³, John², John¹*) was born in Danby, Vermont, March 25, 1803; he married, December 12, 1827, Beulah Wing, daughter of Samuel and Anna [Rogers] Wing, born, February 2, 1803; he died, March 1, 1886, and she, May 13, 1882, at Lynn.

Children, born in Marshfield:

+ 476. Stephen Rogers⁸, b. Sept. 28, 1828.
— 477. Alice Rogers⁸, b. Jan'y 1, 1832 ; d. Ap'l 4, 1836.

He married (2) Elizabeth Russell, June 16, 1883.

350.

VIII. ELISHA FOLGER ROGERS⁷ (*Aaron⁶, Stephen⁵, John⁴, Thomas³, John², John¹*) was born in Danby, Vt., June 20, 1813; he married, December 12, 1835, Elizabeth Mitchell, daughter of Jethro Folder and Anne [Gould] Mitchell, born, June 3, 1813; he died, July 16, 1887, at Rockport, Mass., and she, October 12, 1885.

Children, born in Danby, Vt.:

— 478. Jethro Folger⁸, b. in 1836 ; d. in infancy.
+ 479. James Swift⁸, b. Mar. 28, 1840.

358.

VIII. JANE SOULE ROGERS⁷ (*Thomas⁶, Thomas⁵, Israel⁴, Timothy³, Timothy², John¹*) was born in Marsh-

field, May 15, 1804; she married, May 4, 1826, Hiram
Oakman, son of Constant Fobes and Rachel [Hatch]
Oakman, born, May 3, 1801 ; he died, October 12, 1884,
and she, March 25, 1890.

Children, born in Marshfield:

+   i.   Hiram Abif Oakman[8], b. Ap'l 10, 1827.
+   ii.   Thomas Rogers Oakman[8], b. Mar. 9, 1829 ; see No. 248a—i.
+   iii.   Henry Phillips Oakman[8], b. June 27, 1831.
+   iv.   Otis Briggs Oakman[8], b. July 19, 1833.
+   v.   Nathan Soule Oakman[8], b. Jan'y 20, 1837.
+   vi.   Mary Jane Oakman[8], b. Aug. 7, 1839.
—   vii.   Susanna Adeline Oakman[8], b. May 29, 1842 ; d. unm. Ap'l 21, 1886.

Hiram Abif[8], *Henry Phillips*[8], *Otis Briggs*[8], and *Nathan Soule*[8]
served with credit in the civil war; the first was wounded and the
last two died from disease contracted in the army.

359.

VIII. JUDITH CLIFT ROGERS[7] (*Thomas*[6], *Thomas*[5],
Israel[4], *Timothy*[3], *Timothy*[2], *John*[1]) was born in Marsh-
field, February 23, 1820; she married, May 9, 1849,
Adin Packard Wilde of Braintree, son of Atherton and
Lucy [Packard] Wilde, born, February 12, 1814; he
died, July 3, 1885, and she, November 16, 1854.

Children, born in Marshfield:

—   i.   Adin Wilde[8], d. Ap'l 16, 1850, a few days of age.
—   ii.   Thomas Rogers Wilde[8], b. Dec. 22, 1851 ; d. Aug. 28, 1852.
†   iii.   Roger Henry Wilde[8], b. Oct. 24, 1853.

359—iii.

IX.   *Roger Henry Wilde*[8], married, November 8, 1881, Francis
Gardner Prescott of Quincy, daughter of Josiah Gardner and Caroline
Rebecca [Emery] Prescott, born, Sept. 15, 1856.

Children, born in Atlantic, Mass.:

    i.   Corinna Prescott Wilde[9], b. Aug. 30, 1882.

    ii. Adin Packard Wilde[9], b. Sept. 21, 1884.

—   iii. Lawrence Emery Wilde[9], b. Jan'y 29, 1887 ; d. Feb'y 22, 1887.

    iv. Gertrude Louise Wilde[9], b. Aug. 22, 1890.

363.

VIII. PHEBE GRINNELL ROGERS[7] (*Martin[6], Thomas[5], Israel[4], Timothy[3], Timothy[2], John[1]*) was born in Marshfield, July 22, 1813; she married, December 29, 1835, James Harvey McCrillis, son of James and Jane [Dunham] McCrillis, born, October 16, 1812; they were both lost at sea, with two of their children; they sailed from New York in December, 1866, and the vessel was never heard from.

Children, born in Belfast, Maine:

—   i.   James Martin McCrillis[8], b. May 1, 1840 ; d. Aug. 3, 1843.

—   ii. Edwin Otis McCrillis[8], b. Ap'l 9, 1842 ; lost at sea.

    iii. Emma Lurette McCrillis[8], b. Ap'l 4, 1846.

—   iv. Sarah Phillips McCrillis[8], b. May 5, 1848 ; d. Sept. 9, 1866.

—   v. Isabella Anita McCrillis[8], b. Jan'y 6, 1850 ; lost at sea.

Emma Lurette McCrillis[8], married, Charles F. Thoms of Bangor.

364.

VIII. SARAH PHILLIPS ROGERS[7] (*Martin[6], Thomas[5], Israel[4], Timothy[3], Timothy[2], John[1]*) was born in Marshfield, May 29, 1815; she married, January 17, 1837, Simon Cottrell, son of Joshua and Prudence [Grinnell] Cottrell; he died, December 15, 1839; she married John Phillips Bagley, born, January 15, 1819; she died, August 14, 1846, and he married her sister, Almira Eleanor Rogers.

Child, born in Belfast:

—   i.   Norman Lesley Bagley[8], b. Jan'y 29, 1846 ; d. Sept. 1, 1846.

365.

VIII. MARY ANN ROGERS[7] (*Martin*[6], *Thomas*[5], *Israel*[4], *Timothy*[3], *Timothy*[2], *John*[1]) was born in Marshfield, March 24, 1818; she married, January 10, 1842, Joshua Cottrell, son of Joshua and Prudence [Grinnell] Cottrell; he died, May 20, 1843; she married, January 30, 1845, Axel Hayford, son of Gad and Sally [Bisbee] Hayford, born, April 20, 1814; she died, April 17, 1885, leaving him surviving.

Children, born in Belfast:

By first husband:

— i. Horace Augustine Cottrell[8], b. Aug. 18, 1843; d. in infancy.

By second husband:

— ii. Arvida Evander Hayford[8], b. Oct. 22, 1845; d. unm. June 2, 1879.

iii. William Lloyd Hayford[8], b. Aug. 2, 1848.

366.

VIII. MARTIN CROSBY ROGERS[7] (*Martin*[6], *Thomas*[5], *Israel*[4], *Timothy*[3], *Timothy*[2], *John*[1]) was born in Marshfield, August 28, 1819; he married, June 27, 1843, Emma Jane Doe, daughter of Asa and Nancy Leighton [Sanborn] Doe, born, April 25, 1825; he died, October 6, 1857, and she, October 3, 1849.

Child, born in Searsmont, Maine:

— 480. Edwin Sanborn[8], b. Nov. 23, 1847; d. Jan'y 30, 1854.

367.

VIII. WILLIAM THOMAS ROGERS[7] (*Martin*[6], *Thomas*[5], *Isaac*[4], *Timothy*[3], *Timothy*[2], *John*[1]) was born in Marshfield, October 26, 1821; he married, January 28, 1849, Frances Augusta West, daughter of Asa and Nancy [Piper] West, born, July 25, 1831.

Children, born in Belfast, Maine:
- 481. Charles Augustus[8], b. Jan'y 19, 1850; d. Feb'y 2, 1850.
+ 482. Charles William[8], b. Dec. 3, 1853.
+ 483. Byron Martin[8], b. Dec. 28, 1858.

368.

VIII. ALMIRA ELEANOR ROGERS[7] (*Martin[6], Thomas[5], Israel[4], Timothy[3], Timothy[2], John[1]*) was born in Marshfield, March 12, 1824; she married (as his second wife), December 12, 1847, John Phillips Bagley, born, January 15, 1819; he died, March 20, 1862, leaving her surviving.
Children, born in Belfast, Maine:
- i. Frances Anna Bagley[8], b. Aug. 15, 1848.
† ii. Carrie Lena Bagley[8], b. Ap'l 22, 1858.

368—ii.

IX. *Carrie Lena Bagley[8]*, married, December, 24, 1877, Eugene Promis, son of Leopold Marc and Amanda Amelia [Dunton] Promis, born, May 16, 1847, and they have, born in Philadelphia:
  i. Marion Laithwaite Promis[9], b. Mar. 24, 1891.
  ii. Anita Promis[9], b. July 20, 1894.

369.

VIII. CAROLINE JANE ROGERS[7] (*Martin[6], Thomas[5], Israel[4], Timothy[3], Timothy[2], John[1]*) was born in Belfast, Maine, December 17, 1826; she married, October 7, 1847, Benjamin Sargent, son of Samuel and Mary [Allen] Sargent, born, August 14, 1818; he died, January 28, 1856; she married, October 26, 1862, Adoniram Judson Howard, son of Barnabas and Thirza [Bisbee] Howard, born, May 10, 1831; he died, November 18, 1880, leaving her surviving.
Children, all by first husband, born in Belfast, Maine:
  i. Dudley Allen Sargent[8], b. Sept. 28, 1849.
  ii. Carrie Stacy Sargent[8], b. July 19, 1851.
  iii. Samuel Dayton Sargent[8], b. Nov. 30, 1854.

370.

VIII. MARIA EXPERIENCE ROGERS[7] (*Martin[6], Thomas[5], Israel[4], Timothy[3], Timothy[2], John[1]*) was born in Belfast, Maine, February 18, 1829; married, July 22, 1851, Capt. Richard Pettingill, son of Richard and Mary [Pierce] Pettingill, born, July 13, 1827.

Children, born in Newburyport:

     i. Addie Thayer Pettingill[8], b. Sept. 7, 1852.
— ii. Byron Pettingill[8], b. Oct. 10, 1855 ; d. in infancy.
   iii. Forrest Chester Pettingill[8], b. Aug. 28, 1857.

375 and 356.

VIII. GEORGE HOWLAND ROGERS[7] (*Howland[6], Thomas[5], Israel[4], Timothy[3], Timothy[2], John[1]*) was born, in Marshfield, February 1, 1825; he married, April 22, 1849, EUNICE ANN ROGERS[7], daughter of Abijah and Mercy [Hatch] Rogers, born, August 27, 1826; he died, January 1, 1876, leaving her surviving.

Child, born in Marshfield :

  484. George Calvin[6], b. Oct. 8, 1852.

376.

VIII. WALES ALLEN ROGERS[7] (*Howland[6], Thomas[5], Israel[4], Timothy[3], Timothy[2], John[1]*) was born in Marshfield, August 4, 1826; he married, January 15, 1854, Sarah Ann Tilden, daughter of Wales and Susanna [Little] Tilden, born, February 4, 1825; she died, November 11, 1897.

No children.

377.

VIII. NATHANIEL CLIFT ROGERS[7] (*Howland[6], Thomas[5], Israel[4], Timothy[3], Timothy[2], John[1]*) was born in Marshfield, May 18, 1833; he married, in November,

1859, Sarah Elizabeth Seabury, daughter of William Seabury, born, December 7, 1834; he died, March 1, 1875, leaving her surviving.

Children:

485. Willis[8], b. Aug. 30, 1860, in N. Weymouth.
— 486. Helen Clift[8], b. Aug. 15, 1864, in Weymouth.
487. Parker[8], b. Ap'l 9, 1866, in E. Weymouth.

378.

VIII. PHILENDA ADELAIDE ROGERS[7] (*Howland*[6], *Thomas*[5], *Israel*[4], *Timothy*[3], *Timothy*[2], *John*[1]) was born in Marshfield, May 28, 1835; she married, June 3, 1855, Frederic Hatch, son of Jotham and Rosalina [Hatch] Hatch, born, December 16, 1831; he died, November 2, 1897, leaving her surviving.

Children, born in Marshfield:

— i. Frederic Rogers Hatch[8], b. Aug. 15, 1856 ; d. Feb'y 3, 1857.
 ii. Wilbur Jotham Hatch[8], b. Oct. 27, 1858.
 iii. Roger Howland Hatch[8], b. Sept. 30, 1862.
— iv. Frederic Hatch[8], b. Dec. 13, 1864 ; d. May 24, 1866.
 v. Mary Adeline Hatch[8], b. Sept. 23, 1867.
 vi. Annie Rogers Hatch[8], b. Oct. 12, 1869.
 vii. Clara May Hatch[8], b. Feb'y 24, 1872.
 viii. Herbert Franklin Hatch[8], b. June 29, 1877.

380.

VIII. HENRY WARREN ROGERS[7] (*Warren*[6], *Thomas*[5], *Israel*[4], *Timothy*[3], *Timothy*[2], *John*[1]) was born in Lynn, November 20, 1831; he married, May 18, 1854, Caroline Augusta Bates, daughter of Thomas and Eunice [Danforth] Bates, born, January 1, 1834; she died, June 16, 1875; he married, November 8, 1880, Olive Ann Randall, daughter of Eliphalet and Phebe Chadbourne [Hurd] Randall, born, November 7, 1847.

Children, all by first wife, born in Lynn:

+ 488. Henrietta Eunice[8], b. Mar. 24, 1855.
− 489. Hamilton Everett[8], b. May 9, 1857.
+ 490. Clarence Abel[8], b. May 20, 1859.

382.

VIII. LUCY ANN ROGERS[7] (*Warren[6], Thomas[5], Israel[4], Timothy[3], Timothy[2], John[1]*) was born in Lynn, April 30, 1842; she married, February 23, 1871, Frederick David Mayo, son of John and Lucy [Rumrill] Mayo, born, January 3, 1839.

Children, born in Lynn:

i. Susan Gertrude Mayo[8], b. Nov. 2, 1873.
ii. Henry Rogers Mayo[8], b. Jan'y 19, 1879.

394.

VIII. EDWARD HENRY ROGERS[7] (*Henry[6], Asa[5], Israel[4], Timothy[3], Timothy[2], John[1]*) was born in Medford, September 10, 1824; he married, November 19, 1851, Hannah Susan Blanchard, daughter of Samuel and Rebekah [Merrill] Blanchard, born, May 31, 1827; she died, April 1, 1867; he married, May 27, 1868, Mary Frances Mann, daughter of Enoch and Clarissa [Fisher] Mann, born, May 28, 1830.

No children.

He served a year in the Civil War in the 43d Mass. Regiment; he has been a Representative in the General Court two terms from Chelsea; he was on the Commission of Inquiry, concerning the Hours of Labor. He edited, for the city, the Annals of the War History of Chelsea, and published a history of his Regiment.

His grandfather, ASA ROGERS[5], served two years in the Revolutionary War; he was a Corporal in Col. Thomas's Regiment, and was at West Point under Putnam.

395.

VIII. JAMES BURDETT ROGERS[7] (*Henry[6], Asa[5], Israel[4], Timothy[3], Timothy[2], John[1]*) was born in Medford, September 3, 1826; he married, May 19, 1853, Betsey Ann Hopkins, daughter of William Hutton and Betsey [Higgins] Hopkins, born, November 5, 1834.

Children, born in Chelsea:

— 491. Emma Florence[8], b. July 3, 1857 ; d. April 16, 1862.
    492. William Henry[8], b. Dec. 20, 1863.
= 493. Lizzie May[8], b. May 10, 1869.

397.

VIII. CHARLES EMERY ROGERS[7] (*Henry[6], Asa[5], Israel[4], Timothy[3], Timothy[2], John[1]*) was born in Medford, December 10, 1829; he married, November 1, 1855, Martha Symmes Lothrop, daughter of Isaac and Frances [Symmes] Lothrop, born, September 20, 1835.

Child, born in Charleston, Mass.:

= Isaac Lothrop[7], b. Nov. 16, 1858.

398.

VIII. SIDNEY GREENLEAF ROGERS[7] (*Henry[6], Asa[5], Israel[4], Timothy[3], Timothy[2], John[1]*) was born in South Boston, March 24, 1832; he married, January 12, 1854, Hannah Maria Dill Stoddard.

Children, the first born in Charlestown, and the others in Chelsea:

+ 495. Charles Stoddard[8], b. Dec. 9, 1854.
— 496. Henry[8], b. Mar. 19, 1857 ; d. Oct. 21, 1858.
— 497. Edwin[8], b. Sept. 7, 1858 ; d. Oct. 23, 1858.
+ 498. Franklin Greenleaf[8], b. Jan'y 8, 1860.

399.

VIII. REV. ANDREW JACKSON ROGERS[7] (*Henry[6], Asa[5],*

Israel[4], *Timothy*[3], *Timothy*[2], *John*[1]) was born in Medford, November 10, 1833; he married, January 16, 1873, Gertrude Jennette Barrett, daughter of Horace Willard and Harriet [Newell] Barrett, born, April 2, 1848; he died, May 6, 1876, leaving her surviving.

Child, born in Biddeford, Me.:

— 499. Edith Gertrude[8], b. Feb'y 27, 1875.

408.

VIII. CHARLES BARTLETT ROGERS[7] (*Charles*[6], *Charles*[5], *Zaccheus*[4], *Timothy*[3], *Timothy*[2], *John*[1]) was born in Portland, May 14, 1827; he married, August 20, 1863, Hannah Elizabeth Patten of Bath Me., daughter of David and Elizabeth [Hunter] Patten, born May 9, 1843.

Child, born in Portland:

— 500. Maria Adams[8], b. Oct. 16, 1864.

413.

VIII. CAROLINE AMANDA ROGERS[7] (*Benjamin*[6], *Benjamin*[5], *Zaccheus*[4], *Timothy*[3], *Timothy*[2], *John*[1]) was born in Marshfield, September 14, 1826; she married, January 27, 1847, Francis Standish, son of David and Jane [Hogan] Standish, born, November 24, 1815; he died, November 17, 1875, and she, February 5, 1866.

Children, the first born in Boston, and the others in Brighton, now Boston:

    i. Myles Standish[8], b. Oct. 17, 1851.
— ii. Frank Winter Standish[8], b. Jan'y 13, 1854 ; d. May 12, 1875.
— iii. Mabel Standish[8], b. Ap'l 29, 1856 ; d. Jan'y 12, 1869.
— iv. Clift Standish[8], b. Aug. 10, 1858 ; d. Oct. 11, 1864.

413—i.

IX. *Myles Standish*[8], married April 28, 1890, Louise Marston

Farwell, daughter of Asa and Marcia [Piper] Farwell, born, January 15, 1861, and they have children, born in Boston :

    i.   Barbara Standish[9], b. Mar. 25, 1891.
    ii. Lora Standish[9]. b. Nov. 2, 1892.
    iii. Myles Standish[9], b. Nov. 22, 1893.

414.

VIII. Isabel Ann Rogers[7] (*Benjamin[6]*, *Benjamin[5]*, *Zaccheus[4]*, *Timothy[3]*, *Timothy[2]*, *John[1]*) was born in Marshfield, March 22, 1828; she married, August 26, 1856, John Healey Brownson; he died, December 4, 1858; she resides in Boston.

No children.

415.

VIII. Benjamin Franklin Rogers[7] (*Benjamin[6]*, *Benjamin[5]*, *Zaccheus[4]*, *Timothy[3]*, *Timothy[2]*, *John[1]*) was born in Boston, August 16, 1830; he married, June 7, 1855, Blanche D'Eou.

Children, born in Cambridge :

— 501. Blanche Ella[8], b. July 20, 1856.
— 502. Benjamin[8], b. Dec. 28, 1862 ; d. Jan'y 16, 1877.
— 503. Lillian Clift[8], b. July 28, 1864.

416.

VIII. Fannie Elvira Rogers[7] (*Benjamin[6]*, *Benjamin[5]*, *Zaccheus[4]*, *Timothy[3]*, *Timothy[2]*, *John[1]*) was born in Boston, August 25, 1832; she married, July 16, 1857, George Dunn White, son of George Washington and Mary Ann [Dunn] White, born October 26, 1826; he died, September 17, 1869, leaving her surviving.

Child, born in Brighton :

    i.   Mary Carrie White[8], b. Sept. 25, 1860,

who married, October 31, 1883, Arthur Francis Clapp, son of John and Sarah Ann [Bullard] Clapp, born, October 4, 1859.

417.

VIII. LYSANDER WALDO ROGERS[7] (*Benjamin*[6], *Benjamin*[5], *Zaccheus*[4], *Timothy*[3], *Timothy*[2], *John*[1]) was born in Boston, July 25, 1838; he married, April 25, 1877, Fannie E. Howland, and they have

504. Winnifred[8], b.

418.

VIII. CHARLES ALVAN ROGERS[7] (*Alvan*[6], *Benjamin*[5], *Zaccheus*[4], *Timothy*[3], *Timothy*[2], *John*[1]) was born in Boston, June 7, 1836; he married, April 25, 1861, Sarah Elizabeth Hatch, daughter of Isaac and Sarah [Greenwood] Hatch, born, September 25, 1838; she died, July 25, 1896.

Children, born in Chelsea:

+ 505. Alvan Herbert[8], b. Jan'y 3, 1863.
+ 506. Winthrop Lincoln[8], b. Feb'y 25, 1865.
+ 507. Jennie Louise[8], b. Nov. 23, 1869.
+ 508. Helen Augusta[8], b. July 21, 1873.

421.

VIII. GEORGE EDWIN ROGERS[7] (*Alvan*[6], *Benjamin*[5], *Zaccheus*[4], *Timothy*[3], *Timothy*[2], *John*[1]) was born in Boston, June 15, 1843; he married, June 15, 1865, Mary Ella Harden, daughter of Harlow and Abby Rogers [Newhall] Harden, born in Gardiner, Maine, June 17, 1865.

Children, born in Chelsea:

= 509. Harlow Harden[8], b. Aug. 23, 1867.
= 510. Bradlee[8], b. Feb'y 1, 1869.
= 511. Foster[8], b. Nov. 20, 1871.

422.

VIII. MARY AUGUSTA ROGERS[7] (*Alvan*[6], *Benjamin*[5],

Zacheus⁴, Timothy³, Timothy², John¹) was born in Boston, August 28, 1845; she married, June 5, 1867, William C. Lamkin, born January 14, 1843; he died, January 17, 1890, and she, January 26, 1870.

Children, one born in Chelsea and the other in Worcester:

    i. Walter Rogers Lamkin⁸, b. Feb'y 7, 1868.
    ii. Carrie Augusta Lamkin⁸, b. Nov. 28, 1869.

425.

VIII. CLIFFORD IRVING ROGERS⁷ (*Prince⁶, Benjamin⁵, Zaccheus⁴, Timothy³, Timothy², John¹*) was born in East Boston, January 23, 1839; he married, June 9, 1864, in Perth Amboy, N. J., Elizabeth Barton, daughter of John and Elizabeth Parker [Randolph] Barton, born, November 25, 1840:

Children:

   — 512. A son⁸, b. Nov. —, 1868, in Perth Amboy; d. same day.
   † 513. Barton Clifford⁸, b. Jan'y 28, 1870, in Wyoming.
   — 514. Paul Clayton⁸, b. Mar. 21, 1872, in Colorado.
   — 515. Florence⁸, b. Jan'y 14, 1874, in Colorado; d. Jan'y 14, 1875.

He lives on the old Benjamin Rogers farm in Pembroke; is (1898) Town Collector.

IX. *Barton Clifford Rogers⁸*, married, December 25, 1891, Evie Hinckley, daughter of Frank Hinckley; and they have, born in Marshfield:

   516. Florence Elizabeth⁹, b. Dec. 22, 1892.

431.

VIII. PATIENCE JANE ROGERS⁷ (*Atherton Wales⁶, Samuel⁵, Adam⁴, Timothy³, Timothy², John¹*) was born in Lincolnville, Maine, January 14, 1825; she married, May 8, 1846, Rev. David Perry. No further account received.

432.

VIII. GEORGE ATHERTON ROGERS[7] (*Atherton Wales[6], Samuel[5], Adam[4], Timothy[3], Timothy[2], John[1]*) was born in Lincolnville, Maine, October 25, 1834; he married, August, 1867, Georgiana Cottrill Chapman, daughter of Nathaniel and Mary Permelia [Cottrill] Chapman, born, August 20, 1847.

Child, born in Chelsea:

+   517.   Josephine Mary[8], b. Nov. 9, 1868.

433.

VIII. LUCIUS HENRY CHANDLER ROGERS[7] (*Atherton Wales[6], Samuel[5], Adam[4], Timothy[3], Timothy[2], John[1]*) was born in Lincolnville, Maine, September 14, 1840; he married, June 26, 1864, Laura Juliet Eastman, daughter of Hubbard and Mary [Green] Eastman, born, December 13, 1840.

Children, the first born in Boston, and the others in Chelsea:

—   518.   Bertha Josephine[7], b. Nov. 1, 1865.
—   519.   Atherton Wales[7], b. Sept. 10, 1868.
—   520.   Daniel Eastman[7], b. Ap'l 4, 1875.

436a.

VIII. ALICE ANNIE ROGERS[7] (*Adam[6], Samuel[5], Adam[4], Timothy[3], Timothy[2], John[1]*) was born in Sunbury, Ohio, March 20, 1837; she married, December 16, 1855, Hiram Edmund Paget, son of Hiram and Jane [Symons] Paget, born, February 5, 1835; he died February 2, 1862; she married, September 28, 1868, William Bicknell Fain, son of John and Mary [Bicknell] Fain, born, March 22, 1826; he died, March 23, 1876; she is living at Portland, Oregon.

Children, by first husband, the first born at Drake-ville, and the next two at Chariton, Iowa:

    i.   Olive Sylvina Paget[8], b. Feb'y 21, 1857.
— ii. George Linneans Paget[8], b. Jan'y 11, 1859; d. Nov. 19, 1880.
    iii. Edmund Fitz Winter Paget[8], b. Jan'y 12, 1861.

By second husband, born in Portland, Oregon:

    iv. Achsah Gay Fain[8], b. Ap'l 21, 1870.
    v. Azubah Decrow Fain[8], b. Jan'y 13, 1872.

437.

VIII. SAMUEL WALTER ROGERS[7] (*Elisha[6], Samuel[5], Adam[4], Timothy[3], Timothy[2], John[1]*) was born in Lincolnville, Me., December 9, 1833; he married, in 1867, Amelia Henriette Frohock, daughter of Jeremiah and Henriette [Easton] Frohock, born, April 26, 1849; he died, January 19, 1887, leaving her surviving.

Children, born in Lincolnville:

    521. Lena Almon[8], b. Jan'y 25, 1868.
    522. Ada Myra[8], b. Feb'y 11, 1870.
    523. Abbie Etta[8], b. May 24, 1872.
    524. Carrie Rena[8], b. Oct. 22, 1876.
— 525. Olive Delilah[8], b. Oct. 2, 1880.
— 526. Walter Irving[8], b. Feb'y 14, 1883.

445.

VIII. EDWIN ROGERS[7] (*Walter[6], Walter[5], Adam[4], Timothy[3], Timothy[2], John[1]*) was born in Sudbury, October 1, 1834; he married, February 10, 1857, Maria Louisa Jones, daughter of John and Nancy [Maynard] Jones, born, November 24, 1839.

Children, born in South Sudbury:

+ 527. Fred Waldo[8], b. June 13, 1859.
+ 528. Walter Barstow[8], b. Jan'y 18, 1869.

446.

VIII. ALBERT DANA ROGERS[7] (*Walter*[6], *Walter*[5], *Adam*[4], *Timothy*[3], *Timothy*[2], *John*[1]) was born in Sudbury, September 2, 1838; he married, October 19, 1871, Martha Ward Hollis, daughter of John Warren and Judith Bussie [Ward] Hollis, born, December 23, 1846; she died, January 1, 1887; he married, January 10, 1895, Alice Mary Jones, daughter of Hiram Wilkins and Mary Joanna [Heald] Jones, born, February 27, 1857.

Children, born in Boston:

    529. Ethel Ward[8], b. Nov. 22, 1873.
— 530. Annie Hollis[8], b. July 8, 1875.
— 531. Maud Hayden[8], b. Ap'l 23, 1877.
— 532. Alberta Dana[8], b. Nov. 10, 1881.
— 533. Martha Gertrude[8], b. Dec. 15, 1886.

Ethel Ward Rogers[8], married, October 28, 1897, Daniel Tyler; reside in Brookline.

447.

HOMER ROGERS[7] (*Walter*[6], *Walter*[5], *Adam*[4], *Timothy*[3], *Timothy*[2], *John*[1]) was born in Sudbury, October 11, 1840; he married, January 10, 1868, Ellen Eudora Perry, daughter of Elijah and Mehitable [Battelle] Perry, born, May 13, 1847.

Children, the first six born in South Sudbury, and the others in Allston:

 + 534. Howard Perry[8], b. June 1, 1869.
 + 535. Elliott[8], b. Feb'y 10, 1872.
— 536. Carrie Louise[8], b. Feb'y 10, 1872; d. Aug. 8, 1872.
 + 537. Harland Hayden[8], b. Mar. 3, 1873.
— 538. Emily Battelle[8], b. Sept. 21, 1875; d. Nov. 19, 1875.
— 539. Mark Homer[8], b. May 21, 1877.
— 540. Leon Barstow[8], b. Mar. 4, 1879.
— 541. Louis[8], b. Nov. 30, 1880.
— 542. Marion Leonard[8], b. May 19, 1882.

448.

VIII.   ELIZABETH HUNT ROGERS[7] (*Walter⁶, Walter⁵, Adam⁴, Timothy³, Timothy², John¹*) was born in Sudbury, August 7, 1842; she married, November 23, 1865, George Henry Hall, son of John Clay and Mary U. [——] Hall, born, December 10, 1839; he died, May 26, 1877; she married, October 3, 1880, George Lawrence, son of Ralph and Phebe Lawrence, born, June 15, 1839.

Children, born in South Sudbury:

—   i.   Guy Mannering Hall⁸, b. Sept. 6, 1867 ; d. Dec. 20, 1869.
   ii.   Ralph Hayden Hall⁸, b. Oct. 9, 1869.
—   iii.   Albert Leroy Hall⁸, b. Nov. 18, 1871 ; d. Oct. 19, 1891.
   iv.   Seneca Wilson Hall⁸, b. Sept. 16, 1874.

449.

VIII.   MELVINA AMANDA ROGERS[7] (*Samuel Barstow⁶, Walter⁵, Adam⁴, Timothy³, Timothy², John¹*) was born in Sudbury, February 15, 1840; she married, April 26, 1864, Edward Roland Cutler, M. D., son of Roland and Martha [Richardson] Cutler, born, January 15, 1841.

Children, the first born in Hartford, Conn.; the second, in South Sudbury, and the others, in Waltham ;

   i.   George Washington Cutler⁸, b. Ap'l 2, 1866.
   ii.   Howard Atherton Cutler⁸, b. Sept. 3, 1870.
   iii.   Florence Augusta Cutler⁸, b. Feb'y 20, 1872.
   iv.   Roland Rogers Cutler⁸, b. Oct. 17, 1874.
   v.   Annie Martha Cutler⁸, b. Mar. 31, 1876.
—   vi.   Infant⁸, b. Aug. 19, 1878 ; d. same day.
—   vii.   Infant⁸, b. Sept. 16, 1880 ; d. same day.

452.

VIII.   ATHERTON WALES ROGERS[7] (*Samuel Barstow⁶, Walter⁵, Adam⁴, Timothy³, Timothy², John¹*) was born in Sudbury, August 10, 1848; he married, May 27,

1868, Alcesta Elizabeth Thompson, daughter of Abel
Adeline [Davis] Thompson, born December 30, 1850;
she died, July 2, 1895; he married, September 11, 1896,
Katharine Margaret McKay, daughter of Daniel and
Christy Ann [Robertson] McKay, born March 23, 1862.
Children, born in Sudbury:

By first wife:

— 543. Bessie Florence[8], b. May 5, 1873.
— 544. Isadore Cutler[8], b. Dec. 27, 1877.

By second wife:

545. Katherine Robertson[8], b. Oct. 14, 1897.

456.

VIII. GEORGE WARREN ROGERS[7] (*Elisha*[6], *Elisha*[5],
Adam[4], *Timothy*[3], *Timothy*[2], *John*[1]) was born in Marsh-
field, September 3, 1835; he married, May 15, 1857,
Mary Elizabeth Bowman, daughter of John Whitney
and Abigail [Thomas] Bowman, born, January 29, 1839.
Children, born in Marshfield:

546. Fred Warren[8], b. Aug. 30, 1858.
547. Jennie Elsworth[8], b. Sept. 10, 1861.
548. George Otis[8], b. July 2, 1865.
549. Flora Gilbert[8], b. Feb'y 2, 1868.
550. William Sumner[8], b. Mar. 8, 1870.
— 551. Frank Whitney[8], b. Sept. 28, 1873.

This family live on the old Adam Rogers place in Marshfield.

464.

VIII. LUTHER RODGERS[7] (*Luther*[6], *Simeon*[5], *Samuel*[4],
Samuel[3], *Timothy*[2], *John*[1]) was born in Marshfield, July
2, 1803; he married, April 20, 1834, Lydia Clift, daughter
of Deacon Joseph and Mary [Little] [Rogers] Clift,
born September 23, 1813; he died, April 4, 1853, and
she, July 12, 1866.

Children, born in Marshfield:

+ 552. John Luther[8], b. March 1, 1836.
+ 553. Henry Clift[8], b. June 15, 1839.
− 554. Wales Tilden[8], b. Aug, 4, 1843 ; d. Sept. 15, 1843.
+ 555. Herbert Tilden[8], b. July 15, 1845.
+ 556. Mary Little[8], b. June 30, 1850.

465.

VIII. WALES RODGERS[7] (*Luther[6], Simeon[5], Samuel[4], Samuel[3], Timothy[2], John[1]*) was born in Marshfield, June 20, 1805; he married, June 14, 1829, Hannah Little, daughter of Luther and Hannah [Lovell] Little, born August 29, 1804; he died, February 10, 1890, and she, September 22, 1887.

Children, born in Marshfield:

+ 557. Marcellus Wales[8], b. Ap'l 25, 1831.
558. Hannah Little[8], b. July 16, 1832.
559. Ellen Maria[8], b. Feb'y 16, 1834.
560. Miriam Gray[8], b. Nov. 19, 1835.
561. Emily Jane[8], b. Jan'y 31, 1838.
562. Olive Little[8], b. Nov. 19, 1839.
− 563. James Little[8], b. Ap'l 24, 1842 ; d. Dec. 5, 1842.
564. James Lovell[8], b. July 15, 1844.

466.

VIII. CLIFT RODGERS[7] (*Luther[6], Samuel[5], Samuel[4], Samuel[3], Timothy[2], John[1]*) was born in Marshfield, December 4, 1806; he married, December 27, 1835, Eleanor Baxter, daughter of James and Mary [Phipps] Baxter, born, July 31, 1818; he died, April 13, 1897, and she, March 13, 1893.

No children.

468.

VIII. SARAH LITTLE ROGERS[7] (*Luther[6], Samuel[5], Samuel[4] Samuel[3] Timothy[2] John[1]*) was born in Marshfield, October 11, 1811; she married, January 10, 1842, as his second wife, Nathaniel Phillips, son of Daniel and Abigail [Thomas] Phillips, born, February 19, 1798; he died, June 28, 1884; she is still (1898) living.

Children, born in Marshfield:

   —   i.   Wendell Alvin Phillips[8], b. July 30, 1842.
   —   ii.   Sarah Elizabeth Phillips[8], b. June 12, 1844.
       iii.   Helen Phillips[8], b. Aug. 30, 1848 ; m. Amasa Bartlett.
   —   iv.   Abbie Rogers Phillips[8], b. Nov. 30, 1851.

469.

VIII. AVERY ROGERS[7] (*Luther[6], Samuel[5], Samuel[4], Samuel[3], Timothy[2], John[1]*) was born in Marshfield, June 17, 1814; he married, September 29, 1842, Lucy Jenkins Hall, daughter of Zaccheus Tilden and Polly [Damon] Hall, born October 9, 1824; he died, November 14, 1894, leaving her surviving.

Children, born in Marshfield :

   565.   Lucy Frances[8], b. July 3, 1843.
   566.   Willard[8], b. May 3, 1844.
   567.   Alfred[8], b. Feb'y 5, 1847.

471.

VIII. ALVIN ROGERS[7] (*Luther[6], Simeon[5], Samuel[4], Samuel[3], Timothy[2], John[1]*) was born in Marshfield, February 16, 1818; he married, July 1, 1849, Harriet Augusta Fishley, daughter of William and Hannah [Ayers] Fishley, born July 31, 1828; she died, July 19, 1879.

Children, the first two born in Marshfield, and the others in Quincy;

   568.   William Alvin[8], b. May 20, 1850.
  — 569.   Waldo[8], b. Jan'y 30, 1852 ; d. unm. Sept. 22, 1883.
  — 570.   Luther[8], b. May 10, 1854 ; d. unm. June 12, 1893.
   571.   Frank Elmer[8] b. Aug. 27, 1862.

474.

VIII. ABIGAIL FRANCES ROGERS[7] (*Luther*[6], *Simeon*[5], *Samuel*[4], *Samuel*[3], *Timothy*[2], *John*[1]) was born in Marshfield, September 2, 1825; she married, November 21, 1855, Howard Clapp, son of Elijah and Harriet [Ford] Clapp, born July 6, 1829; he died, September 22, 1894.
Children, born in Boston:

    i.   Abbie Frances Clapp[8], b. Dec. 22, 1856.
† ii.   Clift Rogers Clapp[8], b. Feb'y 10, 1861.

Abbie Frances Clapp[8], married October 28, 1897, Luigi Melano Rossi.

474—ii.

IX. *Clift Rogers Clapp*[8], married, October 6, 1892, Gertrude Blanchard, daughter of John Wheeler and Harriet [Chambers] Blanchard, born, December 30, 1866, and they have, born in Dorchester :

    i.   Howard Rogers Clapp[9], b. July 14, 1893.
   ii.   Emily Blanchard Clapp[9], b. Oct. 27, 1894.

476.

IX. STEPHEN ROGERS ROGERS[8] (*Moses Folger*[7], *Aaron*[6], *Stephen*[5], *John*[4] *Thomas*[3] *John*[2] *John*[1]) was born in Marshfield, September 23, 1828; he married, September 14, 1849, Mary James Little, daughter of Edward Preble and Edy [Rogers] Little, born, November 15, 1827.
Children, the first born in Marshfield, the next two in Sandwich, and the others in Philadelphia :

  — 572.   Mary Ann[9], b. Mar. 21, 1851 ; d. Aug. 18, 1852.
  — 573.   Elizabeth[9], b. Nov. 16, 1853 ; d. Dec. 15, 1853.
      574.   Moses Folger[9], b. Sept. 9, 1855.
      575.   Edward Little[9], b. June 28, 1858.
      576.   Harry Brett[9], b. Feb'y 7, 1861.
      577.   May Beulah[9], b. May 30, 1863.

479.

IX. JAMES SWIFT ROGERS[8] (*Elisha Folger[7], Aaron[6], Stephen[5], John[4], Thomas[3], John[2], John[1]*) was born in Danby, Vt., March 28, 1840; he married, June 26, 1865, Annie Buffum Earle, daughter of Edward and Ann Baxter [Buffum] Earle, born July 28, 1838.

Children, born in Worcester, Mass.:

— 578. Edward Earle[9], b. May 3, 1866; d. Oct. 1, 1884.
— 579. Elliott Folger[9], b. July 28, 1868; d. unm. Oct. 2, 1895.
† 580. Annie[9], b. Mar. 3, 1872.

X. *Annie[9]*, married, June 6, 1895, Charles D. Knowlton, M. D., of Boston, and they have, born in Boston:

   i. Viamia Rogers Knowlton[10], b. Dec. 13, 1896.

358—i.

IX. HIRAM ABIF OAKMAN[8] (*Jane Soule[7], Thomas[6], Thomas[5], Israel[4], Timothy[3], Timothy[2], John[1]*) was born in Marshfield, April 10, 1827; he married, April 25, 1852, LUCINDA HATCH[7] (*Ichabod HATCH[6], Rebekah[5], Israel[4], Timothy[3], Timothy[2], John[1]*) born, January 14, 1830, in Marshfield, where they are now (1898) living.

Children, born in Marshfield:

    i. Edward Hatch Oakman[9], b. Ap'l 29, 1853.
   ii. Celia Jane Oakman[9], b. May 21, 1854.
— iii. Charles Willis Oakman[9], b. June 14, 1856; d. Mar. 21, 1865.
— iv. Martha Louise Oakman[9], b. Oct. 20, 1857; d. unm. Nov. 21, 1886.
—   v. Foster Tillinghast Oakman[9], b. Sept. 5, 1859; d. May 4, 1865.
— vi. Otis Briggs Oakman[9], b. Oct. 27, 1864.

Edward Hatch Oakman[9] married Nellie Turner; they have had one child, which died in infancy.

Celia Jane Oakman[9] married George Frank Wilson, and they have:

    i. Fred Oakman Wilson[10], b. June 9, 1887.

358—iii.

IX. HENRY PHILLIPS OAKMAN⁸ (*Jane Soule⁷, Thomas⁶, Thomas⁵, Israel⁴, Timothy³, Timothy², John¹*) was born in Marshfield, June 27, 1831; he married, March 8, 1853, Arethusa Hatch, daughter of Ichabod and Sela Sylvester [Palmer] Hatch, born, October 11, 1833.

Children, the first three born in Marshfield, and the others in Neponset:

   —   i.   Roxie Fobes Oakman⁹, b. Sept. 19, 1855; d. Mar. 8, 1865.
   —   ii.   Henry Phillips Oakman⁹, b. Oct. 24, 1858; d. Jan'y 9, 1878.
      iii.   Elmer Palmer Oakman⁹, b. May 28, 1866.
      iv.   George Willis Oakman⁹, b. Feb'y 8, 1869.
      v.   Arthur Lincoln Oakman⁹, b. Dec. 18, 1874.

358—iv.

IX. OTIS BRIGGS OAKMAN⁸ (*Jane Soule⁷, Thomas⁶, Thomas⁵, Israel ⁴, Timothy³, Timothy², John¹*) was born in Marshfield, July 19, 1833; he married Sarah Mann Brooks of Hanover, daughter of John and Amy [Mann] Brooks, born, December 12, 1832; he died, June 8, 1864; no children.

358—v.

IX. NATHAN SOULE OAKMAN⁸ (*Jane Soule⁷, Thomas⁶, Thomas⁵, Israel⁴, Timothy³, Timothy², John¹*) was born in Marshfield, January 20, 1837; he married Hannah Eliza Brooks, of Hanover, daughter of John and Amy [Mann] Brooks, born, February 26, 1840; he died, July 4, 1868.

Children, born in Hanover:

    †   i.   Nellie Soule Oakman⁹, b. June 27, 1860.
    —   ii.   Nathan Otis Oakman⁹, b. Oct. 27, 1867.

358—v—i.

X. *Nellie Soule Oakman*⁹ married, January 1, 1884, Edward Lorraine Young, son of William and Zuriel [Towle] Young, born, August 1, 1856.

Children, born in Hanover:

    i. Edward Lorraine Young¹⁰, b. July 6, 1885.
    ii. Donnell Brooks Young¹⁰, b. Ap'l 25, 1888.
    iii. Malcolm Oakman Young¹⁰, b. July 24, 1893.

358—vi.

IX. MARY JANE OAKMAN⁸ (*Jane Soule⁷, Thomas⁶, Thomas⁵, Israel⁴, Timothy³, Timothy², John¹*) was born in Marshfield, August 7, 1839; she married, December 31, 1863, Henry Abiel Turner, son of Abiel and Rebecca [Bates] Turner, born, November 21, 1827.

Children, born in South Scituate, now Norwell:

  — i. Flora Jane Turner⁹, b. Ap'l 16, 1865; d. May 11, 1875.
  — ii. Susie Oakman Turner⁹, b, Jan'y 31, 1867; d. May 21, 1885.
  — iii. John Henry Turner⁹, b. Sept. 2, 1869; d. Aug. 23, 1871.
    iv. Nathan Soule Turner⁹, b. Jan'y 10, 1872.
    v. George Clarence Turner⁹, b. May 21, 1874.
  — vi. Mary Rogers Turner⁹, b. Sept. 6, 1876; d. Mar. 6, 1895.

482.

IX. CHARLES WILLIAM ROGERS⁸ (*William Thomas⁷, Martin⁶, Thomas⁵, Israel⁴, Timothy³, Timothy², John¹*) was born in Belfast, Me., December 3, 1853; he married, July 6, 1879, Ada Isabel Black, daughter of Franklin Hall and Abbie Hepsabeth [Robinson] Black, born, April 19, 1854.

Children, the first born in Hartford, Conn., and the other, in Belfast, Me.:

581. Raymond Francis[9], b. June 6, 1880.
582. Renworth Robin[9], b. Mar. 6, 1882.

483.

IX. BYRON MARTIN ROGERS[8] (*William Thomas[7], Martin[6], Thomas[5], Israel[4], Timothy[3], Timothy[2], John[1]*) was born in Belfast, December 28, 1858; he married, December 30, 1893, Annie Adelia Brier, daughter of Moses Wilson and Ann Eliza [Tasker] Brier, born, October 31, 1849.

Child, born in Belfast, Me.:

583. Donald Brier[9], b. Oct. 28, 1895.

488.

IX. HENRIETTA EUNICE ROGERS[8] (*Henry Warren[7], Warren[6], Thomas[5], Israel[4], Timothy[3], Timothy[2], John[1]*) was born in Lynn, March 24, 1855; she married, March 24, 1886, James Freeman Seavey, son of Shadrach and Lucinda [Edgerly] Seavey, born, December 6, 1842.

No children.

490.

IX. CLARENCE ABEL ROGERS[8] (*Henry Warren[7], Warren[6], Thomas[5], Israel[4], Timothy[3], Timothy[2], John[1]*) was born in Lynn, May 11, 1859; he married, June 8, 1881, Edith Augusta Riley, daughter of Ephraim Henry and Sophia Jewett [Bangs] Riley, born, August 13, 1859.

Children, born in Lynn:

584. Arthur Hamilton[9], b. Mar. 1, 1882.
585. Walter Clarence[9], b. Jan'y 15, 1884.
586. Alice Caroline[9], b. May —, 1886.

495.

IX. CHARLES STODDARD ROGERS[8] (*Sidney Greenleaf[7], Henry[6], Asa[5], Israel[4], Timothy[3], Timothy[2], John[1]*) was born in Charlestown, December 9, 1854; he married, January 12, 1880, Alice Minetta Kane, daughter of James and Elizabeth Celia [Cooper] Kane, born, August 19, 1860.

Children, born in Chelsea, Mass.:

> 587. Charles Edward[9], b. Jan'y 19, 1882.
> 588. Grace Alice[9], b. Aug. 28, 1888.
> 589, Harold Stoddard[9], b. Jan'y 4, 1892.

498.

IX. FRANKLIN GREENLEAF ROGERS[8] (*Sidney Greenleaf[7], Henry[6], Asa[5], Israel[4], Timothy[3], Timothy[2], John[1]*) was born in Chelsea, January 9, 1860; he married, October 24, 1888, Luna Olivia Hebard, daughter of George Lucius and Julia Jemima [Pratt] Hebard, born, July 7, 1867.

Children, born in Barre, Vt.:

> 590. Ralph Hebard[9], b. Ap'l 14, 1892.
> — 591. Carleton Franklin[9], b. July 9, 1895; d. Ap'l 26, 1896.

505.

IX. ALVAN HERBERT ROGERS[8] (*Charles Alvan[7], Alvan[6], Benjamin[5], Zaccheus[4], Timothy[3], Timothy[2], John[1]*) was born in Chelsea, January 3, 1863; he married, January 6, 1890, Linda Starr Chamberlin, daughter of Josiah W. and Linda A. [Bigelow] Chamberlin, born, May 13, 1869.

Children, born in Boston:

> 592. Ellery Wilson[9], b. Jan'y 26, 1891.
> 593. Dorothy[9], b. Feb'y 28, 1893.

506.

IX. WINTHROP LINCOLN ROGERS[8] (*Charles Alvan[7], Alvan[6], Benjamin[5], Zaccheus[4], Timothy[3], Timothy[2], John[1]*) was born in Chelsea, February 25, 1865; he married, November 1, 1892, Mary Louise Kinsley, daughter of Edward Wilkinson and Calista Adelaide [Billings] Kinsley, born, March 6, 1865.

Child, born in Brooklyn, N. Y.:

594.   Calista Kinsley[9], b. Oct. 3, 1893.

507.

IX. JENNIE LOUISE ROGERS[8] (*Charles Alvan[7], Alvan[6], Benjamin[5], Zaccheus[4], Timothy[3], Timothy[2], John[1]*) was born in Chelsea, November 23, 1869; she married, February 21, 1898, Stewart Wrightington, son of Charles Ward and Catharine G. [Schermerhorn] Wrightington, born, March 7, 1866.

508.

IX. HELEN AUGUSTA ROGERS[8] (*Charles Alvan[7], Alvan[6], Benjamin[5], Zaccheus[4], Timothy[3], Timothy[2], John[1]*) was born in Chelsea, July 21, 1873; she married, October 19, 1897, Edward Browning Miles, son of James Browning and Julia Elizabeth [Hurlbut] Miles, born, February 25, 1870.

517.

IX. JOSEPHINE MARY ROGERS[8] (*George Atherton[7], Atherton Wales[6], Samuel[5], Adam[4], Timothy[3], Timothy[2], John[1]*) was born in Chelsea, November 9, 1868; she married, October 20, 1892, William Locke Swan, son of William Russell and Mary Augusta [Noyes] Swan, born, December 16, 1866.

Child, born in Chelsea:

i.   Hester Swan[9], b. Oct. 13, 1894.

527.

IX. FRED WALDO ROGERS[8] (*Edwin[7], Walter[6], Walter[5], Adam[4], Timothy[3], Timothy[2], John[1]*) was born in South Sudbury, June 13, 1859; he married, February 26, 1884, Rosella Smith Mason, daughter of Hibbard Francis and Martha Emily [Parker] Mason, born, August 19, 1862.

No children.

528.

IX. WALTER BARSTOW ROGERS[8] (*Edwin[7], Walter[6], Walter[5], Adam[4], Timothy[3], Timothy[2], John[1]*) was born in South Sudbury, January 18, 1869; he married, July 21, 1891, Emma Frances Paul, daughter of Isaac Dean and Emily Elvira [Hathaway] Paull, born, December 19, 1869.

Children, born in Taunton:

    595. Mabel Dean[9], b. May 18, 1892.
    596. Mildred Louisa[9], b. Oct. 29, 1893.

534.

IX. HOWARD PERRY ROGERS[8] (*Homer[7], Walter[6], Walter[5], Adam[4], Timothy[3], Timothy[2], John[1]*) was born in South Sudbury, June 1, 1869; he married, in Boston, May 4, 1893, Persis Stewart Davis, daughter of Martin Warner and Persis Anne [Stewart] Davis, born, December 14, 1869.

Children, born in Allston, Boston:

    597. Homer[9], b. Feb'y 24, 1894.
    598. Tyler Stewart[9], b. Aug. 4, 1895.

535.

IX. ELLIOT ROGERS[8] (*Homer[7], Walter[6], Walter[5], Adam[4], Timothy[3], Timothy[2], John[1]*) was born in South

Sudbury, February 10, 1872; he married, at Kennebunk, Maine, December 16, 1896, Mary Hackett Thompson, daughter of Nathaniel Lord and Nancy Frances [Hackett] Thompson, born, July 5, 1865.

537.

IX. HARLAND HAYDEN ROGERS[8] (*Homer[7], Walter[6], Walter[5], Adam[4], Timothy[3], Timothy[2], John[1]*) was born in South Sudbury, March 3, 1873; he married, in New York City, Ida Lois Rouse, daughter of Charles William and Elizabeth Wyman [Hayden] Rouse, born, January 31, 1871.

552.

IX. JOHN LUTHER RODGERS[8] (*Luther[7], Luther[6], Simeon[5], Samuel[4], Samuel[3], Timothy[2], John[1]*) was born in Marshfield, March 1, 1836; he married, December 25, 1861, Ellen Maria Webb, daughter of Seth and Eliza [Dunbar] Webb, born, September 13, 1834.

Child, born in Charlestown:

— 599. Fred Webb[9], b. July 12, 1870.

553.

IX. HENRY CLIFT RODGERS[8] (*Luther[7], Luther[6], Simeon[5], Samuel[4], Samuel[3], Timothy[2], John[1]*) was born in Marshfield, June 15, 1839; he married, November 19, 1863, Lucy Adelaide Rodgers, daughter of Horace Goodwin and Lucy Jane [Clapp] Rodgers, born, April 18, 1845.

Children, born in Quincy:

— 600. Luther Henry[9], b. July 18, 1865; d. Feb'y 2, 1881.
— 601. Minnie Morton[9], b. May 2, 1869.
  602. Mary Lucilla[9], b. Nov. 3, 1882.

555.

IX. HERBERT TILDEN RODGERS[8] (*Luther*[7], *Luther*[6], *Simeon*[5], *Samuel*[4], *Samuel*[3], *Timothy*[2], *John*[1]) was born in Marshfield, July 15, 1845; he married, April 30, 1872, Lilla Flora Bass, daughter of John Adams and Mary [Perham] Bass, born February 12, 1848.

Children, born in Quincy:

— 603. Arthur Herbert[9], b. May 20, 1874; d. Jan'y 12, 1882.
— 604. Ralph Bass[9], b. Aug. 10, 1877.

556.

IX. MARY LITTLE RODGERS[8] (*Luther*[7], *Luther*[6], *Simeon*[5], *Samuel*[4], *Samuel*[3], *Timothy*[2], *John*[1]) was born in Marshfield, June 30, 1850; she married, January 20, 1870, Ibrahim Morrison, son of Alvah and Mira [Southworth] Morrison, born, October 21, 1848.

No children.

557.

IX. MARCELLUS WALES ROGERS[8] (*Wales*[7], *Luther*[6], *Simeon*[5], *Samuel*[4], *Samuel*[3], *Timothy*[2], *John*[1]) was born in Marshfield, April 25, 1831; he married, January 1, 1857, Susan Elizabeth Holmes, daughter of William and Susan [Farris] Holmes, born, October 6, 1832.

Children, born in Marshfield:

605. Osborne[9], b. Sept. 2, 1858.
606. Howard[9], b. Ap'l 10, 1862.
607. Mabel[9], b. Oct. 28, 1863.
— 608. Wales[9], b. Ap'l 15, 1865; d. unm. Ap'l 5, 1888.
609. Olive Little[9], b. Oct. 27, 1868.
— 610. Lizzie Farris[9], b. Dec. 3, 1873.

560.

IX. MIRIAM GRAY RODGERS[8] (*Wales*[7], *Luther*[6], *Simeon*[5], *Samuel*[4], *Samuel*[3], *Timothy*[2], *John*[1]) was born in

Marshfield, November 19, 1835; she married, December 25, 1859, Lysander Salmon Richards, son of Lysander and Content [Clapp] Richards, born April 13, 1835; she died, December 19, 1897.

Children, the first two born in Quincy and the other in Boston:

—   i.   Clift Rodgers Richards[9], b. Aug. 20, 1861 ; d. Nov. 19, 1863.
      ii.   Eleanor Rodgers Richards[9], b. Jan'y 9, 1863.
†   iii.   Clift Rodgers Richards[9], b. Oct. 29, 1866.

560—iii.   .

X.   *Clift Rodgers Richards[9]* married *Fannie Olive Bartlett[9]*, daughter of James and Olive Little [Rodgers[8], No. 562] Bartlett, and they have :

      i.   Clift Rodgers Richards[10], b. June 20, 1896, in Montville, Me.
      ii.   James Bartlett Richards[10], b. Dec. 26, 1897, in Washington, D. C.

MEMORANDUM.

Having received a quite full account of the descendants of PRISCILLA ROGERS[5] (*Thomas*[4], *Thomas*[3], *John*[2], *John*[1]), I conclude to give it by itself and continuously.

DESCENDANTS OF PRISCILLA ROGERS[5]:

99—i.

VII.   HULDA ELLIS[6] (*Priscilla*[5]) was born in Hanover, March 3, 1779; she married, May 18, 1805, Nathan Studley, son of Elihab and Betsey [Stetson] Studley, born May 16, 1780; he died, June 27, 1850, and she, July 26, 1829.

Children, born in East Abington, now Rockland:

+   i.   William Studley[7], b. June 19, 1806.
+   ii.   Sophia Studley[7], b. Ap'l 12, 1808.
+   iii.   Andrew Studley[7], b. Feb'y 1, 1810.
+   iv.   Reuben Studley[7], b. Feb'y 3, 1812.
+   v.   Sylvia Studley[7], b. Sept. 10, 1815.
+   vi.   Elizabeth Ellis Studley[7], b. June 26, 1817.
+   vii.   Alvin Studley[7], b. Sept. 25, 1819.
+   viii.   Hulda Studley[7], b. Jan'y 18, 1822.

99—ii.

VII.   REBECCA ELLIS[6] (*Priscilla*[5]) was born in Hanover, March 17, 1781; she married, November 12, 1803, William Gifford, son of Zaccheus and Sarah [Shove] Gifford, born, March 22, 1778; she died, November 13,

1827; he married, October 17, 1844, Elizabeth Jordan; she died, February 23, 1891, and he, February 18, 1865. Children, all by first wife, born in Falmouth:

+   i.   Albert Gifford[7], b. Aug. 31, 1804.
    ii.   Mary Gifford[7], b. Mar. 12, 1806.
    iii.   Seth Kelly Gifford[7], b. Oct. 10, [23] 1807.
    iv.   Phila Gifford[7], b. July 19, 1809.
    v.   William Gifford[7], b. Feb'y 5, 1811.
—   vi.   Rebecca Gifford[7], b. Feb'y 17, 1813 ; d. unm.
+   vii.   David Ellis Gifford[7], b. Feb'y 1, 1815.
    viii.   Lydia Gifford[7], b. Mar. 9, 1817.
—   ix.   Joshua Gifford[7], b. Mar. 6, 1819 ; d. Sept. 29, 1820.
+   x.   Sarah Gifford[7], b. June 15, 1821.
    xi.   Susan Howland Gifford[7], b. Feb'y 21, 1826 ; d. Mar. 20, 1839.

99—iii.

VII. ABIGAIL ELLIS[6] (*Priscilla*[5]) was born in Hanover, October 16, 1782 ; she married, October 13, 1802, John Sherman, son of John and Experience [Kelly] Sherman, born, October 13, 1781 ; he died, July 13, 1865, and she, May 26, 1871.

Children, the first seven born in Longplain, Mass., and the others, in Leon, N. Y.:

    i.   Mary Sherman[7], b. Jan'y 4, 1804.
    ii.   Eliza Sherman[7], b. Aug. 28, 1805.
    iii.   Mordecai Sherman[7], b. May 27, 1807.
    iv.   Daniel Sherman[7], b. Feb'y 15, 1808.
    v.   Deborah Sherman[7], b. Jan'y 23, 1811.
—   vi.   Nathaniel Sherman[7], b. Nov. 9, 1813 ; d. Sept. 16, 1820.
—   vii.   Lydia Sherman[7], b. Aug. 24, 1816 ; d. Sept. 16, 1820.
—   viii.   Sarah Sherman[7], b. July 10, 1818 ; d. Sept. 11, 1820.
    ix.   John Sherman[7], b. July 19, 1820.
    x.   Joseph Sherman[7], b. May 5, 1822.
    xi.   James Rogers Sherman[7], b. May 6, 1824.
    xii.   Henry Sherman[7], b. Aug. 3, 1827.

He was a soldier in the war of 1812 ; in 1818, the family moved
to a place they then called Concord, near Buffalo, N. Y. (but now
Leon), as shown by letters written in 1819 and 1821 and still preserved ; but they left behind part of their children.

99—v.

VII. PRISCILLA ELLIS[6] (*Priscilla[5]*) was born in Hanover, April 30, 1787; she married, November 13, 1804,
Theophilus Gifford, son of Zaccheus and Sarah [Shove]
Gifford, born, March 4, 1784; he died, December 8,
1852, and she, December 20, 1840.

Children, born in Falmouth, now West Falmouth :

+   i. Elizabeth Gifford[7], b. Feb'y 20, 1807.
+   ii. Ellis Gifford[7], b. July 26, 1809.
     iii. Thomas Scattergood Gifford[7], b. July 20, 1811.
+   iv. Azariah Shove Gifford[7], b. Nov. 26, 1813.
     v. Charity Gifford[7], b. Mar. 15, 1816.
     vi. Hannah Gifford[7], b. Feb'y 9, 1818.
     vii. Hulda Gifford[7], b. Nov. 11, 1819.
     viii. Samuel Gifford[7], b. Dec. 12, 1821.
     ix. James Ellis Gifford[7], b. May 15, 1832.

99—vi.

VII. DAVID ELLIS[6] (*Priscilla[5]*) was born in Hanover,
June 19, 1789; he married, January 1, 1817, Maria Loud,
daughter of Daniel and Charity [White] Loud, born,
October 11, 1795; he died, April 18, 1863, and she,
October 13, 1888.

Children, the first two probably born in Hanover, the
next three in Hanover, and the others, in Lynn :

—   i. Maria Ann Ellis[7], b. Nov. 11, 1817 ; d. Mar. 21, 1834.
—   ii. Albert Ellis[7], b. Ap'l 1, 1819 ; d. Oct. 6, 1824.
     iii. Lucinda Loud Ellis[7], b. Oct. 22, 1820 ; living (1898),
         unm.
—   iv. Sophia Dwelly Ellis[7], b. Jan'y 2, 1822 ; d. Ap'l 6, 1824.
—   v. Sophia Dwelly Ellis[7], b. Ap'l 14, 1826 ; d. June 8, 1831.

+ vi. Lydia Davis Ellis[7], b. Feb'y 14, 1827.
— vii. David Ellis[7], b. May 18, 1828 ; d. Mar. 16, 1834.
— viii. Sarah Jane Ellis[7], b. Oct. 7, 1829 ; d. unm. Oct. 1, 1873.
+ ix. Thomas Rogers Ellis[7], b. Ap'l 12, 1831.
— x. Mary Elizabeth Ellis[7], b. Oct. 6, 1833 ; d. unm. Aug. 17, 1896.
— xi. Lucy Ann Ellis[7], b. Feb'y 13, 1835 ; d. unm. July 11, 1889.

99—viii.

VII. OTIS ELLIS[6] (*Priscilla[5]*) was born in Hanover, November 4, 1795; he married, April 12, 1827, Ruth Barker, daughter of Robert and Ruth [Tucker] Barker, born, July 11, 1793; he died, May 22, 1860, and she, May 2, 1860.

Children, born in Hanover:

— i. Rhoda Barker Ellis[7], b. May 10, 1830.
— ii. David Otis Ellis[7], b. Oct. 26, 1832 ; d. Oct. 29, 1832.
+ iii. Priscilla Rogers Ellis[7], b. Ap'l 26, 1835.

Rhoda Barker Ellis[7] is the publisher of this work.

99—ix.

VII. ELIZABETH ELLIS[6] (*Priscilla[5]*) was born in Hanover, July 4, 1797; she married, December 11, 1817, John Pratt, son of John and Lydia [Mower] Pratt, born, January 4, 1794; he died, March 1, 1865, and she, August 21, 1872.

Children, born in Lynn:

+ i. Alfred Adams Pratt[7], b. Sept. 26, 1818.
+ ii. George Otis Pratt[7], b. Aug. 31, 1820.
+ iii. Eliza Ellen Pratt[7], b. Sept. 21, 1824.
+ iv. Mary Emily Pratt[7], b. Sept. 24, 1828.
— v. John Irving Pratt[7], b. Feb'y 11, 1832 ; d. Feb'y 17, 1833.
— vi. John Irving Pratt[7], b. Oct. 15, 1834 ; d. Oct. 19, 1836.
+ vii. Cynthia Frances Pratt[7], b. Sept. 16, 1841.

99—i—i.

VIII. WILLIAM STUDLEY[7] (*Hulda* ELLIS[6], *Priscilla[5]*) was born in East Abington, now Rockland, June 19, 1806; he married, June 10, 1832, Elizabeth Ingersoll Haskell of Ipswich, daughter of Jonathan Haskell, born, January 4, 1811; he died, July 18, 1886, and she, April 6, 1853.

Children, born in East Abington:

    i. William Andrews Studley[8], b. Jan'y 5, 1833.
+ ii. Mary Elizabeth Studley[8], b. May 1, 1834.
— iii. Hannah Maria Studley[8], b. June 21, 1836; d. Jan'y 11, 18—.
    iv. Nathan Francis Studley[8], b. Aug. 6, 1838.
    v. John Alvin Studley[8], b. July 6, 18—.
+ vi. Adaline Augusta Studley[8], b. May 13, 1843.
    vii. Jacob Nash Studley[8], b. July 16, 1845.
— viii. Lucius Alden Studley[8], b. Dec. 17, 1847; d. Feb'y 5, 1848.
+ ix. Charles Eldron Studley[8], b. Ap'l 23, 1852.

99—i—ii.

VIII. SOPHIA STUDLEY[7] (*Hulda* ELLIS[6], *Priscilla[5]*) was born in East Abington, April 12, 1808; she married, April 12, 1829, Jacob Nash, son of Jacob and Rachel [Ramsdell] Nash, born, October 22, 1809; he died, February 25, 1851, and she, April 10, 1895.

Children, born in Abington:

    i. Sophia Elizabeth Nash[8], b. July 13, 1830.
    ii. Rachel Nash[8], b. Sept. 15, 1834.
    iii. Sylvia Augusta Nash[8], b. Sept. 15, 1838.

99—i—iii.

VIII. ANDREW STUDLEY[7] (*Hulda* ELLIS[6], *Priscilla[5]*) was born in East Abington, now Rockland, February 1, 1810; he married, February 10, 1831, Mary Junkins, daughter of Zenas and Mary [Pratt] Junkins, born, April 24, 1810; he died, November 1, 1896, and she, November 10, 1876.

Children, born in East Abington:

+   i.   Mary Andrews Studley[8], b. Ap'l 8, 1831.
+   ii.   Austin Studley[8], b. Ap'l 30, 1833.
+   iii.   Jane Bicknell Studley[8], b. Nov. 22, 1834.
    iv.   Andrew Hilton Studley[8], b. Ap'l 15, 1836.
    v.   Hulda Ellis Studley[8], b. Ap'l 19, 1838.
    vi.   Sarah Ellis Studley[8], b. Oct. 14, 1840.
—   vii.   Ferdinand Studley[8], b. Nov. 10, 1846; d. Sept. 7, 1847.
—   viii.   Isabella Studley[8], b. Nov. 10, 1846; d. June 29, 1847.
    ix.   Elvira Studley[8], b. Aug. 14, 1848.

Andrew Hilton Studley[8] married, October 17, 1857, Betsey Holbrook, daughter of Richard and Annie [Reed] Holbrook, born, September 13, 1831; no children.

Hulda Ellis Studley[8] married, November 15, 1862, Walter L. Davis, son of George and Hannah [Hayden] Davis, born, April 8, 1836; no children.

Sarah Ellis Studley[8] married, February 11, 1866, Nathaniel Barnabas Briggs, son of Joseph and Priscilla Bradford [Ryder] Briggs, born, November 20, 1835; she died, March 19, 1895; no children.

Elvira Studley[8] married, April 25, 1869, Martin L. Holmes, son of Martin W. and Jane [Standish] Holmes, born, October 20, 1843; no children.

99—i—iv.

VIII.   Reuben Studley[7] (*Hulda* Ellis[6], *Priscilla*[5]) was born in East Abington, February 3, 1812; he married, November 28, 1834, Adaline Burgess, daughter of Laomi and Sarah [Whitney] Burgess, born, July 18, 1814; she died, June 8, 1891, leaving him still (1898) surviving.

Children, born in East Abington:

  i. Reuben Whitney Studley[8], b. Sept. 15, 1836.
  ii. George Sylvester Studley[8], b. Dec. 26, 1838.
— iii. Henry Jacobs Studley[8], b. Oct. 18, 1841 ; d. Sept. 18, 1843.
  iv. Horace Walker Studley[8], b. Ap'l 18, 1844.
— v. Charles Henry Studley[8], b. Ap'l 10, 1846 ; d. Nov. 18, 1849.
  vi. Susan Ellen Studley[8], b. Oct. 18, 1848.
  vii. Emily Maria Studley[8], b. Feb'y 23, 1851.
  viii. Charles Nelson Studley[8], b. Dec. 8, 1854.
  ix. John Freeman Studley[8], b. Nov. 3, 1856.

99—i—v.

VIII. SYLVIA STUDLEY[7] (*Huldah* ELLIS[6], *Priscilla*[5]) was born in East Abington, September 10, 1815; she married, July 16, 1835, Bela Smith, born, February 11, 1813; he died, July 30, 1891, and she, January 17, 1891. Children, born in Abington:

  i. Emma Louisa Smith[8], b. Feb'y 16, 1845.
— ii. Bela Hart Benton Smith[8], b. Feb'y 24, 1849; d. Aug. 15, 1868.

99—i—vi.

VIII. ELIZABETH ELLIS STUDLEY[7] (*Huldah* ELLIS[6], *Priscilla*[5]) was born in East Abington, now Rockland, June 26, 1817; she married, July 20, 1843, Stephen Standish, son of Job and Ruth [Witherell] Standish, born, March 22, 1821; he died, January 5, 1890, leaving her still surviving.
  No children.

99—i—vii.

VIII. ALVIN STUDLEY[7] (*Huldah* ELLIS[6], *Priscilla*[5],) was born in East Abington, now Rockland, September 25, 1819; he married, June 11, 1843, Mary Baucome

Estes, daughter of William and Bethiah [Josselyn] Estes, born, December 3, 1824.

Children:

    i.   Clara Loriane Studley[8], b. May 25, 1844; at East Abington.

— ii. Alvin Boyd Studley[8], b. Ap'l 3, 1846, at Hanover.

   iii. Caroline Cutler Studley[8], b. May 15, 1853, at Holliston.

— iv. Alvaretta Studley[8], b. Mar. 24, 1866, at Natick.

Alvin Boyd Studley[8] was a soldier in third Mass. Cavalry and and died in the service, Jan'y 26, 1865.

99—i—viii.

VIII. HULDAH STUDLEY[7] (*Huldah* ELLIS[6], *Priscilla*[5]) was born in East Abington, now Rockland, January 18, 1822; she married, June 1, 1843, Nehemiah Porter Baker, son of Allen and Abigail [Joyce] Baker, born, June 4, 1820; both still (1898) living.

Children, born in East Abington:

    i.   Abbie Ellen Baker[8], b. Aug. 18, 1843.

    ii. Susan Allen Baker[8], b. Aug. 26, 1848.

— iii. Andrew Herbert Baker[8] b. Feb'y 24, 1852; d. Oct. 9, 1864.

† iv. George Otis Baker[8], b. Ap'l 8, 1856.

    v. Maria Ellis Baker[8], b. Aug. 1, 1859.

IX. *George Otis Baker*[8], married, Sept. 18, 1877, Alice Warren; he died, Aug. 15, 1893.

Child, born, in Hanover:

— i. Grace Herbert Baker[9], b. July 10, 1878.

99—ii—i.

VIII. ALBERT GIFFORD[7] (*Rebekah* ELLIS[6], *Priscilla*[5]) was born in Falmouth, August 31, 1804; he married, August 3, 1836, Rhoda Barker, daughter of Robert and Ruth [Tucker] Barker, born, August 12, 1799; he died, September 9, 1852, and she, April 21, 1883.

Children, the first born in Dartmouth, and the others
in New Bedford:

- i.   Rebecca Chase Gifford[8], b. May 21, 1837 :
- ii. Robert Barker Gifford[8], b. Feb'y 22, 1839 ;
- iii. William Gifford[8], b. Sept. 26, 1840 ;
- iv. Lydia Gifford[8], b. Mar. 12, 1842 : d. unm., July 15,
  1865.

99—ii—vii.

VIII. DAVID ELLIS GIFFORD[7] (*Rebecca* ELLIS[6], *Priscilla*[5]) was born in Falmouth, February 1, 1815; he
married, November 16, 1845, Mary Jordan, daughter of
James and Hannah [Jordan] Jordan, born, December
3, 1818; he died, April 3, 1884, and she, January 19,
1879.

Children, the first two born in Rahway, N. J., and the
others in West Falmouth:

Hannah Louise Gifford[8], b. Mar. 20, 1847.
James Henry Gifford[8], b. Nov. 10, 1851.
Helen Mar Gifford[8], b. Ap'l 10, 1855.
Elizabeth Carny Gifford[8], b. Nov. 11, 1857.
—   Annie Maria Gifford[8]. b. Oct. 2, 1861 ; d. unm., Nov.
17, 1889.

99—ii—x.

VIII. SARAH GIFFORD[7] (*Rebecca* ELLIS[6], *Priscilla*[5])
was born in Falmouth, June 15, 1821; she married,
October 20, 1847, Charles Miller, son of Abraham and
Elizabeth [Griffen] Miller, born, March 23, 1821 ; they
now (1898) reside in West Falmouth, Mass.:

Children, born in New York City:

- + i.   Susan Emily Miller[8], b. Feb'y 11, 1851.
- + ii. Lillian Sarah Elizabeth Miller[8], b. Aug. 12, 1855.
- + iii. Charles William Miller[8], b. Sept. 19, 1857.

99—v—i.

VIII. ELIZABETH GIFFORD⁷ (*Priscilla* ELLIS⁶, *Priscilla*⁵) was born in (now) West Falmouth, February 25, 1807; she married, June, 1831, (as his second wife) Stephen Dillingham, son of Joseph and Esther [Rogers] Dillingham, born, October 26, 1799; he died, October 31, 1871, and she, December 31, 1896.

Children, born in West Falmouth:

+ i. James Thomas Dillingham⁸, b. Feb'y 12, 1833.
+ ii. Hannah Gifford Dillingham⁸, b. Ap'l 27, 1836.
— iii. Henry Dillingham⁸, b. May 1, 1838; d. unm., Mar. 3, 1859, in Sacramento.

99—v—ii.

VIII. ELLIS GIFFORD⁷ (*Priscilla* ELLIS⁶, *Priscilla*⁵) was born in (now) West Falmouth, July 26, 1809; he married, September 29, 1836, Abby Chase, daughter of Edmund and Phebe [Slade] Chase, born April 26, 1816; he died, October 22, 1866, and she, February 17, 1895.

Children, born in Fall River:

— i. Charles Ellis Gifford⁸, b. Feb'y 28, 1838; d. Mar. 16, 1838.
+ ii. Phebe Slade Gifford⁸, b. Nov. 13, 1839.
+ iii. Charles Ellis Gifford⁸, b. Dec. 16, 1842.
— iv. Edmund Chace Gifford⁸, b. Jan'y 13, 1845; d. Oct. 29, 1845.
— v. Benjamin Slade Chace Gifford⁸ b. Sept. 17, 1846; d. Aug. 14, 1848.
+ vi. Benjamin Slade Chace Gifford⁸, b. Aug. 5, 1849.
+ vii. Edmund Chace Gifford⁸, b. Mar. 10, 1852.
— viii. Thomas Willis Gifford⁸, b. Jan'y 10, 1854; d. May 2, 1854.
— ix. Abbie Elizabeth Gifford⁸, b. Sept. 10, 1855.
— x. Marianna Gifford⁸, b. Nov. 17, 1858.

99—v—iv.

VIII. AZARIAH SHOVE GIFFORD[7] (*Priscilla* ELLIS[6], *Priscilla[5]*) was born in Falmouth, now West Falmouth, November 26, 1813; he married, May 5, 1848, Lois Bean, daughter of James and Hannah [Roberts] Bean, born, March 30, 1823; he died, September 6, 1866, and she, January 8, 1871.

Children, born in West Falmouth:

+   i.   James William Gifford[8], b. Sept. 21, 1850.
−   ii.   Seth Gifford[8], b. Mar. 20, 1853; d. Ap'l 7, 1854.
+   iii.   Seth Kelley Gifford[8], b. July 29, 1854.
+   iv.   John Henry Gifford[8], b. Feb'y 6, 1858.

99—vi—vi.

VIII. LYDIA DAVIS ELLIS[7] (*David* ELLIS[6], *Priscilla[5]*) was born in Lynn, February 14, 1827; she married, November 27, 1854, Isaac Francis Galloupe, M. D., son of Isaac and Annis [Allen] Galloupe, born, June 27, 1823.

Children, born in Lynn, Mass:

i.   Francis Ellis Galloupe[8], b. Oct. 3, 1855.
ii.   Charles Williams Galloupe[8], b. May 12, 1858.

Francis Ellis Galloupe[8], married, June 4, 1889, Frances Baker Clark, son of Horace and Sophronia Parsons [Greenleaf] Clark, born. April 8, 1860; and they have, born in Lynn:

i.   Chauncey Adams Galloupe[9], b. Nov. 24, 1891.

Dr. Galloupe served in the Civil War as Regimental, Brigade and Division Surgeon; was captured, Feb'y 1, 1864, at Newbern while operating on a wounded officer, and sent to Libby Prison; he was brevetted Lt. Colonel "for faithful and meritorious service during the war."

99—vi—ix.

VIII. THOMAS ROGERS ELLIS[7] (*David* ELLIS[6], *Priscilla[5]*) was born in Lynn, April 12, 1831; he married, June 8, 1858, Frances Elizabeth Burrill, daughter of

Alanson and Betsey [Mudge] Burrill, born, November 12, 1834.

Children, born in Lynn:

—   i. David Alanson Ellis[8], b. July 20, 1859; d. unm., Aug. 13, 1882.
—   ii. Henrietta Maria Ellis[8], b. Mar. 13, 1862; d. Aug. 23, 1862.
     iii. Mary Clark Ellis[8], b. July 6, 1865.

Mary Clark[8], married, Jan'y 31, 1889, Thomas Coleman McDonald and they have

     i. Jessie McDonald[9], b. Dec. 27, 1889.

99—viii—iii.

VIII. PRISCILLA ROGERS ELLIS[7] (*Otis* ELLIS[6], *Priscilla*[5]) was born in Hanover, April 26, 1835; she married, June 11, 1876, as his second wife, Dr. Henry Watson Dudley, son of John Kimball and Betsey Harvey [Gilman] Dudley, born, November 30, 1831; she died, October 19, 1886, leaving him surviving.

No children.

99—ix—i.

VIII. ALFRED ADAMS PRATT[7] (*Elizabeth* ELLIS[6], *Priscilla*[5]) was born in Lynn, September 26, 1818; he married, November 11, 1842, Mary Hubbard Marsh, daughter of Benjamin and Mary [Whitney] Marsh, born, April 16, 1820; he died, December 30, 1896, and she, October 15, 1888.

Child, born in Lynn:

—   i. Henry Blanchard Pratt[8], b. Aug. 22, 1843; d. Sept. 3, 1846.

99—ix—ii.

VIII. GEORGE OTIS PRATT[7] (*Elizabeth* ELLIS[6], *Priscilla*[5]) was born in Lynn, August 31, 1820; he married, November 30, 1847, Mary White Whitmore, daughter of Major and Lydia [Plummer] Whitmore; he died, February 2, 1855, and she, November 20, 1896.

Children:

+   i.   George Emerson Pratt[8], b. May 7, 1849.
+   ii.   John Irving Pratt[8], b. Feb'y 18, 1851.

99—ix—iii.

VIII.   Eliza Ellen Pratt[7] (*Elizabeth* Ellis[6], *Priscilla*[5]) was born in Lynn, September 21, 1824; she married, December 24, 1848, John Lewis Robinson, son of Christopher and Eliza [Spinney] Robinson, born in Lynn, April 9, 1828; she died, January 31, 1885, leaving him surviving.

Children, born in Lynn:

      Adelaide Herbert Robinson[8], b. Nov. 25, 1850.
—   Elizabeth Tyler Robinson[8], b. May 25, 1852 ; d. May 25, 1852.
—   Elizabeth Tyler Robinson[8], b. July 29, 1853 ; d. Sept. 23, 1853.
—   George Otis Robinson[8], b. Jan'y 20, 1855 ; d. Jan'y 20, 1855.
      George Tyler Robinson[8], b. Ap'l 25, 1859.

99—ix—iv.

VIII.   Mary Emily Pratt[7] (*Elizabeth* Ellis[6], *Priscilla*[5]) was born in Lynn, September 24, 1828; she married, April 4, 1867, George Washington Armstead, son of Samuel Larkin and Sarah [Norcutt] Armstead, born, January 20, 1829, in Charlestown; he died, February 12, 1872, and she, January 4, 1871.

No children.

99—ix—vii.

VIII.   Cynthia Frances Pratt[7] (*Elizabeth* Ellis[6], *Priscilla*[5]) was born in Lynn, September 16, 1841; she married, November 30, 1871, William Lewis Estes, son of William and Jane D. [Lewis] Estes, born in Rockland, Mass., August 22, 1845.

No children.

99—i—i—ii.

IX. MARY ELIZABETH STUDLEY[8] (*William* STUDLEY[7], *Huldah* ELLIS[6], *Priscilla[5]*) was born in East Abington, May 1, 1834; she married, May 19, 1853, Davis Cushing, son of David and Hannah Collamore [Whiting] Cushing, born, April 27, 1830.

Children, born in East Abington (now Rockland):

—   i.   Walter Davis Cushing[9], b. Feb'y 23, 1856; d. unm., May 1, 1896.
—   ii.   Elizabeth Ingersoll Cushing[9], b. Dec. 1, 1858; d. May 25, 1875.
     iii.   Fred Louette Cushing[9], b. Mar. 16, 1860.
     iv.   Maud Neville Cushing[9], b. Dec. 1, 1862.
     v.   Nettie Sherman Cushing[9], b. Dec. 21, 1865.

99—i—i—vi.

IX. ADALINE AUGUSTA STUDLEY[8] (*William* STUDLEY[7], *Huldah* ELLIS[6], *Priscilla[5]*) was born in East Abington, May 13, 1843; she married, December 8, 1865, Micah Gibbs Shurtleff, son of Seth and Mercy [Gibbs] Shurtleff, born, December 8, 1839.

Children:

     i.   Louis Erland Shurtleff[9], b. Sept. 20, 1866, in (now) Rockland.
—   ii.   Minnie Reed Shurtleff[9], b. July 12, 1868, in No. Carver; d. Oct. 24, 1869.
     iii.   Mattie Helen Shurtleff[9], b. Sept. 8, 1874, in No. Carver.
     iv.   Carroll Kent Shurtleff[9], b. Mar. 3, 1878, in Raynham.

X. *Louis Erland Shurtleff[9]*, married, June 14, 1893, Alice Raymond, daughter of Micajah K. and Mary Esther [Davis] Raymond, born in New Bedford, December 13, 1873.

Child, born in New Bedford.

  i. Erland Raymond Shurtleff[10], b. Feb'y 7, 1897; d. June 19, 1897.

99—i—i—ix.

IX. CHARLES ELDRON STUDLEY[8] (*William* STUDLEY[7], *Huldah* ELLIS[6], *Priscilla*[5]) was born in East Abington, April 25, 1852; he married, December 31, 1882, Grace Thaxter Hunt, daughter of Benjamin Lincoln and Othalia Kingman [Soule] Hunt, born, January 25, 1855.

Child, born in Abington:

  i. Amelia Baylies Studley[9], b. June 9, 1883.

99—i—iii—i.

IX. MARY ANDREWS STUDLEY[8] (*Andrew* STUDLEY[7], *Huldah* ELLIS[6], *Priscilla*[5]) was born in East Abington, now Rockland, April 8, 1831; she married, November 23, 1853, John Flavel Keene, son of Freeman and Abigail [Robinson] Keene, born, October 6, 1830; he died, January 7, 1889, and she, April 6, 1890.

Child, born in East Abington:

  — i. Hattie Austin Keene[9], b. July 14, 1858; d. Sept. 13, 1859.

99—i—iii—ii.

IX. AUSTIN STUDLEY[8] (*Andrew* STUDLEY,[7] *Huldah* ELLIS[6], *Priscilla*[5]) was born in East Abington, April 30, 1833; he married, November 21, 1858, Lydia Whiting Shaw, daughter of Elijah and Mary Noyes [Wales] Shaw, born, January 31, 1838.

Child, born in East Abington:

  † i. Frederic Austin Studley[9], b. Nov. 30, 1860.

99—i—iii—ii—i.

X. *Frederic Austin Studley*[9], married, January 22, 1888, Sara

Alma Burrell, daughter of Charles Mann and Rhoda Luthern [Hibbard] Burrell, born, October 30, 1861.

Children, born in Rockland:

    i. Beatrice Alma Studley[10], b. Sept. 6, 1889.

    ii. Ralph Austin Studley[10], b. Sept. 3, 1891.

99—i—iii—iii.

IX. JANE BICKNELL STUDLEY[8] (*Andrew* STUDLEY[7], *Huldah* ELLIS[6], *Priscilla*[5]) was born in East Abington, November 22, 1834; she married, November 26, 1854, Edward Wilson Whiting, son of Piam Collamore and Sarah Dunbar [Brooks] Whiting, born, December 9, 1833.

Children, born in East Abington (now Rockland):

  † i. George Clellan Whiting[9], b. Aug. 27, 1861.

  † ii. Grace Norwood Whiting[9], b. Feb'y 21, 1863.

  — iii. Hittie May Whiting[9], b. Oct. 19, 1871 ; d. May 25, 1873.

99—i—iii—iii—i.

X. *George Clellan Whiting*[9], married, February 13, 1881, Jennie Sampson Swift, daughter of Martin and Louisa Sampson [Ames] Swift, born, April 28, 1859.

Child, born in Rockland :

    i. Jennie Louisa Whiting[10], b. May 26, 1882.

99—i—iii—iii—ii.

X. *Grace Norwood Whiting*[9], married, June 27, 1888, Edwin Starr Tirrell, son of Edwin Starr and Emeline [Lane] Tirrell, born, February 9, 1863.

Children, born in Spencer :

  — i. Edwin Whiting Tirrell[10], b. Oct. 9, 1889 ; d. Dec. 11, 1889.

    ii. Ethel Norwood Tirrell[10], b. Dec. 3, 1892.

99—ii—x—i.

IX. SUSAN EMILY MILLER[8] (*Sarah* GIFFORD[7], *Rebecca* ELLIS[6], *Priscilla*[5]) was born in New York City,

February 18, 1851; she married, October 21, 1873, Gilbert Hopkins Swezey, son of Van Rensselaer and Dorothy Catherine [Davis] Swezey, born, April 22, 1842; they now (1898) reside at Yaphank, L. I., New York.

Children, the first born in New York City and the others in Yaphank:

  — i. Lillian Cometa Swezey⁹, b. July 10, 1874.
  — ii. Dora Catharine Swezey⁹, b. Dec. 22, 1875.
  — iii. Van Rensselaer Swezey⁹, b. Feb'y 11, 1878.
  — iv. Sarah Ellis Swezey⁹, b. Aug. 28, 1880.
  — v. Florence Swezey⁹, b. Dec. 30, 1881.
    vi. Charlotte Powell Swezey⁹, b. July 21, 1883.
    vii. Charles Miller Swezey⁹, b. Sept 12, 1888.
   viii. Frank Robinson Swezey⁹, b. Dec. 30, 1897.

99—ii—x—ii.

IX. LILLIAN SARAH ELIZABETH MILLER⁸ (*Sarah* GIFFORD⁷, *Rebecca* ELLIS⁶, *Priscilla⁵*) was born in New York City, August 12, 1855; she married, April 25, 1889, Daniel Benedict Phillips, son of Philetus and Hannah [Van Horn] Phillips, born, March 11, 1860: they now (1898) reside in North Falmouth, Mass.

Children, born in North Falmouth:

   i. Leonie Phillips⁹, b. Ap'l 12, 1892.
   ii. Charles Lawrence Phillips⁹, b. Mar. 12, 1896.

99—ii—x—iii.

IX. CHARLES WILLIAM MILLER⁸ (*Sarah* GIFFORD⁷, *Rebecca* ELLIS⁶, *Priscilla⁵*) was born in New York City, September 19, 1857; he married, September 19, Delia Mary Austin Walsh, daughter of Edward and Mary [O'Donnell] Walsh, born, February 2, 1857; she died, September 3, 1893.

Children, born in New York City:

—   i.   Gertrude Adelaide Miller⁹, b. Sept. 2, 1886 ; d. Aug. 14, 1888.

      ii.   Charles Frederick Miller⁹, b. July 14, 1889.

     iii.   Elizabeth Beatrice Miller⁹, b. Sept. 30, 1892.

99—v—i—i.

IX.   JAMES THOMAS DILLINGHAM⁸ (*Elizabeth* GIFFORD⁷, *Priscilla* ELLIS⁶, *Priscilla*⁵ (was born in West Falmouth, February 12, 1833; he married, August —, 1855, Caroline Frances Swift, daughter of Joseph and Wing [Gifford] Swift, born, November 26, 1832; be died, April 15, 1889, at Sheboygan, Wis., leaving her surviving.

No children.

99—v—i—ii.

IX.   HANNAH GIFFORD DILLINGHAM⁸ (*Elizabeth* GIFFORD⁷, *Priscilla* ELLIS⁶, *Priscilla*⁵) was born in West Falmouth, April 23, 1836; she married, February 22, 1868, George Plummer, son of Joseph C. and Mary Jane [Wood] Plummer, born, April 24, 1837; living in West Falmouth.

No children.

99—v—ii—ii.

IX.   PHEBE SLADE GIFFORD⁸ (*Ellis* GIFFORD⁷, *Priscilla* ELLIS⁶, *Priscilla*⁵) was born in Fall River, November 13, 1839; she married, November 22, 1876, Henry Clay Aydelott, son of Stuart and Sarah [Stuart] Aydelott, born, August 2, 1834.

Child, born in Fall River:

     i.   Laura Belle Aydelott⁹, b. Ap'l 1, 1878.

99—v—ii—iii.

IX.   CHARLES ELLIS GIFFORD⁸ (*Ellis* GIFFORD⁷, *Priscilla* ELLIS⁶, *Priscilla*⁵) was born in Fall River, Decem-

ber 16, 1842; he married, October 3, 1871, Elna Viettie
Soule, daughter of Resolved and Sophia Turner [Giff-
ord] Soule, born, September 1, 1851; she died, December 28, 1878; he married, November 8, 1881, Ella Tabor,
daughter of George Washington and Mary Ingraham
[Livermore] Tabor, born, November 29, 1854.

No children.

99—v—ii—vi.

IX. BENJAMIN SLADE CHACE GIFFORD[8] (*Ellis* GIF-
FORD[7], *Priscilla* ELLIS[6], *Priscilla*[5]) was born in Fall
River, August 5, 1849; he married, June 2, 1887, Mary
Lee French, daughter of Hiram and Mary [Long]
French, born, July 10, 1858.

Children, born in Fall River:

—   i.   Edith Gifford[9], b. May 10, 1889 ; d. Mar. 22, 1894.
    ii.   Paul Gifford[9], b. June 30, 1890.

99—v—ii—vii.

IX. EDMUND CHACE GIFFORD[8] (*Ellis* GIFFORD[7],
Priscilla ELLIS[6], *Priscilla*[5]) was born in Fall River,
March 10, 1852; he married, March 31, 1880, Edith
Heywood Miles, daughter of William T. and Isabella
Jane [Reed] Miles, born, June 11, 1858; she died, July
26, 1888; he married, June 2, 1892, Alice Josephine
Flagg, daughter of Ira Chandler and Sarah Elizabeth
[Shapleigh] Flagg, born, December 8, 1862.

Children, born in Fall River:

By first wife :

    i.   Ellis Gifford[9], b. Ap'l 19, 1884.
    ii.   Marjorie Belle Gifford[9], b. Aug. 19, 1885.

By second wife :

    iii.   Dorothy Gifford[9], b. Dec. 22, 1893.
    iv.   Helen Gifford[9], b. Mar. 25, 1895.
    v.   Hilda Gifford[9], b. May 25, 1897.

99—v—iv—i.

IX. JAMES WILLIAM GIFFORD[8] (*Azariah Shove* GIF-
FORD[7], *Priscilla* ELLIS[6], *Priscilla*[5]) was born in West
Falmouth, September 21, 1850; he married, January 3,
1876, Annie Elizabeth Brown, daughter of Alexander
and Margaret [Miller] Brown, born, August 22, 1851.

Children, the first born in Fall River, and the others
in Attleboro:

      i.   James William Gifford[9], b. Jan'y 30, 1878.
      ii. Charles Henry Gifford[9], b. Feb'y 28, 1880.
      iii. Lois Annie Gifford[9], b. Ap'l 24, 1881.
      iv. Ethel May Gifford[9], b. Jan'y 20, 1889.

99—v—iv—iii.

IX. SETH KELLEY GIFFORD[8] (*Azariah Shove* GIF-
FORD[7], *Priscilla* ELLIS[6], *Priscilla*[5]) was born in West
Falmouth, July 29, 1854; he married, July 15, 1878,
Sarah Elma Winslow; she died in March, 1881; no
children; he married, June 28, 1883, Mary Amy Collins,
daughter of Amos Wilbur and Lucy Thurber [Fry]
Collins, born, November 18, 1849.

Children, the first born in Lynn, and the other in
Haverford, Pa.:

      i. Margaret Amy Gifford[9], b. July 24, 1888.
      ii. Philip Collins[9], b. Sept. 22, 1891.

99—v—iv—iv.

IX. JOHN HENRY GIFFORD[8] (*Azariah Shove* GIF-
FORD[7], *Priscilla* ELLIS[6], *Priscilla*[5]) was born in West
Falmouth, February 6, 1858; he married, September
14, 1886, Phebe Elizabeth Newton, daughter of James
and Elizabeth Slade [Anthony] Newton, born, September 21, 1859.

Children, born in Fall River:

—   i.   Edward Shove Anthony Gifford⁹, b. Sept. 2, 1889 ; d. Mar. 9, 1890.
     ii.   Newton Rogers Gifford⁹, b. Dec. 17, 1890.

99—ix—ii—i.

IX.   George Emerson Pratt⁸ (*George Otis* Pratt⁷, *Elizabeth* Ellis⁶, *Priscilla*⁵) was born May 7, 1849; he married, January 1, 1872, Emma Alma Conner, daughter of Henry Clay and Ann Sarah [Cobbett] Conner, born, March 18, 1852.

Children, born in Elmira, N. Y.:

     i.   Jessie Maud Pratt⁹, b. Aug. 19, 1872.
—   ii.   Frederic Huntington Emerson Pratt⁹, b. Aug. 27, 1874; d. Ap'l 10, 1882.
—   iii.   Ernest Wey Pratt⁹, b. Sept. 16, 1876; d. Jan'y 27, 1885.
     iv.   Alice Henrietta Pratt⁹, b. Jan'y 19, 1879.
     v.   Grace Emily Pratt⁹, b. Oct. 10, 1883.

99—ix—ii—ii.

IX.   John Irving Pratt⁸ (*George Otis* Pratt⁷, *Elizabeth* Ellis⁶, *Priscilla*⁵) was born, February 18, 1857; he married, Oct. 13, 1875, Mary Lizzie Jennings, daughter of Thomas Dean and Sarah [Hilton] Jennings, born in Lynn, June 30, 1854.

Child, born in Lynn:

     i.   Mabel Jennings Pratt⁹, b. Ap'l 10, 1879.

ADDITIONS AND CORRECTIONS.

I.

PARTIES OF THE NAME NOT IDENTIFIED.

We have found the names of a few whom we have not identified:

1. There was a *William Rogers* in Scituate in 1671, but very certainly not of this family; no record of his family has been found, but he probably had descendants.

2. The Marshfield records gave the birth of Abiah, child of *Stacy Rogers*, born March 11, 1728/9, but no further mention of them is found in church, town or probate records.

3. *Jennet Rogers*, daughter of William and Jennet Rogers was baptized, May 29, 1720, Scit. Ch. Rec.

4. *Elisha Rogers* of Marshfield, married, December 2, 1741, Margaret McFarland; he died soon after; she had daughter, Orphan, born, February 26, 1742/3. "Orphin, daughter of Margaret Rogers, widow, baptized March 26, 1742." Orphan married a White and died May 25, 1816, aged 73. Margaret was appointed Adm'x of the estate of Elisha, January 15, 1742/3.

5. *William Rogers* (see p. 47) was probably of the same family as Elisha.

6. Will of Jesse Thomas of Pembroke, dated June 5, 1762, gives to James Cox, *alias* Rogers, son of Abigail Rogers of Pembroke, thirty pounds at his arrival to the age of twenty-one. Vol. xix, p. 59.

II.

WANTON AND ROGERS BURYING GROUND.

On the farm of Edward Wanton, in old Scituate, close by North River, about a mile above Union Bridge, was a burying ground, which had been fenced and used before 1707, and probably for

many years; in fact, it is believed that it was set apart as early as
1661, when Edward Wanton purchased the farm and that John
Rogers[1] was buried in it that year. Wanton conveyed the farm to
his son in 1705, and in 1707 the son conveyed to Edward Wanton
of Scituate and John Rogers, Senior, of Marshfield [John[2]] the
burying ground as then and theretofore fenced and used, to be used
only as a burying ground by Wanton and Rogers, their heirs, assigns,
families and "posterityes," with a passage way to the road. When
the son sold the farm, he reserved the burying ground; but, as
generally in such cases, after the farm passed out of the possession
of the family, the burying ground was neglected and trees grew
upon it until it became a thicket and all appearance of a burying
ground disappeared, save one headstone and the fragment of another
as mentioned on p. 21.

III.

FAMILIES REWRITTEN OR CORRECTED BY ADDITIONS.

1. The family of MARY DOGGETT[3] (p. 21) was taken from an
erroneous authority. The children were:

—   i.   Samuel Doggett[4], b. Dec. 24, 1683; d. in infancy.
     ii.   Samuel Doggett[4], b. Ap'l 7, 1685.
    iii.   Mary Doggett[4], b. Ap'l 16, 1687.
     iv.   Sarah Doggett[4], b. Ap'l 7, 1689.

2. As already stated (p. 38) the statement of the second marriage of John[3] (No. 15, p. 24) is erroneous; the widow Turner
married her cousin, John[3] (No. 25, p. 29); to avoid confusion
corrected accounts of both families are given;

15.

IV.   JOHN ROGERS[3] (*Joseph[2], John[1]*) was born in that
part of Duxbury which became Pembroke; he married,
March 6, 1722/3, Leah Lincoln, daughter of Daniel and
Sarah [Nichols] Lincoln of Hingham, born, December
9, 1695; she died, at the house of her uncle, Moses
Lincoln of Hingham, March 11, 1728/9.

Children, born in Pembroke:

— 47.   Leah⁴, b. Ap'l 27, 1724; d. June 9, 1736.
  48.   Abigail⁴, b. Oct. 4, 1725.
  49.   Daniel⁴, b. Oct. 2, 1727.

No further information has been obtained in relation to this family; they do not seem to be mentioned in any of the Pembroke records.

25.

IV.   JOHN ROGERS³ (*Timothy²*, *John¹*) was born in Marshfield; he married, December 11, 1700, Hannah Sprague, daughter of Hon. Samuel and Sarah [Chilling-worth] Sprague; she died and he married (2) Sarah [Wing] Turner, widow of ——— Turner and daughter of Elisha and Mehitable [Butler] Wing of Wareham, born, May 4, 1708; she died about 1748, and he, in 1762.

Children, born in Marshfield:

By first wife:

+ 69.   Hannah⁴, b. Feb'y 9, 1701-2.
+ 70.   Sarah⁴, b. Sept. [Dec.] 26, 1705.
  70a. Stephen⁴, b.

By second wife:

+ 49a. Elizabeth⁴, [Betty] b. Feb'y [Ap'l] 5, 1731.
— 49b. Daughter⁴, probably died young.

It is probable that there other children by the first wife, but none have been identified.

Thomas Stockbridge was appointed his Admʳ, June 7, 1762; there was no real estate; the papers describe him as a tailor, as his father was before him; his estate was insolvent.

An indenture, dated Oct. 17, 1710, shows that Hannah Rogers, wife of John Rogers of Marshfield, was the daughter of Samuel and and Sarah Sprague and was then living.

Several deeds from John Rogers of Marshfield, tailor, between 1710 and 1744, have been found, to none of which was his wife,

Hannah, a party; among them is a deed in 1732, to his son, Stephen of Marshfield. B. XXVII, p. 180.

Deeds, one dated June 18, 1743, and one July 12, 1744, are signed by his wife, Sarah. B. XXXVIII, p. 203: B. XXXVII, p. 14.

Deed, dated Feb'y 18, 1746, but not acknowledged till Oct. 5, 1748, is signed by wife, Sarah. B. XL, p. 278.

In a deed given in 1744, he mentions his son, Stephen. B. XXXVII, p. 77.

In 1748, he conveyed land to Moses Rogers, but the deed was not acknowledged, and was proved in court in 1763, after his death; Sarah's name is not in this deed. B. XLVII, p. 227.

Stephen[4] has not been traced. The only mention of him that has been found, other than in his father's deeds, is in a deed from Stephen, in which his wife, Sarah, joins, to his father, "John Rogers of Marshfield, Tailor." B. XXXVI, p. 166.

There were two children by the second wife.

Phillip Turner ("son of Sarah Rogers, the wife of John Rogers, of Marshfield, and grandson to Elisha Wing") and Rebekah Jenney, daughter to Nathan Jenney and Priscilla, his wife, were married "7 mo. 7th, 1750." Sandwich Fr. Rec.

Elisha Wing of Wareham, in his will (1752) mentioned "Philip Turner, the son of my daughter, Sarah," "and the two children my daughter, Sarah, left by her husband, John Rogers," giving them one-third of his household stuff.

And Elizabeth Wing, daughter of Elisha, in her will (1756) gave a legacy to Philip Turner, son of her sister, Sarah Rogers, and also, to "Betty Hoxie, wife of Silas Hoxie, and daughter to my said sister, Sarah Rogers." Vol. XIV, p. 199, 326.

The identification of the *John*[3], who married the widow, Sarah [Wing] Turner, was established by a deed from Betty [Rogers] Hoxie and court records, which the accidental discovery of the deed led to finding.

Betty [Rogers] Hoxie conveyed real estate which came to her as the heir of Stephen Stockbridge[5], son of Thomas and Hannah [Rogers[4]] Stockbridge; see p. 50 How she could have been his heir, was a decided puzzle; but it was found that under the law as then existing (which was soon after changed) when a man died without children, father or mother, brothers or sisters, nephews or nieces, his *surviving* uncles and aunts inherited his property to the exclusion of the children of *deceased* uncles and aunts. The nearest relatives which Stephen left (besides Betty Hoxie) were cousins; therefore, as Betty inherited his property, she must have been his aunt, which she could be only as the half-sister of his mother, Hannah Rogers[4] (*John*[3], *Timothy*[2]) and the John whom Betty's mother married, must have been Hannah's father.

3. *Abigail Rogers*[3] (No. 21, p. 26), the second wife of Thomas Parris, died, December 11, 1713, and he married for his third wife, Grace Record, January 31, 1714/15; the will of Abigail's father, dated April 10, 1716, speaks of her as then deceased; no account of Thomas Parris that I have seen mentions the third wife, but the Pembroke records have it as just stated.

4. *Abel Rogers*[3] (No. 145, p. 43) is said to have lived at Castine.

5. *Thomas Tirrell* (No. 62, p. 45) was born in Weymouth, July 7, 1699.

6. *Ebenezer Rogers*[4] (No. 67, p. 48). His wife was Sarah Stetson, daughter of Isaac and Elizabeth Stetson.

The estate of Hannah Berry was settled May 7, 1759; as her real estate could not be divided, her brother, Peleg Stetson, took it at the appraisal and paid "unto his mother and brothers and sisters, their ratable parts" * * * "to his mother Elizabeth Hatch & to his brothers & sisters, viz., Cornelius Stutson, John Stutson, Nathaniel Stutson, Jenne Thomas, Sarah Rogers and Mary Spear" &c. Vol. XV, p. 160.

The Pembroke records give Cornelius, Nathaniel, Jeannett, Peleg and John as children of Isaac and Elizabeth "Studson."

7. No. 86, p. 53. *Rebecca Stetson*[6] was married, Nov. 27, 1796, and *Lydia*[6] was born Feb'y 28, 1779.

8. *Eunice Rogers*[6] (No. 232, p. 61) late in life, married Levi Curtis, as his second wife.

9. Page 15, line 4. Hon. JOSEPH W. PORTER of Bangor, thinks that Elizabeth Hudson married Jonathan Vickery of Hull and Chatham.

IV.

CLERICAL AND OTHER ERRORS.

It is well known that the record of the same fact in different records (family, town or church) is not always the same, and it often is difficult to determine to which to give the preference. Persons also, especially those without experience, in copying names and dates, unconsciously make mistakes. As it was impossible for me or Miss ELLIS to examine personally all the records from which the foregoing facts were taken, or to send proofs to the different parties, I have sent out the sheets of this pamphlet to parties interested for the purpose of noting the errors. The result is that more were noted than I had expected, but very many of them were in the papers which came into the hands of the editor; while others are his, and others were printers' errors which escaped notice in reading proof.

P. 7, line 31. "Posy" and "Posye," which have heretofore been given in certified copies of this will, are now after a very careful examination, believed to be "Gorg" and "Gorge," meaning "George" which was the real name of the boy.

P. 9, line 21. "Samuel Niles" should be "Samuel Arnold"; the name on the record is almost illegible, but as Samuel Arnold was the minister at the time, the name is quite certainly "Samuel Arnall."

P. 14, line 23. For "Hannah Torrey" read "Honour Torrey."

P. 15, line 32. "Anna" is a misprint for "Annis."

P. 25, line 25. The authority for "Jeannette, second daughter," proves to be erroneous; it should be "Penelope, daughter."

P. 32, line 24. A re-examination of the record shows that "House" should be "Hewes," "Huse" or "Hughs."

P. 35, last line. "Nov. 5, 1671" should be "July 11, 1671"; some one read "11-5-1671" erroneously.

P. 39, lines 4 and 10. "1767" should be "1747," and "1740" should be "1750."

P. 40, line 12. For "Kent" read "Hunt."

P. 59, line 13. For "1863" read "1864."

P. 64, line 14. The Family Bible gives "Nov. 24, 1860," but I am satisfied that the correct date is "Nov. 20, 1859."

P. 65, line 6. For "*Isaiahs*" read "*Israels*."

P. 71, lines 14, 15. For "Nov. 30, 1865," read "May 29, 1845."

P. 72, line 10. For "Austress" read "Anstress."

P. 101, lines 19 and 21. For "1853" read "1863," and for "September 26, 1863" read "December 26, 1879."

P. 104, line 21. For "Dilloway" read "Dillaway."

P. 106, third line from bottom. For "1857" read "1897."

P. 114, line 5. For "Belfast" read "Camden."

P. 115, line 2. For "1880" read "1888."

P. 115, lines 35 and 37, and p. 116, line 2. For "Wilson" and "Willson" read "Millson."

P. 116, line 20. For "Aaron" read "Anson."

P. 116, line 21; p. 117, lines 6, and 28, p. 118, line 2. For "Huntingdon" read "Huntington."

P. 118, line 24. Omit "two," and line 25 for "other" read "others."

P. 125, line 2. After "she" insert "married."

P. 127, No. 463. For "Mary" read "Nancy."

P. 130, line 1. For "May 15, 1804" read "August 31, 1803."

P. 132, line 29. For "*Isaac*" read "*Israel*."

Trieste Publishing has a massive catalogue of classic book titles. Our aim is to provide readers with the highest quality reproductions of fiction and non-fiction literature that has stood the test of time. The many thousands of books in our collection have been sourced from libraries and private collections around the world.

The titles that Trieste Publishing has chosen to be part of the collection have been scanned to simulate the original. Our readers see the books the same way that their first readers did decades or a hundred or more years ago. Books from that period are often spoiled by imperfections that did not exist in the original. Imperfections could be in the form of blurred text, photographs, or missing pages. It is highly unlikely that this would occur with one of our books. Our extensive quality control ensures that the readers of Trieste Publishing's books will be delighted with their purchase. Our staff has thoroughly reviewed every page of all the books in the collection, repairing, or if necessary, rejecting titles that are not of the highest quality. This process ensures that the reader of one of Trieste Publishing's titles receives a volume that faithfully reproduces the original, and to the maximum degree possible, gives them the experience of owning the original work.

We pride ourselves on not only creating a pathway to an extensive reservoir of books of the finest quality, but also providing value to every one of our readers. Generally, Trieste books are purchased singly - on demand, however they may also be purchased in bulk. Readers interested in bulk purchases are invited to contact us directly to enquire about our tailored bulk rates. Email: customerservice@triestepublishing.com

You May Also Like

Treatise on Water Supply, Drainage, and Sanitary Appliances of Residences. Including Machinery, Lighting and Cookery Apparatus

Frederick Colyer

ISBN: 9780649540754
Paperback: 140 pages
Dimensions: 6.14 x 0.30 x 9.21 inches
Language: eng

The Influence of Correct Food Quantities Upon Human Life

Theron C. Stearns

ISBN: 9781760579609
Paperback: 130 pages
Dimensions: 6.14 x 0.28 x 9.21 inches
Language: eng

www.triestepublishing.com

You May Also Like

"Ladies from Hell".
Illustrated
with Photographs

R. Douglas Pinkerton

ISBN: 9781760573447
Paperback: 290 pages
Dimensions: 6.0 x 0.61 x 9.0 inches
Language: eng

Gelibene
Shrifen

Ivan Sergeevich
Turgenev &
Leon Kobrin

ISBN: 9780649540143
Paperback: 302 pages
Dimensions: 6.14 x 0.63 x 9.21 inches
Language: eng

www.triestepublishing.com

You May Also Like

Shut Your Mouth and Save Your Life

George Catlin

ISBN: 9781760570491
Paperback: 118 pages
Dimensions: 6.14 x 0.25 x 9.21 inches
Language: eng

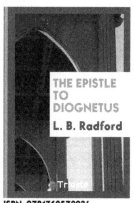

The Epistle to Diognetus

L. B. Radford

ISBN: 9781760570934
Paperback: 106 pages
Dimensions: 6.14 x 0.22 x 9.21 inches
Language: eng

www.triestepublishing.com